Preventing Money Laundering and Terrorist Financing

Preventing Money Laundering and Terrorist Financing

A Practical Guide for Bank Supervisors

Pierre-Laurent Chatain
John McDowell
Cédric Mousset
Paul Allan Schott
Emile van der Does de Willebois

THE WORLD BANK
Washington, DC

ISBN: 978-0-8213-7912-7
eISBN: 978-0-8213-7913-4
DOI: 10.1596/978-0-8213-7912-7

Library of Congress Cataloging-in-Publication Data

Preventing money laundering and terrorism financing : a practical guide for bank supervisors / by Pierre-Laurent Chatain . . . [et al.].
    p. cm.
  Includes bibliographical references and index.
   ISBN 978-0-8213-7912-7 — ISBN 978-0-8213-7913-4 (electronic)
1. Money laundering—Prevention. 2. Banks and banking—Corrupt practices. 3. Terrorism—Finance—Prevention. I. Chatain, Pierre-Laurent, 1961-
  HV6768.P74 2009
  364.16'8—dc22
                                                                                        2009007464

Contents

Boxes

Figures

Foreword

The current financial crisis poses many challenges to all countries. The need for enhanced transparency and financial integrity in national financial systems is more important than ever. It is therefore critically important to have in place strong anti-money laundering/combating the financing of terrorism (AML/CFT) oversight mechanisms, not only to protect the integrity of the financial system, but also to ensure that public funds mobilized to address the financial crisis will not be misused or misappropriated.

Money laundering is a serious crime that affects the economy as a whole, impeding the social, economic, political, and cultural development of societies worldwide. Over the last decades, globalization has been accompanied by the growth of cross-border and national underground economies fueled by illegal businesses. Such criminal activities as drug trafficking, human trafficking, migrant smuggling, traffic in body organs and firearms, as well as prostitution and racketeering, have generated immense profits that boost demand for money laundering. Fighting money laundering involves combating the recycling of illegally gained proceeds and providing additional tools to detect and go after the underlying crime.

Terrorism and its financing are also affecting both the national and the international economies.[1] As do money launderers, terrorists raise their funds through various profitable activities that mainly stem from criminal acts, such as kidnapping, extortion, large-scale smuggling, narcotics trafficking, robbery, and theft. Terrorists need to use the financial infrastructure to mobilize and channel their funds.

One central objective of supervisors and regulators is to bolster confidence in the financial system, and to use all available tools to ensure that financial institutions are not owned by criminals or being misused for criminal purposes.

As countries around the world adopt AML/CFT legislation, effective supervision is pivotal to the success and impact of a country's AML/CFT system. In this respect, devising methods of supervising compliance by the banking sector is central to any AML/CFT regime. Every bank has the obligation to know its customers and to report

---

[1] Financial Action Task Force on Money Laundering, 2002. See also R. Barry Johnston, and Oana M. Nedelescu, "The Impact of Terrorism on Financial Markets", *Journal of Financial Crime*, vol. 13, 2006.

suspicious transactions. Although these obligations sound straightforward, they have proved challenging to implement. What can banks do to gather specific information about their customers? How should it be recorded? When does the bank have to file a Suspicious Transaction Report? It is here that a supervisor can play a crucial role in helping supervised institutions: First, in understanding the full extent of the obligations of Customer Due Diligence and Suspicious Transaction Reports and, second, in ensuring that those obligations are not just words on paper but are applied in practice, backed by sanctioning mechanisms against non-compliance.

In this regard, field work in both developed and developing countries has shown an overall low compliance in the area of supervision of banks and other financial institutions. Indeed, supervisory compliance is generally lower than the average level of compliance with all Financial Action Task Force recommendations. By providing examples of good practices, this book aims to help countries better conform to international standards.

This book is specifically designed for bank supervisors, some of whom may be looking for ways to devise a program of AML/CFT supervision. Others may have encountered difficulties in elements of their systems of supervision and are looking for alternatives. Supervisors may also come to recognize even more efficient ways to carry out AML/CFT supervision. The objective of this book is therefore to provide a "how to" reference for practitioners of financial regulation and supervision.

The authors have attempted to conceive a *practical* guide, with the purpose of resolving strategic and operational supervisory issues. They cover the entire spectrum of supervision, ranging from supervision objectives to the design and carrying out of onsite and offsite inspection programs, and from cooperation with other domestic and international AML/CFT authorities to sanctions and enforcement.

The international community recognizes that under-regulated or unsupervised entities have the potential to undermine confidence in financial markets and hamper economic recovery. Better transparency, enhanced oversight, and stronger cross-border cooperation among regulators and supervisors in all areas of risks, including money laundering and terrorist financing, are necessary to ensure that financial institutions always remain sound, sustainable, and vigilant. This task is even greater during difficult times.

It is our hope that this book will serve this ultimate goal.

Michael U. Klein
Vice President
Finance and Private Sector Development
World Bank–IFC
Chief Economist, IFC

Acknowledgments

This publication was written by Pierre-Laurent Chatain (Team Leader), John McDowell, Cédric Mousset, Paul Allan Schott, and Emile van der Does de Willebois, with the participation of Kamil Borowik. The authors are especially grateful to Latifah Merican-Cheong, Program Director, Financial Market Integrity, World Bank, for her guidance and comments in producing this book.

The peer reviewers for the paper were Colin Powell, Chairman of the Jersey Financial Services Commission; Lisa D. Arquette, from the Federal Deposit Insurance Corporation; Jean-Pierre Michau, Special Advisor to the Governor of the Bank of France; Alain Vedrenne-Lacombe, from the International Monetary Fund (IMF); Professor Louis de Koker, Director of the Centre for the Study of Economic Crime (CenSEC); Jody Ketteringham, from the UK Financial Service Authority; Raymond Chan, from the Hong Kong Monetary Authority; Carlos Correa and his team from the US Department of the Treasury, Office of Technical Assistance. Their comments, discussion, and follow-up sharpened the paper, and we thank them greatly. These inputs were further enhanced by the insight of the General Secretary of the French Banking Commission, in particular by Violaine Clerc and Nick Burbidge from Canada's Office of the Superintendent of Financial Institutions.

The authors would like to express their gratitude to Edouard Fernandez-Bollo and Errol Kruger, the co-chairs of the Basel Committee's AML/CFT Expert Group and to Stephane Mahieu, member of the Secretariat of the Basel Committee, who provided valuable input and recommendations. Also, we would like to show our appreciation for the work of all members of the AML/CFT Expert Group (AMLEG).

The labors of our editors, Peter Maitland and Dawn Amott, are also highly appreciated, as is the assistance of Seung Beom Koh (FPDFI) and support staff Thelma Ayamel, Oriana Bolvaran, Nicolas de la Riva, Maria Orellano, and Susana Coca.

The authors would also like to express their gratitude to Tim Lyman, from the Consultative Group for the Poor (CGAP), for his collaboration on the issue of implementing a risk-based approach on AML/CFT in poor countries. In this respect, the authors would like to thank Professor Louis de Koker who contributed to the book by providing his perspective on how to implement AML/CFT supervision without hampering financial inclusion.

The fieldwork for this book was done in several markets: Hong Kong, China; Malaysia, South Korea, Singapore, Italy, Belgium, the Netherlands, Spain, and Jersey. The time spent by people in these locations will not be forgotten. Although the following list is not nearly exhaustive, we would like to highlight some of the organizations and people without whom we could not have produced this paper:

Belgium: Commission Bancaire, Financière et des Assurances, Banque Nationale de Belgique, Cel voor Financiële Informatieverwerking (CFI-Belgian FIU), Association Belge des Banques, Belgian Financial Federation, ING, CPH Banque, Petercam.

Hong Kong, China: The Government of the Hong Kong Special Administrative Region; Hong Kong Monetary Authority; Hong Kong Police Forces, Joint Financial Intelligence Unit; Hong Kong Association of Banks; Standard Chartered Bank; HSBC; Bank of China; DBS.

Italy: Ufficio Italiano dei Cambi,[1] Banca d' Italia.

Jersey: Jersey Financial Services Commission, Joint Financial Crimes Unit of the States of Jersey Police, Jersey Bankers Association, BNP-Paribas, Capita Fiduciary Group.

Malaysia: Bank Negara Malaysia and Dato' Zamani Abdul Ghani, Deputy Governor, Bank Negara Malaysia; Malayan Banking Berhad (Maybank); CIMB Group; Association of Banks in Malaysia (ABM); Citigroup, HSBC, and Standard Chartered.

Malaysia, Offshore Center of Labuan: LOFSA (the Labuan Offshore Financial Services Authority), Public Bank Ltd, Standard Chartered, Bank of Tokyo-Mitsubishi UFJ, CALYON.

Netherlands: De Nederlandsche Bank, FIU-Nederland, GarantiBank, ABN Amro.

Singapore: Monetary Authority of Singapore, ABS (Association of Banks of Singapore), Singapore Police Force, Institute of Defense and Strategic Studies, Deutshe Bank, BNP-Paribas.

Spain: Comisión de Prevención de Blanqueo de Capitales e Infracciones Monetarias (SEPBLAC), Banco de España, BBVA, Grupo Santander, La Caixa, Caja Laboral, Caja Madrid.

South Korea: Ministry of Strategy and Finance (former Ministry of Finance and Economy), Bank of Korea; Financial Supervisory Service; Korean Financial Intelligence Unit; Korea Exchange Bank, Shinhan Bank, Kookmin Bank; Korea Federation of Banks. The authors would also like to express their appreciation to the Executive Director in the office for Korea at the World Bank and the staff of the office for their active support.

The Authors
Washington, DC
March 2009

---

[1] Ufficio Italiano dei Cambi is now part of the Banca d'Italia and is called the Banca d'Italia - Unita di Informazione Financiaría (UIF).

About the Authors

Pierre-Laurent Chatain is lead financial sector specialist at the World Bank's Financial Market Integrity Unit. Since he joined the Bank in September 2002 as senior financial sector specialist, he has led several anti-money laundering assessment missions as part of the Financial Sector Assessment Program in anglophone, francophone, and Spanish-speaking countries, and has designed and delivered many technical assistance programs and outreach events in Africa, the Middle East, Latin America, and Southeast Asia. Before joining the World Bank, Mr. Chatain worked for the Bank of France for more than 15 years. He held several positions in succession within the legal and inspection departments. He was auditor from 1992 to 1996, then was promoted to inspector. He also served as mission chief at the French Banking Commission, where he led multidisciplinary on-site inspection teams in commercial banks in France and overseas. He also exercised managerial responsibilities at the Bank of France as deputy-director of the On-site Control Department. Mr. Chatain has published widely on issues of mediation, conflict resolution, and civil bankruptcy. He holds a master's degree in law from the University of Paris 1 Panthéon-Sorbonne and is a graduate of the French Political Science Institute.

John McDowell is a senior financial sector specialist with the Financial Market Integrity Department at the World Bank. He has contributed to the creation and implementation of the World Bank strategy for the provision of anti-money laundering assistance to client countries and assists in the adoption of high-quality supervisory and risk management standards in financial institutions. Some of his responsibilities encompass providing guidance to World Bank units responsible for country programs; developing a dialogue with international rule-setting bodies and other organizations; contributing to the dissemination of international best practices; providing technical assistance in response to client requests; and participating in financial sector assessment missions. Prior to joining the World Bank, Mr. McDowell served for more than four years as a senior policy advisor for the U.S. Department of State where he was responsible for the development and implementation of a global anti-money laundering strategy to combat money laundering, terrorist financing, and financial crime.

Mr. McDowell spent most of his career with the U.S. Comptroller of the Currency (OCC) where he held several positions involved with directing bank supervisory activities. While at the OCC he also developed bank examination policies and procedures and formulated banking regulations and policies covering money laundering and financial crimes for the National Banking System. Mr. McDowell holds a master's degree in government and business from Harvard University, Cambridge, Massachusetts, and a B.S. degree in business administration from the University of Florida.

Cédric Mousset joined the World Bank in 2005 as a senior financial sector specialist. He took part in Financial Sector Assessment Programs in Asia, the Middle East, and Africa. During those missions, he reviewed the soundness of financial systems and assessed countries' compliance with Financial Action Task Force (FATF) recommendations and the Basel core principles for effective banking supervision. He also assisted several jurisdictions in Asia, Latin America, and Africa to design and implement anti-money laundering and combating the financing of terrorism (AML/CFT) risk-based supervision through training, technical assistance, and regulatory drafting. In addition, he has been involved in studies on Basel 2 implementation and loan loss provisioning, as well as market discipline. Mr. Mousset was also involved in the review of the effects of the subprime crisis on European banking systems undertaken by the Committee of European Banking supervisors in late 2007. Before joining the World Bank, he worked in the on- and off-site supervision departments of the Banque de France and was directly responsible for the supervision of some of the largest French financial groups. He is a graduate of the Ecole Supérieure de Commerce de Rouen (Business School) and from the Institut d'Etudes Politiques de Paris.

Paul Allan Schott is an attorney in private practice in Washington, D.C. He also serves as a consultant to the World Bank. He is a nationally recognized expert in bank regulatory matters, having served as chief counsel of the Office of the Comptroller of the Currency, assistant general counsel at the U.S. Department of the Treasury, and senior attorney at the Federal Reserve Board. He has written books on anti-money laundering and the federal regulation of bank holding companies; published numerous articles; and spoken at many professional seminars. Currently, he works with foreign governments on enhancing anti-money laundering and bank supervisory programs; he works with private clients on AML, bank and holding company powers, capital, and various compliance issues. He also serves as an expert witness for litigation matters involving bank regulatory and supervisory issues. Mr. Schott received his B.A. degree from Kent State University, his J.D. degree from Boston University School of Law, and his LL.M. degree from Georgetown University Law Center.

Emile van der Does de Willebois has degrees in law and philosophy. He started his career in 1997 working for the Office of the Prosecutor at the International Criminal Tribunal for the former Yugoslavia in the Hague, following a few months with the defense in the *Tadic* case (1996). He then moved to private practice in a law firm specializing in banking and securities law. Mr. van der Does de Willebois joined the Dutch Ministry of Finance in mid-2002, drafting AML legislation and regulations and implementing the latest Financial Action Task Force 40 Recommendations in Dutch legislation. He joined the World Bank in December 2004; since then he has been assisting countries in the Eastern Europe region and more recently in Eastern Asian Pacific countries with legislative drafting, awareness raising, and other AML/CFT-related areas.

Acronyms and Abbreviations

ACH	automated clearing house
ADB	Asian Development Bank
AIVD	Dutch General Information and Security Service
AFECEI	Investment Firms and Credit Institutions Association (France)
AML/CFT	anti-money laundering and combating the financing of terrorism
AMLEG	AML/CFT Expert Group
AMLO	Anti-Money Laundering Office (Thailand)
BCCI	Bank of Credit and Commerce International
ATM	automated teller machine
AUI	Archivo Unico Informatico (Italy)
BCBS	Basel Committee on Banking Supervision
BCP	Basel Core Principles for effective banking supervision
BIS	Bank for International Settlements
BNM	Bank Negara Malaysia
BoI	Bank of Italy
BoP	Bank of Portugal
BoS	Bank of Scotland
BoT	Bank of Thailand
BSA	Bank Secrecy Act (US)
BSAAG	Bank Secrecy Act Advisory Group
CAMEL	capital adequacy, asset quality, management factors, earnings and liquidity
CB	Commission bancaire (France)
CBFA	Banking, Finance, and Intelligence Commission
CDD	customer due diligence
CGAP	Consultative Group for the Poor
CECEI	Credit Institutions and Investment Firms Committee (France)
CenSec	Centre for the Study of Economic Crime
CIP	customer identification program
CO	compliance officer
CTR	currency transaction report

DNB	De Nederlandsche Bank
DNFBPs	Designated nonfinancial businesses and professions
EC	Essential Criteria
EAMEAP	Executives' Meeting of East Asia Pacific
FATF	Financial Action Task Force
FDIC	Federal Deposit Insurance Corporation (U.S.)
FEC	Financial Expertise Center (The Netherlands)
FIRM	Financial Institutions Risk Analysis Method ((The Netherlands)
FFIEC	U.S. Federal Financial Institutions Examination Council
FINCEN	Financial Crimes Enforcement Network (US)
FINTRAC	Financial Transaction and Reports Analysis Centre of Canada
FIU	financial intelligence unit
FSA	financial services authority (UK)
FSAP	Financial Sector Assessment Program
FSRBs	Financial Action Task Force Style Regional Bodies
FSS	Financial Supervisory Service (South Korea)
FT	financing of terrorism
GIANOS	Generatore Indici di Anomalia per Operazioni Sospette (Generator of Abnormality Indexes for Suspicious Transactions) (Italy)
HIDTA	high-intensity drug trafficking areas
HIFCA	high-intensity financial crime area
HKMA	Hong Kong Monetary Authority
IBC	International Business Corporations
IDB	Inter-American Development Bank
IFC	International Finance Corporation
IFIs	International Financial Institutions
IMF	International Monetary Fund
INCSR	International Narcotics Strategy Report (US)
IT	information technology
JFSC	Jersey Financial Services Commission
JMLSG	Joint Money Laundering Steering Group
KoFIU	Korean Financial Intelligence Unit (South Korea)
KYC	Know Your Customer
LCR	large cash reporting
LOFSA	Labuan Offshore Financial Services Authority (Malaysia)
MAS	Monetary Authority of Singapore
M-FS	mobile phone financial services
MIS	management information system
ML	money laundering
MLRO	money laundering reporting officer
MOU	memorandum of understanding

NCCT	Non-Cooperative Countries and Territories
NRA	non-resident alien
OCC	Office of the Comptroller of the Currency (U.S.)
OFAC	Office of Foreign Assets Control (U.S.)
OFC	offshore center
OSFI	Office of the Supervisor of Financial Institutions (Canada)
OTS	Office of Thrift Supervision (U.S.)
PEP	politically exposed person
PIC	private investment company
PTA	payable-through accounts
QLB	Questionnaire de Lutte Contre le Blanchiment (France)
RBS	Royal Bank of Scotland
SAR	special administrative region
SBIF	Superintendencia de Bancos e Instituciones Financieras (Chile)
SEPBLAC	Comisión de Prevención de Blanqueo de Capitales e Infracciones Monetarias (Spain)
SR	supervision and regulation
SRO	Self-Regulatory Organization
STR	Suspicious Transaction Report
TF	terrorist financing
TPO	Tripartete Overleg (Netherlands)
TRACFIN	Traitement du Renseignement et Action contre les Circuits Financiers Clandestins (France)
UFI	Unita di Informazione Financiera
UIC	Ufficio Italiano dei Cambi
UNODCCP	United Nations Office for Drug Control and Crime Prevention
WB	World Bank

Introduction

Background

Money laundering has a major impact on a country's economy because it affects economic growth. Both money laundering and terrorist financing can weaken individual banks, and they are also a threat to a country's overall financial sector reputation.[1] Combating money laundering and terrorist financing is, therefore, a key element in promoting a strong and sound financial sector.

The adverse consequences for institutions are generally described as

- *Reputational:* Clients that provide a stable deposit base and make reliable borrowers lose confidence in an institution connected with money laundering and take their business elsewhere.
- *Transactional:* Impaired internal processes or relations with other banks impede the institution, or raise its operating and funding costs.
- *Legal:* There is a risk of lawsuits, adverse judgments, unenforceable contracts, fines, and penalties, which may include license withdrawal and management dismissal (and possibly a lifetime ban from participation in the banking industry).

A key imperative for governments around the globe is to ensure that the banking system cannot be used for the purposes of money laundering/terrorist financing, and it is impossible to achieve this goal without the active involvement of bank supervisors. Difficulties with implementation, supervision, and enforcement of AML/CFT policies, procedures and rules have become an increasing concern for both developed and developing countries. Indeed, as the 2002 to 2008 Financial Sector Assessment Programs (FSAPs) reports and Financial Action Task Force[2] Style Regional Bodies (FSRBs[3]) mutual assessments show, AML/CFT supervision, in the vast majority of cases, is one of the weakest sectors of national regimes (see figure 1).

At the same time, developing countries have been increasingly asking the World Bank, the IMF, the Inter-American Development Bank (IDB), the Asian Development Bank (ADB), and other international/regional bodies, for technical

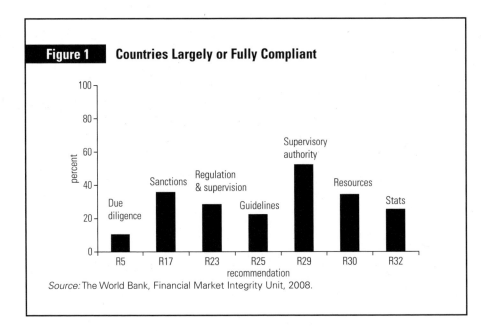

Figure 1 **Countries Largely or Fully Compliant**

Source: The World Bank, Financial Market Integrity Unit, 2008.

assistance in establishing an effective and comprehensive supervisory apparatus compliant with AML/CFT international standards. This has become a major challenge, both at national and regional levels.

The World Bank reviewed about 56 assessment reports prepared by the FATF, FSRBs, and International Financial Institutions to take stock of the implementation of AML/CFT international standards in both developed and developing countries. From the analysis of these reports, several lessons can be drawn. As shown in figure 1, supervisory compliance is generally lower than the average level of compliance with all FATF Recommendations. With the exception of Recommendation 29, the level of compliance with all Recommendations relevant to supervision matters is low (FATF Recommendations are listed in annex 9)

Objectives

This guide aims to support implementation of international standards as established by the FATF, the Basel Committee on Banking Supervision (BCBS), and other bodies, by, among other things

- Providing examples of AML/CFT supervisory regimes in both developed and developing countries
- Describing best practices that have been implemented
- Giving practical advice on how a particular jurisdiction might incorporate AML/CFT into its supervisory regime (one system is not right for all countries)

This guide also presents key elements for an effective AML/CFT on-site and off-site supervisory system and proposes appropriate tools and methodologies.

It is important to note that the examples given represent practices the authors believe can provide useful guidance to bank supervisors. They should not be regarded as definitive models, nor should it be inferred that the countries from which they are drawn are fully compliant with all applicable AML/CFT standards.

Scope

The scope of the guide is banks and does not address the securities, insurance, and microfinance sectors. The guide, therefore, encompasses the following topics:

- AML/CFT international standards that specifically apply to bank supervisors
- Objectives of a supervisory regime
- Types of risks faced by banks with regard to ML/TF (money laundering/terrorist financing) that justify implementation and enforcement of preventive measures
- Patterns of high-risk transactions and sectors that require enhanced due diligence and monitoring
- Different jurisdictional approaches to supervision (for example, the U.S., Europe, Asia)
- Licensing process, and suitable and proper tests
- On-site examination procedures and processes (preparation of the mission, scope, breakdown of tasks, and so forth.)
- Examples of methodologies and tools used by supervisors to conduct AML/CFT on-site examinations
- Off-site supervision procedures and processes (breakdown of activities, information to be collected, and so on.)
- Examples of methodologies and tools used by supervisors to conduct AML/CFT off-site supervision
- Feedback from, and useful communication with, supervised banks
- Examples of sanctions to be applied to banks with compliance deficiencies
- Sanctioning process (basic steps to be followed by the supervisor before sanctioning a bank, role of the legal department, publication of sanctions)
- Interaction between supervisors and other preventive and law enforcement agencies (FIU, prosecutor, foreign supervisory bodies)

Methodology

The core research of this guide is based on fieldwork conducted in a selection of countries where there has been significant AML/CFT supervision. The authors have made use of their own expertise and knowledge and have conducted additional research. Representation from both developing and developed countries has provided insight into varying worldwide practices and supervisory models.

The team comprised six experts from the World Bank: Pierre-Laurent Chatain, lead financial sector specialist and task team leader; Cédric Mousset and Emile van der Does de Willebois, senior financial sector specialists; and John McDowell and Paul Allan Schott, consultants. Kamil Borowik, financial analyst, was also a participant.

The team designed a list of key questions to be asked during interviews and meetings with foreign authorities so as to follow a uniform method for collecting information and data during their fieldwork. Members of the team visited the USA, four European jurisdictions (Belgium, Italy, the Netherlands, and Spain), and four Asian jurisdictions (Malaysia; South Korea; Singapore; and Hong Kong, China) as well as the offshore centers of Jersey and Labuan.

The word "bank" in this guide specifically refers to the Basel definition. The use of this definition does not prohibit a country from applying the principles of this guide to other financial institutions or to other entities covered by AML/CFT requirements. The term "AML/CFT supervisors," unless otherwise described, refers to persons supervising the compliance of banks with the requirements of AML/CFT; they might not necessarily be the primary bank supervisors. Other terminology is used in a manner that is consistent with the definitions contained in the Glossary to the FATF Methodology for Assessing Compliance with the FATF 40 Recommendations and the FATF 9 Special Recommendations (updated February 2008).

Notes

1. See Brent L. Bartlett, International Development group: Dewey Ballantine, LLP, *The Negative Effects of Money Laundering on Economic Developmen*, (Asian Development Bank, 2002)

2. The FATF is an intergovernmental body whose purpose is the development and promotion of national and international policies to combat money laundering and terrorist financing. The FATF is therefore a "policy-making body" created in 1989 that works to generate the necessary political will to bring about legislative and regulatory reforms in these areas. The FATF has published 40 + 9 Recommendations in order to meet this objective.

3. The FATF-style regional bodies have similar form and functions to those of the FATF, though on a regional basis. FSRBs, however, do not set international standards, unlike the FATF. Some FATF members are also members of these bodies. For FSRBs, see: Asian Pacific Group on Money Laundering (APG, http://apgml.org), Financial Action Task Force on Money Laundering in South America (GAFISUD, http://www.gafisud.org),

Caribbean Financial Action Task Force (CFATF, http://www. cfatf.org/), Eurasian Group (EAG, http://www.eurasiangroup.org/), Eastern and Southern Africa Anti-Money Laundering Group (ESAAMLG, http://www.esaamlg.org/), Intergovernmental Action Group against Money-Laundering in Africa (GIABA, http:// www.giabasn.org/), Middle East and North Africa Financial Action Task Force (MENAFATF, http://www.giabasn.org/)

CHAPTER 1

Designing an Effective AML/CFT Supervisory Framework

Contents

CHAPTER 1

1 Overview

A country's[1] regime to counter money laundering and the financing of terrorism has three primary objectives. The first is to deter money launderers and terrorist financiers from using a country's financial system for illicit purposes. The second is to detect money laundering (ML) and terrorist financing (TF) when and where they occur, and the third is to prosecute and punish those involved in such schemes.

There are varied reasons that an anti-money laundering (AML) and counter terrorist financing (CFT) regime is important in any country. The relevant stakeholders from a country's public sector are likely to have slightly different priorities because the stakeholders include policy makers from the legislative and governmental authorities, the judiciary, law enforcement agencies, the financial intelligence unit (FIU),[2] and from financial regulatory and supervisory authorities. But, among other things, the reasons will encompass the need to advance the domestic agenda, will enhance safe-and-sound banking practices, and will avoid or minimize negative international implications. Political will is the most important prerequisite for achieving these three objectives. A national government demonstrates its clear political commitment to establish a robust AML/CFT regime by passing appropriate laws and regulations, by granting suitable powers, by dedicating necessary resources to relevant ministries and agencies, and by prosecuting cases and obtaining convictions.

Clearly, an effective AML/CFT regime requires significant collaboration and cooperation from the country's stakeholders in the public sector. Also crucial to the success of the regime, however, are relevant stakeholders from the private sector, namely the financial institutions and designated nonfinancial businesses and professions (DNFBPs)[3] subject to compliance obligations. These should also be included in the collaborative process.

The primary responsibilities of any AML/CFT supervisor are:

• Monitor AML/CFT compliance in the banking industry
• Enforce AML/CFT regulations set out by policy makers
• Ensure a level playing field to promote fair competition in the financial sector
• Work with the industry to build an effective AML/CFT regime

AML/CFT supervision should, first, promote the overall safety and soundness of the banking system, and should help protect it from criminal acts by money launderers and terrorist financiers. While it is not usually the AML/CFT supervisor's primary role to identify and investigate individual ML/TF cases, transaction testing may be part of the supervisory process. As well, bank examiners often have to take investigative steps either to show that a transaction is suspicious or that an employee is involved in money laundering. Supervisors should also have the authority to conduct inspections (including on-site inspections) of financial institutions to ensure compliance. The inspections should include a review of customers' files and of bank policies, procedures, and books and records, and should also extend to sample testing.

There are essentially three organizational approaches to AML/CFT supervision: supervision by a bank supervisor, supervision by the FIU or other entity, and supervision shared between the FIU and the bank supervisor. In addition, there are at least eight principles policy makers need to address in order for supervisors to be able to implement an effective system. Supervisors should have adequate resources, sufficient independence, access to information, and the power both to make rules and to impose sanctions; they also should, of course, be held accountable. They should adopt either a standardized or a risk-based approach, and they should make use of both on-site and off-site supervision. Chapter 1 is broken into five main sections aimed at discussing the key considerations involved in designing and implementing an effective supervisory framework for AML/CFT. Section 1.2 discusses why AML and CFT should concern supervisors and, more generally, policy makers. Section 1.3 discusses the need for a country to demonstrate political will. Section 1.4 emphasizes the importance of a collaborative and coordinated process that should be undertaken when establishing an AML/CFT regime. Section 1.5 describes the three basic organizational models for supervision. Finally, section 1.6 discusses the different principles that should be taken into account to establish an effective AML/CFT supervisory system.

2 The Importance of AML/CFT to Policy Makers and Supervisors

This section discusses the major banking issues connected with ML and TF. While the importance of different considerations is likely to vary from country to country, policy makers and supervisors should take each of them seriously in establishing an AML/CFT supervisory framework.

2.1 International Implications

Most compliance matters for banks are domestic in nature, and, as a result, it may seem that adverse consequences for compliance failures go no further than the borders of the jurisdiction. This is not, however, the case. When a country develops a reputation for AML/CFT measures that do not meet international standards, or for lax enforcement of its regime, the result will be, at the least, an increase in the cost of doing business. Foreign institutions are highly likely to subject transactions with such countries to added scrutiny, and may even decide to terminate their relationships with business partners from those countries. Thus, the failure to have in place an effective AML/CFT regime that meets international standards could have adverse cost implications both for domestic institutions and for international trade.

2.2 Advancing the Domestic Agenda

AML and CFT both help advance a country's domestic agenda. Because ML and TF are separate crimes from the underlying criminal activity (known as the predicate offense), authorities have a separate and additional avenue for investigation and prosecution. In these cases, when the proceeds generated by the predicate offense are laundered, the subsequent investigation leads to the charge of ML. For example, if corruption, drug trafficking, trafficking in human beings or counterfeit medicines, or illegal logging are predicate offenses in a jurisdiction, the AML regime can, where relevant, be used in the fight against them and, indeed, against any other serious crime. Similarly, in a country where terrorist acts are a concern, these acts have been financed, and CFT can be brought into play as an additional means of combating such offences.

2.3 Criminal Implications

In addition to the establishment of various AML/CFT compliance obligations for banks, such as customer identification, suspicious transaction reporting, and record-keeping requirements, international standards require that the acts of ML and TF be made crimes under the laws of each jurisdiction.[4] Thus, in any individual bank, its directors, management officials, and employees can all be subject to

1

criminal prosecution and receive criminal penalties for engaging in ML or TF activities. As a result, a bank must be concerned with more than just its compliance obligations. It must also make sure that neither its directors nor its employees become engaged in criminal acts, whether accidentally or deliberately. This criminal dimension adds to the complexity and difficulty of dealing with AML/CFT issues.

2.4 Enhancing Safe and Sound Banking Practices

Certain aspects of AML obligations help reduce the incidence of criminal activity in banks. The Basel Committee on Banking Supervision (Basel Committee)[5] has issued a set of principles on bank supervision, *Core Principles for Effective Banking Supervision* (BCP), and an ancillary document, the Core Principles Methodology.[6] The Core Principles require a bank to have appropriate policies and processes in place. These include strict "know-your-customer" rules that promote high ethical and professional standards in the financial sector and that prevent the bank from being used, intentionally or unintentionally, for criminal activities.[7] In this regard, international AML/CFT standards for customer identification and due diligence[8] work to ensure that banks know and monitor their customers' records, thus decreasing the likelihood of criminal activities such as fraud.

In addition, FATF (Financial Action Task Force) Recommendation 10 (which requires banks to maintain detailed records for at least five years) helps to guarantee that a bank has reliable records in the event of litigation between a customer and a bank.

Finally, FATF Recommendation 15 requires a bank to have adequate screening procedures in place to exclude criminals and untrustworthy persons from gaining or regaining employment in banks. These procedures minimize the likelihood that employees will use the bank to further criminal activities such as fraud.

2.5 Qualitative Nature of the Risk

Unlike most prudential risks, such as liquidity, credit, or market risks, ML/TF risks are perceived from a qualitative rather than a quantitative standpoint. As a consequence, supervision of AML/CFT can be complex and difficult. For example, most banks can tolerate a certain amount of credit loss for certain types of loans, provided the overall performance for such loans remains profitable. With AML/CFT, however, there is no acceptable level of risk (except for isolated incidents) even though it is recognized that the most robust compliance program cannot prevent all ML/TF. Thus, AML/CFT supervisors must devise and apply effective mechanisms both to evaluate the quality of a bank's policies and to prevent and detect ML/TF, and also to enforce improvements in areas of identified weaknesses.

2.6 Banks Are Gatekeepers of the Financial System

In most countries, and in particular developing ones, banking is the most important part of the financial system. It is key to facilitating domestic and international payments, it serves as the intermediary for depositors and borrowers, and it provides other financially related products and services. In this regard, a country's AML/CFT regime needs to start with its banks. Because of their crucial role in the financial system, any banks not having effective AML/CFT programs are the ones most likely to be exposed to ML/TF risks, and hence can most easily be exploited by domestic and international criminals. In order to protect the integrity of its financial system, therefore, a country must have an effective AML/CFT regime that satisfies international standards.

On the other hand, some countries, particularly developing ones, must impose this regime without simultaneously making banking access too difficult or costly for their poorer citizens. These citizens may not, for example, be able to provide the required identification documents, or meet the higher costs that result from the AML/CFT. The FATF recommendations do provide sufficient flexibility to accommodate different sets of national domestic conditions and can also allow access-expanding innovations like branchless banking. It is also noteworthy that, if these citizens do find themselves discouraged from using the formal banking system, they will find alternative systems that, by definition, are subject to no controls.[9]

1

1

3   Demonstrated Political Will Is the Key to Success

In order to have a successful AML/CFT regime, any national government must have the political will to undertake all the necessary steps to establish and implement it, and having done so, the government must then demonstrate a clear commitment to the process it has put in place. This means that the government must pass and enforce appropriate laws and regulations, must dedicate the necessary resources to the task, must grant suitable powers to relevant agencies, and must prosecute cases and obtain convictions. Without such political commitment from the highest governmental levels, there is little chance for success for any AML/CFT regime. Indeed, without it, there is little incentive for officials to develop an effective AML/CFT supervisory system. That is because other stakeholders are unlikely to commit themselves either to contribute or participate effectively in the process.

4 Importance of Collaboration and Cooperation

Money laundering and terrorist financing are complex crimes and, for this reason, multiple national agencies must be involved in the various aspects of preventing, detecting, and prosecuting them. The specific agencies involved may vary from country to country, but the collaboration of the following areas is needed for an effective, overall AML/CFT regime:

- Legislature
- Executive Branch or Ministries
- Judiciary
- Law Enforcement, including police, customs, and so forth
- FIU
- Supervisors of banks, including the central bank, of other financial institutions, and of DNFBPs

Where there are different national agencies involved, there are likely to be different objectives and priorities. It is important, nevertheless, to establish a unified set of objectives and priorities for the overall regime, and to have collaboration and coordination among the various public sector constituencies.

Even so, while collaboration among the relevant public sector constituencies is necessary, it is not sufficient to assure effectiveness for a country's regime. There must also be collaboration with those private sector stakeholders (such as banks, other financial institutions, and DNFBPs), that are required to comply with the country's AML/CFT obligations. This group has specialized perspectives on the regime's objectives, as well as on the practicability of the timeframes for achieving them. In addition, the regime will be more effective overall, and the level of compliance will be higher, if the concerns of the private sector are addressed.

4.1 National Strategy

In order to establish an AML/CFT regime that meets international standards, or to strengthen an existing regime, a national strategy should have clear objectives. Most countries find this is best achieved through coordination groups comprising both public sector ministry/agency heads and representatives of the relevant private sector. The coordination group's role is to establish specific objectives and assign responsibility for achieving them, to set timeframes within which each specific objective is to be attained, and to monitor progress.

4.2 Interagency Coordination

Within the same government, different agencies often have different objectives and priorities, and this creates the potential for conflicts of interest. For example, a bank's

1

financial well-being could be seriously damaged if there were unnecessary adverse publicity from law enforcement about possible violations. Therefore, the competent authorities should strive to enhance the effectiveness of the overall regime by avoiding unwarranted repercussions.

Where compliance duties and responsibilities overlap, they cause confusion for those involved because there is potential for conflicts in the way responsibilities are interpreted. To avoid such confusion, ministries/agencies should work together to assign clear lines of responsibility under the country's AML/CFT regime. The avoidance of duplication and wasted resources is an added benefit.

Where two or more ministries/agencies have potential conflicts, procedures should be in place to resolve them if they arise. There is no single best procedural method of addressing them. Often, the agencies involved can resolve their differences by referring them to higher levels of their organizations. Other times, the coordination group itself might be asked to serve as the intermediary. In any event, it is preferable to have a resolution mechanism in place in advance to deal with any real conflict.

4.3 Implementation

Once the national strategy has been established, and areas of responsibility clarified and potential conflicts minimized, a country should establish an action plan for implementation. Many countries form implementation working groups, usually comprising lower level officials from both the public and private sector constituencies. Their role is to guide and coordinate the specific actions needed. Of course, in many cases, individual ministries/agencies are solely responsible for implementing rules and regulations, and they can independently finalize them and make them effective. Nonetheless, wherever there is collaboration and coordination, and wherever differing perspectives are taken into account, the AML/CFT regime will be more effective. This is particularly true regarding the private sector, which has the responsibility of actually carrying out the various compliance obligations.

4.4 Mutual Trust

A successful AML/CFT regime is one in which the private and public sectors have developed mutual trust. While the two have different views and priorities, they share common goals and, therefore, recognize that it is necessary to cooperate if they are to achieve an AML/CFT regime that benefits both. If the public sector is trusted by the private sector, then the private sector is encouraged to participate fully and actively in the regime. This is particularly important for suspicious transaction reporting, given the sensitive nature of the information that members of the private sector are required to submit to the public sector. This information must necessarily be accurate, effective, and of a high quality. When a regime is operating without the active and full participation of the private sector, or is characterized by mistrust between the public and private sectors, it will never be effective as it could be.

5 Organizational Approaches for Effective AML/CFT Supervision

Each jurisdiction devises and establishes its own organizational framework for AML/CFT supervision. Neither the BCPs nor the FATF international standards provide any guidance on which type of model or supervisory arrangements a country should use or which type is more effective than any other. Decisions to adopt a particular model or supervisory arrangement flow from individual national criteria, and these might be features of the domestic banking system, and/or the powers and resources of existing agencies, and/or priorities in the fight against ML and TF.

In general terms, however, based upon a review of many AML/CFT supervisory frameworks, three models exist, as shown in box 1.1:

- Supervision by the bank supervisory body
- Supervision by the FIU
- Shared supervision

BOX 1.1 **Examples of Supervisory "Business Models"**

The bank supervisory body supervises banks for AML/CFT in the cases, for example, of the Commission Bancaire Financière et des Assurances in Belgium, the Commission bancaire in France, De Nederlandsche Bank (DNB) in the Netherlands, and the Jersey Financial Services Commission in Jersey, in the Channel Islands. In Spain, this responsibility is handled by the Financial Intelligence Unit (FIU), the Comisión de Prevención de Blanqueo de Capitales e Infracciones Monetarias (SEPBLAC). In the US, multiple supervisors share supervision. These are the Federal Reserve Board, the Office of the Comptroller of the Currency (OCC), the Federal Deposit Insurance Corporation (FDIC), and the Office of Thrift Supervision (OTS). In Canada, the Financial Intelligence Unit, the Financial Transaction and Reports Analysis Centre of Canada (FINTRAC), has responsibility for AML/CFT supervision, but it relies also on the work of the Office of the Superintendent of Financial Institutions (OSFI), which is responsible for supervision of Canada's federally regulated financial sector, including banks and insurance companies.[a]

a. In Italy, the Ufficio Italiano dei Cambi formerly handled AML/CFT supervision; however, this agency was abolished on January 1, 2008, and its functions were assumed by a new, independent FIU operating under the umbrella of the Banca d'Italia.

1

5.1 Supervision by the Bank Supervisor

Supervision of AML/CFT compliance in banks by the bank supervisor is probably the most common organizational model, and it produces a number of benefits. First, supervisory bodies are usually both highly skilled and knowledgeable about assessing risks in banks, as well as about the policies and procedures to manage those risks. Second, ML/FT risks are monitored like other types of compliance risks for which bank supervisors are responsible. Third, supervisors are knowledgeable about how banks operate and about the products and services they offer. Fourth, supervisors understand the differences between the ways small local banks and large international banks operate. This international dimension to the supervisor's responsibilities is particularly useful in cross-border supervision.

Finally, most bank supervisors have at least some experience in enterprise-wide, consolidated supervision. Many banking institutions are part of large financial organizations, and these include securities firms, insurance companies, and other types of financial entities. Such organizations often adopt an enterprise-wide approach to AML/CFT compliance, just as they do to risks in consolidated credit, market, or general operations. This approach requires a consolidated understanding of the entire organization's risk exposure for ML/TF across all activities, business lines, and legal entities. Such a centralized function often includes the ability for the organization to comprehend the enterprise-wide, indeed worldwide, exposure of a given customer, particularly one considered to be high risk. It is a complex undertaking, but bank supervisors are well equipped to understand the capabilities and limitations of such a system.

This model does have some disadvantages. Bank supervisors, because of prudential concerns, may not give AML/CFT the same priority as governments do, or may not have sufficient resources to do so. In consequence, compliance issues may get neither the quantity nor quality of attention that is necessary. As well, supervising compliance with the AML/CFT regime is not a traditional prudential supervisory responsibility. It is a new concept to some extent, not only for bank staff, but also for the supervisory body, which must learn new skills. This situation may initially be reflected in staff difficulties.

5.2 Supervision by the FIU or Other Entity

As an alternative to the bank supervisory model, AML/CFT compliance supervision may be conducted by the FIU or another governmental agency. Under this model, it is the FIU (or alternative), not the bank supervisory body, which must be authorized, first, to have access to all relevant bank information and, second, to conduct examinations. Such authority is needed to enable the FIU or governmental supervisor to determine a bank's compliance with its AML/CFT obligations.

This model has a number of benefits. First, because collection of information and analysis are the core of its duties, the FIU has expertise in certain AML/CFT matters. Second, AML and CFT are its only responsibilities. Third, the FIU has direct access to suspicious transactions reports (STRs) and related information. According to FATF Recommendation 26, the FIU should have timely access, directly or indirectly, to the financial, administrative, and law-enforcement information required for it to undertake its functions properly, and these include the analysis of STRs.

This model also presents several drawbacks. If the FIU is the supervisor, it may well be inexperienced both in financial inspections and in bank supervisory matters. As well, the FIU is not likely to be sufficiently well equipped to undertake AML/CFT supervision on an enterprise-wide basis. On the other hand, if a body other than the FIU is the supervisor, that body may well not have access to STR information. Examinations are likely to become more limited in scope and expertise, and multiple regulators and different approaches to compliance supervision may generate some confusion for banks.

5.3   Supervision Shared between the FIU and the Bank Supervisor

The third model is to have AML/CFT supervision responsibilities shared between the FIU and the bank supervisor (see box 1.2). This model has one important potential benefit. Because it may well facilitate the sharing of personnel, information, expertise, and other resources between the two entities, the overall quality of AML/CFT supervision should eventually be enhanced.

BOX 1.2   **Example of Shared Supervision**

In Canada, the FIU (FINTRAC) retains accountability for ensuring compliance, but the OSFI (the federal banking/insurance regulator) carries out day-to-day AML/CFT assessments. OSFI and FINTRAC are authorized to share information with each other on entities regulated by OSFI that are subject to the Canadian AML requirement. To operate this authority, OSFI and FINTRAC have entered into a memorandum of understanding laying out precisely which information each will share with the other. OSFI and FINTRAC meet regularly to discuss the results of OSFI's work and FINTRAC's analysis of STR and other filings made by OSFI-supervised entities. The arrangement ensures that duplication of effort is avoided and also provides a forum for discussing emerging AML supervisory issues to ensure that both agencies form a broad and shared view of acceptable risk management practices.

1

This model could, however, produce some difficulties because it requires clear delineations of responsibilities and coordination of supervisory activities, as well as a mechanism for resolving conflicts. Unless the lines of responsibility are clearly delineated, duplicate supervision can result in overlaps that waste resources for both banks and supervisors. Conversely, but for the same reason, there may be gaps in supervision, where each agency wrongly believes the other agency is responsible for a particular area. It is also possible that the two agencies will interpret a bank's AML/CFT obligations differently.

6 Principles for an Effective AML/CFT Supervisory Framework

1

In addition to adopting a supervision model, policy makers, in establishing and subsequently implementing an effective supervisory framework, need to be guided by a number of principles. The following list is not exhaustive, but reflects the best practices observed in many countries.

Supervisors should be

- Granted sufficient independence to be effective,
- Held accountable,
- Granted powers to access information,
- Authorized to make rules,
- Authorized to impose appropriate sanctions, and
- Provided with adequate resources.

The framework should

- Adopt either a standardized or risk-based approach and
- Use both on-site and off-site supervision.

6.1 Independence[10]

While the organizational structure surrounding AML/CFT supervision may vary from country to country, the AML/CFT supervising authority, whether it is the bank supervisor, the FIU, or some other government agency, must have independence. Unless provisions are already in place to guarantee this, such independence for the AML/CFT supervisor should be made clear in the mandate of responsibilities, possibly with a specific grant of authority.

Independence, in general, means that the day-to-day activities of the supervisor are not subject to external direction or control by, for example, the government or by the banking industry. This means that these outside agencies cannot influence particular matters, such as examination decisions or enforcement actions for particular banks. On the other hand, it does not mean that the supervisor's overall direction and policy cannot be influenced by either the legislature or by government policy makers. In other words, the supervisor is not free to act irresponsibly. Nor does independence mean that the supervising authority should not be held accountable for its actions.

Independence should apply to all the different supervisory activities. These include issuing budgets and regulations, exercising enforcement authority, conducting examinations, and setting specific supervisory policies and procedures. Supervisory staff themselves are not independent, but report to the heads of the AML/CFT

1

supervisory body. In France, for example, the general secretariat of the Banking Commission is an independent administrative authority, and the board of the Commission comprises two independent magistrates from the highest national jurisdictions (Court of Cassation and State Council). In the US, the heads of all five bank regulatory agencies and their respective board members serve for specific terms of five or seven years, rather than at the discretion of the President.

6.2 Accountability

Policy makers are faced with the challenge to balance the supervising authority's independence with its accountability to the public good, to the government, and to the banks the supervisor regulates. While the AML/CFT supervisor's independence is of paramount importance, therefore, it is vital that the agency be well governed and accountable for fulfilling its responsibility effectively and efficiently.[11] A review by the legislature, an external audit by competent authorities, and disclosure and external oversight providing, for example, a regular public report of activities, are all effective methods of assuring accountability. Accountability also plays a significant role building trust between the public and that part of the private sector that has compliance obligations. The private sector (as well as the general public) is more likely to have confidence in governmental institutions that are accountable both for their actions and the manner in which they carry out their responsibilities. High integrity in staff and good practices in governance both contribute to the accountability of the AML/CFT supervisor.[12]

In France, for example, the Governor of the Banque de France (the Central Bank), who is also the head of the independent supervisory body for AML/CFT, the Commission bancaire, reports the Central Bank's activities to the public annually through the Parliament. The Central Bank is also subject to independent institutions, the Cour des Comptes and the Inspection Générale des Finances, which are responsible for the oversight of public systems. In addition, the Commission bancaire is required to disclose an overview of its operations to the public. The overview takes the form of an annual report, which includes, for example, the number of on-site visits, of sanctions imposed on noncompliant financial institutions, and of follow-up letters sent about bank inspections. Bank inspections primarily serve two purposes: first, assessing the agency's internal organization and, second, evaluating its efficient use of public funding.

In the United States, all bank regulatory agencies are required to file publicly available annual reports. These provide a detailed description of the agencies' initiatives; financial management results; enforcement actions; and their outreach to industry, community, and consumer organizations.

In Canada, both OSFI and FINTRAC are legally required to present Parliament annually with reports on their activities as specified in their legislated mandates, and also on their plans and priorities for the coming fiscal year.

6.3   Access to Information

International standards to combat ML/TF provide that the supervisory body should have adequate powers to monitor and ensure compliance by banks, including the authority to compel the banks' production of any information relevant to monitoring such compliance.[13] To fulfill its mandate, therefore, a supervisory body must have unfettered access to complete bank information. The supervisor must not be hampered by any kind of bank secrecy laws that could restrict access to relevant information provided in a timely manner.[14] Similarly, access to customer information should be granted, without limitation, about lines of business, geography, customer category, or type of operation.

As part of the monitoring process, the supervisor must determine if the bank's process for filing STRs adequately meets its reporting obligations. Supervisors, therefore, require on-site access to STR files.[15]

The supervisor may also need to ask the FIU for access to certain kinds of information such as reports on trends, typologies, and alerts. These are helpful both to bank regulators and to commercial banks and do not compromise the confidentiality set out in a country's money laundering laws.

6.4   Authority to Make Rules

The AML/CFT supervisor, as the body that evaluates bank compliance, is in the best position to determine bank compliance requirements and, therefore, to issue rules, regulations, and other forms of guidance. The supervisor, however, may require specific authority to do this, and the jurisdiction should, therefore, take appropriate measures, including legislative action, to provide it.

Rules and regulations should be issued in a clear, precise, manner, so the meaning of such rules can be easily understood by those that have to comply with them. Insufficient clarity may jeopardize effective implementation and prevent a level playing field. This in turn will lead to confusion and to an uneven application of the rule, hampering the supervisory body from attaining its ultimate compliance objective. Both the public and private sector benefit when supervisors and banks collaborate to produce clear rules and regulations.

6.5   Sanctioning Powers

International standards require a country to establish effective, proportionate, and dissuasive sanctions, criminal, civil and/or administrative, to deal with relevant financial institutions, and with DNFBPs that fail to abide by their compliance obligations.[16] The same standards specifically provide that the AML/CFT supervisor be lawfully vested with adequate power both to monitor and to ensure compliance, as well as to impose administrative sanctions on noncompliant institutions.[17]

1

For banks, administrative sanctions include remedial action as well as money penalties and other disciplinary measures, and they apply to directors, officers, and employees. These sanctions could include the imposition of a lifetime ban on employment at any bank. Such administrative action can usually be applied with more promptness and efficiency than can civil proceedings, even though civil suits may be used to appeal it. The aim is to cure the deficiencies, rather than penalize the bank, and it is the supervisor who is in the best position to recognize the need for corrective action.

The sanctions imposed should be proportionate to the severity of the compliance deficiency, and they should have a deterrent effect on the banking industry as well as on the subject bank. These penalties, moreover, may differ from and be in addition to those that may be imposed by criminal courts.

Finally, the sanctioning mechanism must comply with the legal system of the jurisdiction, and must provide for all of the rights of any person or entity accused of violating civil or criminal AML/CFT laws or regulations.

6.6   Adequate Resources

International standards require a country to provide AML/CFT supervisors with the financial, human, and technical resources they need. These resources should correspond with the size, level of risk, and quality of AML/CFT controls in the banking sector.

Unfortunately, scarcity of resources is a widespread problem in almost all jurisdictions. The scarcity can be multifaceted, limiting both the numbers of technically skilled persons and the funds to train them. It can limit resources that would supply, for example, computers and programming. Even in developed, well-resourced economies, because of the complexity and sophistication of the banking systems, the resources are often deemed inadequate to meet the need for highly experienced staff and analytical tools. It is vital that AML/CFT regimes be effective, and for this, sufficient funding must be provided. As shown in box 1.3, the use of external auditors can be an option.

Finally, human and technical resources must include adequate resources for the appropriate training of supervisory staff. Employees at all levels need continual training on the application of new laws and preventive measures, as well as on new interpretations of existing matters. In addition, training programs need to keep abreast of ever-changing ML/FT techniques and tactics.

6.7   Standardized and Risk-Based Approaches

AML/CFT supervision is similar to other types of supervision with respect to approaches to examinations, including prudential and other compliance issues. In general, there are two approaches: the standardized approach and the risk-based approach.

1

> ### BOX 1.3 The Use of External Auditors
>
> In some countries, the AML/CFT supervisor commissions external auditors to conduct on-site work. This may be a reasonable option in jurisdictions where the supervisor does not have the in-house resources to do such work, although it may be difficult to find auditors with specific expertise in AML/CFT evaluations.
>
> Although the experts' products may provide the supervisor with valuable information, they do not, by any means, discharge the supervisor from the responsibility of assessing the bank's compliance with its AML/CFT obligations. In any case, it is useful if external auditors, when permitted by the law, report any compliance deficiencies or evidence of inadequate ML/TF risk management to the supervisor, even if the auditor is not part of the examination process. In Belgium, external auditors have to assess internal control frameworks and must report any shortcoming to the Banking, Finance, and Insurance Commission (CBFA). In Spain, since 2005, external auditors are required to review the structure and effectiveness of the AML frameworks of banks and report their conclusions to the Spanish FIU (SEPBLAC).

The standardized approach has two basic versions. The first is a "one size fits all" concept and is predicated upon the idea that all banks within the jurisdiction, regardless of their size, geographic location, or nature of business, should be inspected under the same procedures in the same given time period (usually one to three years). The second version is similar, but uses a separate, but identical, procedure for banks having a certain size, geographic location, type of business, or other category. Both of these versions are simple and uniform (and can be combined as shown in box 1.4).

The risk-based approach is predicated upon a prioritization of time and resources in the examination process and is based upon an assessed risk of ML and/or TF in a given bank. The assessment can be based upon a number of factors, such as geography, bank products and services, types of customers, or banks with prior AML/CFT deficiencies. The key advantage of this approach is that resources, which may be limited, are used more efficiently because they concentrate on those banks perceived by the supervisor as being riskier than others. The assessment of risk also helps the supervisor to develop the scope of examinations, staffing and expertise, as well as to determine whether a comprehensive or focused inspection should be conducted.[18]

6.8 On-Site and Off-Site Supervision

Under international standards, a country is required to empower the AML/CFT supervisor to monitor and ensure that banks and other financial institutions comply

1

BOX 1.4 **Example from Canada**

The Office of the Superintendent of Financial Institutions (OSFI) has implemented an approach that essentially combines features of the standardized and the risk-based approach. Based on its analysis of the ML risk profile of each bank or life insurance company, OSFI assigns one of three risk rankings to the financial institutions it supervises. The risk levels are based on a combination of factors: size; number of branches; existence of foreign operations; and products offered that are generally considered more susceptible to laundering (such as wire transfer services and single premium policies). Based on the analysis against these criteria, each entity or group is ranked as High- Medium- or Low-risk. High-risk entities are put in a planned assessment cycle of every three years, with ongoing monitoring and updating. Medium- and Low-risk entities are subject to four- and five-year cycles, again subject to review if the results of monitoring indicate a change is merited.

---

with their obligations under the country's regime.[19] Most countries carry out their monitoring responsibilities through the examination process. In addition, the Basel Committee emphasizes that an effective banking supervisory system should include both on-site and off-site supervision as well as regular contacts with bank management.[20] Similarly, an effective AML/CFT supervisory system applies both on- and off-site supervision.[21] The percentage of time dedicated to either on- or off-site supervision depends on a number of factors, including the quantity and quality of information available from external sources, the data provided by the banks, prior examination reports, and the sophistication of existing analytical models.

In many countries, accurate analytical models are still in development and are not widely available. In addition, where it is still a developing concept, off-site AML/CFT supervision is largely ancillary to on-site supervision.

Notes

1. The terms "country" and "jurisdiction" are used interchangeably in this handbook, and such terms also mean a territory or other political subdivision of a country or jurisdiction.

2. According to the Egmont Group, which is the international body for FIUs, an FIU is "a central, national agency responsible for receiving (and, as permitted, requesting), analyzing and disseminating to the competent authorities, disclosures of financial information: (i) concerning suspected proceeds of crime and potential financing of terrorism, or (ii) required by national legislation or regulation, in order to counter money laundering and terrorism financing." See www.egmontgroup.org.

3. FATF defines DNFBPs to be casinos; real estate agents; dealers in precious metals or stones; lawyers, notaries, other independent legal professionals and accountants (under certain circumstances); and trust company service providers (with respect to certain services). See Glossary of FATF Forty Recommendations on Money Laundering for more specific details. www.fatf-gafi.org.

4. FATF recommendation 1.

5. The Basel Committee on Banking Supervision is a committee of banking supervisory authorities that was established by the central bank Governors of the G10 countries in 1975. It is made up of senior representatives of banking supervisory authorities and central banks from Belgium, Canada, France, Germany, Italy, Japan, Luxembourg, the Netherlands, Spain, Sweden, Switzerland, the United Kingdom, and the United States. It usually meets at the Bank for International Settlements in Basel, where its permanent secretariat is located.

6. www.bis.org/list/bcbs/tid_25/index.htm.

7. BCP principle 18.

8. FATF recommendations 5 and 6.

9. These aspects are fully discussed in annex 1.

10. See Basel Committee Core Principles, Methodology, principle 1(2).

11. The FATF international standards do not specifically address governance and accountability but do embrace the BCPs. Principle 1 of the BCP states that the bank supervisor should have sound governance and be accountable for the discharge of its duties. See www.bis.org/publications.

12. FATF recommendation 30 requires a country to have processes in place to ensure that the staffs of all competent authorities involved with AML/CFT are of high integrity.

13. FATF recommendation 29.

14. FATF recommendation 4: "Countries should ensure that financial institution secrecy laws do not inhibit implementation of the FATF Recommendations."

15. It is recognized that in some countries, privacy legislation may prohibit the supervisor from having access to individual STR files.

16. FATF recommendation 17.

1

17. See chapter 6 for further details.
18. For further details, see FATF guidance on the Risk-Based Approach to combating Money Laundering and Terrorist Financing, High Level Principles and Procedures, June 2007, available at http://www.fatf-gafi.org/dataoecd/43/46/38960576.pdf.
19. FATF recommendation 29.
20. BCP principle 20.
21. Discussed in chapters 4 and 5, respectively.

Risk Management in Combating Money Laundering and Terrorist Financing

Contents

CHAPTER 2

1 Overview

In their efforts to combat money laundering and terrorism financing, banks can approach the management of risk either from the perspective of the individual bank or from the perspective of the bank supervisor. Ideally, these two perspectives should be, but in fact may not be, essentially the same. Both the bank and the bank supervisor, however, are able to benefit from the other's point of view.

A number of specific risks to banks are inherent in money laundering and terrorist financing. These risks are not mutually exclusive and, indeed, are often interrelated. The risks concern

- Compliance and legal issues,
- Reputation,
- Operational or transaction issues,
- Strategic issues, and
- Liquidity.

From the perspective of the individual bank, a risk assessment is a crucial part of the risk management process. The first step in the assessment is to understand the main types of criminal activity likely to generate proceeds that could then be the subject of money laundering at that bank. These types of activity are likely to differ in different local circumstances, but banks should look for direction to their fellow bankers and to neighboring countries with similar products and services, customers, and locations.

Examples of criminal activity include drug trafficking, arms smuggling, and corruption. Part of the risk management process is to identify vulnerable areas, such as specific

- Products,
- Services,
- Customers (both natural and legal persons), and
- Geographic locations.

The second step is to analyze the data applicable to specific risk categories and to reach some conclusions about the bank's vulnerabilities. There are a number of factors to be considered in this aspect of the analysis, which should include statistical assessments. Among these factors are the purpose of the customer's account, the nature of the customer's business, and the types of transactions involved. Banks that understand these risks are in a better position to establish appropriate controls and procedures to mitigate them.

From the perspective of the bank supervisor, the first move is to review the individual bank's risk assessment process to determine if the assessment performed by the bank reasonably identifies money laundering and terrorist financing risks. In doing so, the supervisor will need to evaluate all relevant factors, including those that should have been considered by the bank, such as total asset size, customer base, products and services offered, and branch locations. The supervisor should apply a personal awareness of the risks associated with these factors and with the particular bank and use the expertise of other competent authorities knowledgeable about money laundering and terrorist financing, such as the financial intelligence unit (FIU) and law enforcement agencies. An understanding of the most current typologies and trends is helpful.

The supervisor must then decide whether the individual bank's risk assessment is adequate, so as to determine whether modifications to it are needed. If the bank has not performed its own risk assessment, the supervisor will need to develop a preliminary risk profile based on the analysis of the above-mentioned factors.

The supervisor should establish the scope of examinations based upon the risk profile determined either by the bank or as established by the supervisor. The on-site examination should, in part, be used to determine the accuracy of the individual bank's risk profile and the adequacy of its mitigating controls.

This chapter is broken into four main sections. Section 2.2 introduces the anti-money laundering and combating the financing of terrorism (AML/CFT) risk management process. Section 2.3 discusses the specific risks associated with money laundering, terrorist financing, and related compliance issues. Section 2.4 reviews the risk assessment process from the individual bank's perspective. Finally, section 2.5 presents the expected outcomes of the ML/FT risk assessment.

2 Introduction to Money Laundering/Terrorist Financing Risk Management

Banks should have effective programs in place to combat money laundering and the financing of terrorism (AML/CFT). Such programs address the risks posed by money launderers and terrorists attempting to gain access to, and make use of, the financial system, and they enhance the ability of banks to identify, monitor, and assist in deterring such activities. These programs help banks to maintain the sound reputation they need to compete successfully both domestically and internationally.

A successful program of this kind will include a mechanism to identify those potential areas of vulnerability that should be effectively addressed by the bank. Identifying and taking appropriate actions to mitigate these vulnerabilities is a critical element of a bank's overall program, and helps to control the risks associated with money laundering and financing of terrorism (ML/FT). Bank supervisors will then review the bank's processes and evaluate the level of risk the bank faces and the bank's effectiveness in addressing it. When assessing a bank's risk evaluation processes for AML/CFT, bank supervisors will assess the ability of management and the directors to measure, monitor, and control the risks assumed by the bank.

2

3 Overview of the Risks Associated with Money Laundering, Terrorist Financing, and Related Compliance Issues

Money laundering and terrorist financing can pose numerous risks to the bank. There are five major areas of risk to consider:

- Compliance and legal risk
- Operational or transaction risk
- Reputational risk
- Credit risk
- Liquidity risk

Far from being mutually exclusive, these risks are often inter-related, and each can have a direct influence upon any of the others. Effectively managing them is important to the stability both of the banking environment and of an individual bank.

3.1 Compliance and Legal Risk

Compliance and Legal risk,[1] which is associated with poor practices such as ineffective internal control policies and procedures or with ineffective ethical standards, can adversely affect both capital and earnings. A bank faces increased compliance and legal risk when it violates or ignores laws, rules, and regulations designed to prevent either money laundering or terrorist financing. The bank's risk can also increase if its laws and/or rules governing bank products, activities, or clients are either ambiguous or untested. When countries are serious about combating money laundering and terrorist financing, such violations or non-conformance may result in bank fines, civil financial penalties, payments of damages, or litigation of various kinds.

Compliance/legal risk often blends with and increases operational risks and risks associated with transaction processing.

3.2 Operational or Transaction Risk

Operational or transaction risk[2] arises when fraud and errors are not successfully controlled, and, in consequence, an adverse effect occurs, first, on a bank's ability to deliver either products or services and, second, on the bank's ability to maintain a competitive position within the banking system. This risk can arise in any product or service that can be used to launder money or finance terrorism. Such products and services can include deposit-taking, lending, correspondent banking activities, trust department activities, electronic banking processes, or private banking activities, and many others. Bank management can effectively control operational or transaction risk through a system of sound internal controls and information systems and by implementing policies that enhance employee integrity and effective operating processes.

3.3 Reputational Risk

A country can grow and prosper only within a sound economic environment, and the reputation of a country's banks, both domestically and internationally, is vital to maintaining such an environment. A bank that does not have sound anti-money laundering and anti-terrorist financing programs in place may become tainted by such activities and will thus increase its reputation risk (see box 2.1). A bank's ability to service existing relationships or to establish new ones is easily damaged by adverse publicity and opinions.

To protect its national and international reputation, a bank must exercise caution when transacting business both with customers and with the communities in which they operate. As a bank's vulnerability to adverse public reaction increases, its ability to offer competitive products and services may also be adversely affected, causing an overall decline in the condition of the bank.

2

BOX 2.1   Reputational Damage: The Case of Riggs Bank

Riggs National Bank, in Washington, DC, was fined more than $40 million because of serious deficiencies in its AML program, including in its private banking practice. Riggs opened multiple private banking accounts for former Chilean dictator Augusto Pinochet, among other politically exposed persons, accepting millions of dollars in deposits under various corporate and individual account names and paying little or no attention to suspicious activity in these accounts. As a consequence, many customers terminated their business relationships with the bank. The reputational damage prevented the bank from attracting new business. Management was distracted from normal business activities. Although not closed by regulators, the bank lost earnings and could not succeed in profitable banking. It was soon purchased by another banking organization.[a]

a. For a complete analysis, see Money Laundering and Foreign Corruption: Enforcement and Effectiveness of the Patriot Act, a case study involving Riggs Bank, report prepared by the minority staff of the permanent subcommittee on investigations, United States Senate, July 15, 2004.

3.4 Credit Risk

Credit risk is present in all lending activities and comes into play when bank funds are extended through actual or implied contractual agreements. The risk itself lies in a borrower's potential failure to meet the terms or conditions of the lending contract. When a bank extends credit to those engaged in criminal activities, such as money laundering or the terrorist financing, its overall credit risk will increase substantially.

Money launderers and those who finance terrorist activities may have little or no intention of repaying the borrowed funds. They frequently establish credit through identity theft or other criminal means, and their guarantors and counter-parties are very likely to be nonexistent.

In any event, banks involved in international lending face heightened credit risk as a matter of course. Effective customer identity policies and procedures, both for domestic and international lending, are critical to controlling credit risk to the bank.

3.5 Liquidity Risk

An increase in liquidity risk occurs when a bank is no longer able to meet its obligations as they come due without incurring unacceptable losses. Among these risks, for example, is the inability to manage unplanned decreases or changes in sources of funding. Liquidity risk can arise from the failure of the bank's management to recognize or address market condition changes that affect the bank's ability to liquidate assets quickly with minimal loss.

A bank's liquidity can be detrimentally affected by adverse publicity related either to money laundering violations or to involvement in terrorist financing activities. Customers, upon hearing of the bank's involvement, may decide to withdraw funds or to discontinue using the bank's services. Additionally, other financial institutions, such as correspondent banks, may cut off funding sources that would otherwise have been available. Agreements between borrower and lender banks generally include clauses that enable the funding bank to withhold funds if the borrowing bank violates certain laws or otherwise puts the bank's solvency at risk. While alternative funding sources may be available, they are likely to be from nontraditional sources and at a higher cost. The results can be extremely detrimental to the overall stability of the bank. The ongoing financial turmoil makes this risk even greater.

4 The ML/FT Risk Assessment Process from the Bank Perspective

4.1 Bank's Risk Assessment Process

As part of its risk management, and as the first step of any ML/FT risk assessment, a bank should understand the main criminal threats to which it might be exposed, for example, drug trafficking, arms smuggling, and corruption. Only banks with effective analyses of the risks involved are sufficiently well equipped to take the appropriate actions to mitigate them. A reasonably designed risk-based approach will provide a framework for identifying the degree of potential money laundering risks associated with specific customers and transactions, and allow an institution to focus on those customers and transactions that potentially pose the greatest risk of money laundering.[3] Having analyzed the money laundering or terrorist financing risk, bank management should then communicate those risks to all business lines, to other management, to the board of directors, and to all appropriate staff. To communicate the risk effectively, the assessment should, wherever possible, be written in language that can be easily understood by those who will use it, including the bank's supervisors.

Some jurisdictions have a mandatory requirement for banks to conduct self-assessments. Canada, for example, recently added this requirement to its anti-money laundering legislation. Banks must have compliance programs in place, and must initiate and document a review of relevant policies and procedures, risk assessment processes, and training programs in order to evaluate their effectiveness. An internal or external auditor must carry out this review every two years.

4.2 Identifying Specific Risk Categories

The bank, then, must first identify the specific products, services, customers, entities, and geographic locations that pose a money laundering risk to the bank. Such threats, arising from attempts to conduct illegal activities through a bank, can come from many different sources throughout the system. Certain products, services, customers, and geographic locations in which the bank operates may be particularly vulnerable, or may have been historically used by criminals for money laundering or terrorist funding activities.

The risks vary depending on the specific characteristics of these sources of illegal activity. When preparing risk assessments, banks should consider factors such as the number and volume of transactions, the nature of the customer relationships, and whether, for example, interaction with customers is face-to-face or via electronic banking (for example, internet banking, mobile banking).

An effective risk assessment is an ongoing process. Risk levels may change as new products are offered, as new markets are entered, as high-risk customers open or close accounts, or as the bank's products, services, policies, and procedures change. The bank should therefore update its risk assessment periodically to take account of these changes.

4.2.1 Products and Services Evaluation

Some bank products and services, as noted above, may pose a higher risk of money laundering or terrorist financing at one bank than at another. A higher degree of risk may exist in cases where, for example, a bank's products and services allow the customer to be treated anonymously, or involve international transactions, or involve high volumes of currency (or currency equivalent) transactions. These categories can include the following:[4]

- Electronic funds payment services: electronic cash such as stored value cards or payroll cards, domestic and international funds transfers, payable upon proper identification (PUPID) transactions, and third-party payment processors; remittance activity; automated clearing house (ACH) transactions; automated teller machines (ATMs); and Mobile Phone Financial Services (M-FS)[5]
- Electronic banking
- Foreign exchange and funds transfers
- Domestic and international private banking
- Trust and asset management services
- Monetary instruments
- Foreign correspondent accounts, such as pouch activity; payable through accounts (PTAs); and foreign currency denominated accounts
- Trade finance or letters of credit
- Special use, or concentration, accounts
- Lending activities, particularly loans secured by cash collateral and marketable securities
- Account services such as nondeposit investment products or insurance products

4.2.2 Individual Customers and Entities

All types of account or customers may, in certain circumstances, become vulnerable to money laundering or terrorist financing. Certain customers and entities may pose specific risks depending on the nature of the business, the occupation of the customer, or the nature of anticipated transaction activity. Though, of course, not all categories of customers pose the same level of risk, banks must always use sound judgment to determine and define the level of risk for each individual customer. To assess customer risk accurately, banks should consider such variables as the customers' geographical location and the services they seek. The following list, although not exhaustive, indicates the customers and entities that are likely to pose a higher level of risk to the bank:[6]

- Foreign financial institutions, including banks and foreign money services providers such as bureaus de change, currency exchanges, and money transmitters
- Nonbank financial institutions such as money services businesses, casinos and card clubs, brokers/dealers in securities, and dealers in precious metals, stones, or jewels
- Senior foreign political figures, which can include their immediate family members and close associates, collectively known as politically exposed persons (PEPs)
- Nonresident aliens (NRAs) and accounts held by foreign individuals
- Foreign corporations and domestic business entities, particularly offshore corporations such as domestic shell companies, private investment companies (PICs) and international business corporations (IBCs) located in high-risk geographic locations
- Deposit brokers, particularly foreign deposit brokers
- Cash-intensive businesses, including, for example, convenience stores, restaurants, retail stores, liquor stores, cigarette distributors, privately owned ATMs, and vending machine operators
- Foreign and domestic nongovernmental organizations and charities
- Professional service providers such as attorneys, accountants, or real estate brokers

4.2.3 Geographic Locations

While a bank must identify domestic and international geographic locations that may pose a higher risk to its AML/CFT compliance program, it also should understand that geographic risk alone does not necessarily mean a customer's or transaction's risk level is either high or low. Banks should evaluate cases individually when assessing the risks associated with doing business, such as opening accounts or facilitating transactions, in certain geographic locations.

A country's bank supervisors should assist the banks they supervise in identifying geographic areas of concern both inside and outside the country. To help guide banks, supervisors should work with law enforcement agencies, the FIU, as well as others, such as local and regional AML/CFT organizations, to develop a list of high-risk areas (see box 2.2.). This listing will vary depending upon the country.

4.3 Analysis of Specific Risk Categories

The second step of the bank's risk assessment process is a detailed analysis of the data obtained during the identification stage, allowing the bank to assess ML/FT

2

BOX 2.2 **Example of the U.S. Guidance for High-Risk Geographic Locations**

- Countries subject to the US Department of the Treasury Office of Foreign Assets Control (OFAC) sanctions, including state sponsors of terrorism
- Countries identified as supporting international terrorism under section 6(j) of the United States Export Administration Act of 1979, as determined by the United States Secretary of State
- Jurisdictions determined to be "of primary money laundering concern" by the United States Secretary of the Treasury, and jurisdictions subject to special measures imposed by the Secretary of the Treasury, through the Financial Crimes Enforcement Network (FinCEN), pursuant to section 311 of the USA PATRIOT Act
- Jurisdictions or countries identified as noncooperative by the Financial Action Task Force on Money Laundering (FATF)[a]
- Major money laundering countries and jurisdictions identified in the United States Department of State's annual International Narcotics Control Strategy Report (INCSR), in particular, countries identified as jurisdictions of primary concern
- Other countries identified by the bank as high risk because of its prior experiences or other factors such as legal considerations or allegations of official corruption

Domestic high-risk geographic locations may include, but are not limited to, banking offices doing business within, or having customers located within, a government-designated high-risk geographic location, including those designated by the United States. Domestic high-risk geographic locations can include

- High Intensity Drug Trafficking Areas (HIDTA),
- High Intensity Financial Crime Areas (HIFCA).

a. As of March 2009, there are no Non-Cooperative Countries and Territories on the FATF list.

---

risk more accurately. The bank evaluates data pertaining to its activities, which should be considered in relation both to the bank's Customer Identification Program (CIP) and to customer due diligence (CDD) information.

The data includes, but is not limited to the following:

- The number of domestic and international funds transfers
- Private banking customers
- Foreign correspondent accounts

- Payable through accounts (PTAs)
- Domestic and international geographic locations of the bank's business area and customer transactions

This more detailed analysis is important as a step in the assessment process because individual account holders will pose varying levels of risk within any type of product or category. It also provides management with a better understanding of the bank's risk profile and will assist management in developing appropriate policies, procedures, and processes to mitigate the overall risk to the bank. While the level and sophistication of the specific risk categories will vary from bank to bank, analysis of the data pertaining to the bank's activities should specifically take into account, as appropriate, the following:

- Purpose of the account
- Actual or anticipated activity in the account
- Nature of the customer's business
- Customer's location
- Types of products and services a customer uses

The value of this two-step risk assessment process can be illustrated by the following examples. In the first step of the process, the collected data may indicate that a bank processes an average of 100 international funds transfers per day. In the second step, the analysis may show that approximately 90 percent of the funds transfers are recurring, well-documented transactions for long-term customers. On the other hand, it may show that 90 percent of these transfers are nonrecurring or are for noncustomers. While the numbers are the same for these two examples, the overall risks are quite different.

4.4 Bank Supervisor's Analysis

Bank supervisors then review a bank's risk assessment process for AML/CFT activities to determine whether the bank has adequately identified the level of risk it has assumed.[7] They will use the information reviewed, and the conclusions they have reached about the bank's process, to determine the scope of the AML/CFT examination. Supervisors must complete their own risk analysis in cases where the bank has done an inadequate one or failed to do one at all. This analysis will be undertaken for the sole purpose of the on-site examination.[8] They will determine the bank's risk profile and, following identification of a shortcoming, will seek appropriate corrective action. The supervisors will use all relevant information available in order to determine the risk to the bank, and they will expand the scope of the AML/CFT examination appropriately. Additionally, if they find that the bank's process is not acceptable in any category, the supervisors must discuss appropriate corrective action with bank management.

The bank supervisor performing the analysis of the bank's process must be knowledgeable about AML/CFT in general, and must have sufficient knowledge of the bank's risks to determine whether the bank's program is adequate and whether it provides the controls needed to mitigate money laundering and terrorist financing risks. In some cases, the supervisor may determine that the bank has a high-risk profile during the examination planning process, but may find through the examination process that the bank adequately addresses those risks through its compliance program. In other cases, the supervisor may think the bank's risk profile is low, but may find during the examination that the bank's compliance program does not adequately mitigate or control the risks identified.

2

5 Expected Outcomes of the ML/FT Risk Assessment

5.1 Banks' Areas of Responsibility

5.1.1 Using the Risk Assessment to Develop the Bank's AML/CFT Programs

An effective risk management process will enable bank management and the board of directors to develop AML/CFT programs that both address and mitigate any gaps in the bank's controls. Accordingly, bank management uses the risk assessment results to develop appropriate policies and procedures that address the risks posed to the bank by potential money laundering and terrorist financing activities. The bank's monitoring system should then focus on those high-risk products, services, customers, and geographic locations that have been identified through its ML/FT risk assessment.

A bank with well-developed and sound risk assessment processes generally should validate its effectiveness by including an independent review of its compliance program. When putting its AML/CFT programs in place, bank management should have considered staff resources and the level of training needed to promote compliance. Should a bank assume higher ML/FT risk profiles, management should provide more in-depth programs that specifically monitor and control those higher levels of risk. The internal or external auditor should, as part of the audit, independently test the bank's policies, procedures, and overall compliance with its AML/CFT programs.

5.1.2 Updating the Risk Assessment

An up-to-date AML/CFT compliance program helps control the risks associated with the bank's activities as they relate to its products, services, customers, and geographic locations. To keep the bank's programs current, management should subject them to periodic review and make appropriate changes that reflect the bank's true risk profile. In addition, bank management should review the program's adequacy when the bank adds new products or services, opens or closes accounts with high-risk customers, or expands through mergers or acquisitions. In the absence of such changes, bank management should reassess the AML/CFT programs every 12 to 18 months to assure that the risk assessment is current.

5.1.3 System-Wide ML/FT Risk Assessment

Banks that are affiliated with other institutions or holding companies often use system-wide ML/FT compliance programs and risk assessment techniques. In such cases, the bank should assess individual risk within business lines and the consolidated risk across all activities and legal entities. The lead banking institution or holding company should frequently update and reassess the ML/FT risks throughout the organization and should communicate any changes to appropriate business units, functions, and legal entities. A risk or deficiency that exists in one part of the organization may increase concerns in other parts, and bank management should quickly and diligently address these concerns throughout the organization.

5.2 The Bank Supervisor's Areas of Responsibility

5.2.1 Getting a General Understanding of the Bank's ML/TF Risk Exposure

Bank supervisors, through reviewing the bank's internal processes, should determine whether management has performed an effective risk assessment, identifying the significant risks posed to the bank by money laundering or terrorist financing.[9] They should also review the bank's written programs addressing AML/CFT and should confirm that the appropriate levels of management have approved them. In addition, supervisors should review the bank's internal controls, including those related to the opening of accounts, to suspicious activity monitoring and reporting, and to other relevant policies and procedures.[10] The bank's internal control program should include dual control and segregation of duties over accounts that could be used for money laundering or terrorist financing activities. Supervisors also should review board and management reports to determine whether the bank complies with stated policies, whether written or practiced.

Some banks, as already noted, may not have performed or completed adequate ML/FT risk assessments. In such cases, the bank supervisors must complete a risk analysis based on all information available. They should also document information relating to the bank's risk assessment, or lack of a risk assessment, and document any deficiencies in the bank's process.

Supervisors performing the risk analysis should have a general understanding of the bank's money laundering and terrorist funding risks, and should document those risks. This documentation helps determine the scope of the examination the supervisors must perform. To help the bank develop or improve its ML/FT risk assessment, supervisors should share any information they use with bank management.

The risk analysis process that bank supervisors develop will generally not be as comprehensive as the risk assessment that ought to have been developed by the bank. Supervisors, however, will obtain the same information on the bank's products, services, customers, and geographic locations, including the volume and trend of transactions, and will use this information to make a determination about potentially high-risk areas within the bank. The process will include an analysis of the following:

- The bank's AML database for reporting possible suspicious transactions or for tracking those transactions that are a normal course of business
- Prior examination or inspection reports and any work papers developed from those examinations or reports
- Responses to governmental entities that relate to AML/CFT
- Discussions with bank management and appropriate regulatory oversight personnel
- Any regulatory required reports of condition or income or other reports that the bank is required to submit to government entities that might be relevant to the bank's AML/CFT efforts

Bank supervisors will review levels and trends of information that could affect the bank's ML/FT risk levels and should review information pertaining, among other things, to the following:

- Funds transfers
- Foreign exchange
- Private banking
- Monetary instrument sales
- Foreign correspondent accounts and PTAs
- Branch locations
- Domestic and international geographic locations of the bank's business area
- Suspicious transaction and currency transaction reporting

Bank supervisors will also evaluate all relevant information related to such factors as the bank's total asset size, customer base, products, services, and geographic locations. They should apply their knowledge of the risks associated with these factors to help determine a bank's ML/FT risk profile.

After identifying potential high-risk areas within a bank, the bank supervisor should be able to form preliminary ML/FT risk profiles and determine the adequacy of the bank's programs. This preliminary profile serves as the basis for the scope of the initial examination. The supervisor, through the assessment, may determine that an individual bank is engaging in potentially high-risk activities, and the supervisor should then evaluate whether the bank is appropriately measuring, monitoring, and controlling the specific risks through effective AML/CFT compliance programs.

Bank supervisors should develop examination scopes based on preliminary ML/FT risk profiles and should identify additional procedures that must be completed during the examination to address any specific areas of concern. Although the initial scope may change during the examination as supervisors review other aspects of the bank's program, the preliminary risk profile should help provide a reasonable scope for the AML/CFT review.

5.2.2 Determination of the Bank's ML/FT Overall Risk Profile

At the conclusion of the analysis, bank supervisors will reach an overall conclusion about the adequacy of the bank's system and controls for its ML/FT compliance programs. This conclusion will take into account the initial risk profile as developed by the bank or, as the case may be, by the bank supervisor, and will include whether or not the bank is able to manage the risk posed by potential money laundering or terrorist financing appropriately. The conclusion should also take into account the bank's aggregate risk profile as developed by the bank or the bank supervisors.

The existence of ML/FT risk should not be a serious concern to bank supervisors as long as the bank's programs adequately identify, measure, monitor, and control those risks. When banks do not appropriately control the risks of money laundering or terrorist financing, supervisors must discuss their concerns with bank management and with the board of directors, and they should expect management to take timely and appropriate corrective action.

Notes

1. *Legal risk* is the potential for lawsuits, adverse judgments, unenforceable contracts, fines and penalties generating losses, increased expenses for a bank, or even closure of the institution (Basel Committee); see www.bis.org/publ/bcbs85.pdf.

2. According to the Basel Committee definition, *operational risk* is the risk of loss resulting from inadequate or failed internal processes, people, and systems or from external events.

3. See Wolfsberg Statement: Guidance on a Risk Based Approach for Managing Money Laundering Risks. See www.wolfsberg-principles.com/pdf/risk-based-approach.pdf

4. For further details, see annex 6.

5. M-FS or mobile banking is the use of financial services through means unique to a mobile telephone. For a comprehensive analysis of ML/TF risks associated to mobile banking and related mitigation measures, see P.L. Chatain and others, "Integrity in Mobile Phone Financial Services: Measures for Mitigating Risks from Money Laundering and Terrorist Financing," World Bank Working Paper 146, June 2008.

6. "Banks should develop graduated customer acceptance policies and procedures that require more extensive due diligence for higher risk customers. For example, the policies may require the most basic account-opening requirements for a working individual with a small account balance. It is important that the customer acceptance policy is not so restrictive that it results in a denial of access by the general public to banking services, especially for people who are financially or socially disadvantaged. On the other hand, quite extensive due diligence would be essential for an individual with a high net worth whose source of funds is unclear." (From Basel CDD document, 2001, par 20.)

7. For complete details, see chapter 5.

8. In jurisdictions where they are provided for in law, the supervisor should impose/recommend appropriate sanctions in cases where the bank fails to complete a risk assessment or where its assessment is inadequate.

9. For complete details, see chapter 5.

10. See chapter 6.

2

CHAPTER 3

The Licensing Process and AML/CFT Due Diligence

Contents

1 Overview

A banking institution controlled by criminals, or with a criminal or criminals in key managerial positions, is at significantly greater risk of being used for money laundering or terrorist financing purposes. International standards, therefore, provide that a jurisdiction should take the necessary legal or regulatory measures to prevent criminals or their associates from holding or being the beneficial owner of a significant or controlling interest, or holding a management function, in a bank.[1] Key to the success of such measures is a properly designed and enforced licensing mechanism.

The Basel Committee on Banking Supervision has established a set of minimum licensing criteria for ensuring that banks will be established and operated in a safe and sound manner. These minimum requirements should be implemented through domestic law and regulation and, where appropriate, complemented by additional requirements to take into account risks specific to the jurisdiction.

The licensing process must be clearly structured, transparent, and based on reliable information. Further, the licensing authority needs to have adequate resources to discharge its duties. Finally, if the licensing authority and the anti-money laundering and combating the financing of terrorism (AML/CFT) supervisor are not the same, the views of the supervisor should be taken into account by the licensing authority as part of the licensing process.

This chapter is arranged into two sections. Section 3.2 gives an overview of the licensing requirements for banks, while section 3.3 discusses considerations for an effective licensing process.

3

2 Summary of the Licensing Requirements for Banks

2.1 General

No AML/CFT framework can be effective where criminals control or manage banks. The examples in box 3.1 illustrate how banks controlled by criminals were able to engage actively in money laundering (ML) and terrorist financing (TF) while circumventing banking regulations designed to prevent such behaviors. These

---

BOX 3.1 **Two Examples of Money Laundering Schemes in Banks Controlled by Criminals**

Bank of Credit and Commerce International (BCCI)

"BCCI's unique criminal structure—an elaborate corporate spider-web with BCCI's founder, Agha Hasan Abedi and his assistant, Swaleh Naqvi, in the middle—was an essential component of its spectacular growth and a guarantee of its eventual collapse. The structure was conceived by Abedi and managed by Naqvi for the specific purpose of evading regulation or control by governments. It functioned to frustrate the full understanding of BCCI's operations by anyone.

"Unlike any ordinary bank, BCCI was from its earliest days made up of multiplying layers of entities, related to one another through an impenetrable series of holding companies, affiliates, subsidiaries, banks-within-banks, insider dealings and nominee relationships. By fracturing corporate structure, recordkeeping, regulatory review, and audits, the complex BCCI family of entities created by Abedi was able to evade ordinary legal restrictions on the movement of capital and goods as a matter of daily practice and routine. In creating BCCI as a vehicle fundamentally free of government control, Abedi developed in BCCI an ideal mechanism for facilitating illicit activity by others, including such activity by officials of many of the governments whose laws BCCI was breaking.

"BCCI's criminality included fraud by BCCI and BCCI customers involving billions of dollars; money laundering in Europe, Africa, Asia, and the Americas; BCCI's bribery of officials in most of those locations; support of terrorism, arms trafficking, and the sale of nuclear technologies; management of prostitution; the commission and facilitation of income tax evasion, smuggling, and illegal immigration; illicit purchases of banks and real estate; and a panoply of financial crimes limited only by the imagination of its officers and customers."

Source: Senator John Kerry and Senator Hank Brown (1992), *the BCCI Affair: Report to the Committee on Foreign Relations of the United States Senate.*

(Continued)

> **BOX 3.1** **Two Examples of Money Laundering Schemes in Banks Controlled by Criminals (*Continued*)**
>
> **Russian federation in the 1990s**
>
> According to the United Nations Office for Drug Control and Crime Prevention ("UNODCCP"), "the Russian federation law enforcement agencies estimated that by the end of 1998, organized crime controlled about half of commercial banks, 60 percent of public and 40 percent of private businesses."
>
> "The control over banks enables an easy generation of illicit proceeds. It significantly simplifies criminal actions (for example, extortion or kidnapping for ransom) against the bank's customers. It also facilitates the criminal penetration into other sectors of the economy, as it simplifies the financial servicing of criminal operations. For money laundering activities, the control provides a long term advantage and considerable protection in the event that banking regulations are imposed. When the criminal organization itself owns and runs a bank, even the most stringent regulation would not contribute much to curbing money laundering. "It is not necessary to worry about suspicious reports when one owns the bank."
>
> *Source:* UNODCCP (2001), *Russian capitalism and money laundering.*

examples also illustrate how useful banks can be to criminals for laundering the proceeds of their criminal activities.

The proper design and implementation of licensing requirements therefore constitutes a key building block of an effective AML /CFT regime. The licensing process is typically undertaken either by the banking supervisor or by a specific licensing authority. In the latter case, the AML /CFT supervisor has to have adequate cooperation arrangements with the relevant authority[2] to have its views taken into account and to have access to adequate information.

The prohibition of criminal involvement in banking must apply to direct control through direct ownership and to indirect control, through beneficial ownership, of a significant or controlling interest in a bank. Furthermore, this prohibition must apply to holding a management function in a bank.

2.2 The Basel Committee on Banking Supervision Sets Minimum Licensing Requirements

Principle 3 of the Basel Core Principles for Effective Banking Supervision (BCP) sets out minimum criteria for the licensing of banks. The principle states that the licensing authority must have the power to set criteria and reject applications for institutions that do not meet the standards. The licensing process, at a minimum, should also consist of an assessment of the ownership structure and governance of the bank and its wider group, including the fitness and propriety of board members and senior management, its strategic and operating plan, internal controls and risk management, and its projected financial condition, including its capital base. Finally, where the proposed owner or parent organization is a foreign bank, the prior consent of its home country supervisor should be obtained.

To implement principle 3, the Basel Committee established a methodology containing 13 essential criteria for a jurisdiction's licensing process.[3] These essential criteria are as follows:

- The licensing authority could be the banking supervisor or another competent authority. If the licensing authority and the supervisory authority are not the same, the supervisor has the right to have its views considered on each specific application. In addition, the licensing authority provides the supervisor with any information that may be material to the supervision of the licensed institution.
- The licensing authority has the power to set criteria for licensing banks. These may be based on criteria set in laws or regulations.
- The criteria for issuing licenses are consistent with those applied in ongoing supervision.
- The licensing authority has the power to reject an application if the criteria are not fulfilled or if the information provided is inadequate.
- The licensing authority determines that the proposed legal, managerial, operational, and ownership structures of the bank and its wider group will not hinder effective supervision on both a solo and a consolidated basis.
- The licensing authority identifies and determines the suitability of major shareholders, including the ultimate beneficial owners, and others that may exert significant influence. It also assesses the transparency of the ownership structure and the sources of initial capital.
- A minimum initial capital amount is stipulated for all banks.
- The licensing authority, at authorization, evaluates proposed directors and senior management as to expertise and integrity (the fit and proper test) and any potential for conflicts of interest. The fit and proper criteria include (1) skills and experience in relevant financial operations commensurate with the intended activities of the bank and (2) no record of criminal activities or adverse regulatory judgments that make a person unfit to hold important positions in a bank.
- The licensing authority reviews the proposed strategic and operating plans of the bank. This includes determining that an appropriate system of corporate governance, risk management and internal controls, including those related to the detection and prevention of criminal activities, as well as the oversight of

proposed outsourced functions, will be in place. The operational structure is required to reflect the scope and degree of sophistication of the proposed activities of the bank.

- The licensing authority reviews pro forma financial statements and projections for the proposed bank. This includes an assessment of the adequacy of the financial strength to support the proposed strategic plan as well as financial information on the principal shareholders of the bank.
- In the case of foreign banks establishing a branch or subsidiary, before issuing a license, the host supervisor establishes that no objection (or a statement of no objection) from the home supervisor has been received. For purposes of the licensing process, as well as ongoing supervision of cross-border banking operations in its country, the host supervisor assesses whether the home supervisor practices global consolidated supervision.
- If the licensing, or supervisory, authority determines that the license was based on false information, the license can be revoked.
- The board, collectively, must have a sound knowledge of each of the types of activities the bank intends to pursue and the associated risks.

3

3 Considerations for an Effective Licensing Process

3.1 The Approach Taken by a Jurisdiction Must Take into Account Potential Risks

The licensing process must take into account the risks posed by a natural or legal person that proposes to own or control a significant portion of bank shares (see box 3.2). Similarly, the licensing process needs to consider risks posed by natural persons proposed to hold directorships and senior management positions. The following factors should be considered in assessing such risks:

- The nature and extent of influence that the position concerned (that is, director/senior manager or shareholder, including a beneficial owner) would hold over the bank
- The rationale for the person's assuming the position or shareholding role
- In the case of a natural person, whether that person is fit and proper based upon prior business experience and demonstrated competency (see box 3.3.)
- Whether the person possesses any sort of criminal record, and if so, the nature and seriousness of the offenses
- In the case of a legal person, whether that entity is fit and proper based upon prior business experience and other activities, the transparency of its governance, the rationale for its proposed ownership, sources of income, and the countries where it operates, where appropriate
- The main features of the domestic environment such as the level of disclosure and the quality of financial information, group structures (for example, groups organized through individual connections rather than shareholdings), the "maturity" of the banking system,[4] the criminal environment, the prevalence of cash in the economy[5] and other checks and balances in the system

Licensing requirements should be proportionate to risks so they effectively address higher risks without unduly barring persons from entering the banking industry. Shareholders may be subject to licensing requirements when they propose to control more than a certain percentage of a bank's shares or voting rights, as determined by the jurisdiction. As well, the licensing authority may reject applications where a bank would be controlled by multiple holding companies.[6] Some countries also require that banks be listed and subject to the related disclosure requirements.

3.2 An Effective Licensing Process Must Be Transparent and Based on Reliable Information

The licensing process should include (1) clear information requirements, which should be publicly available; (2) proper checks to ensure that the information submitted is reliable; (3) adequate analysis capacity; and (4) regular review of the process to assure that it remains adequate for the domestic and international

BOX 3.2 **The United Kingdom Regime for Controlled Persons[7]**

Persons performing certain functions (known as "controlled functions") are required to be approved by the Financial Services Authority (FSA), the financial supervisor in the United Kingdom. Controlled functions fall into three broad categories covering the exercise of a significant influence on the conduct of the firm's affairs, dealing with the firm's customers, and dealing with the property of customers.[a]

The basic criterion for the approval of a particular person to perform a particular controlled function is that the FSA is satisfied he is a fit and proper person to perform a controlled function. The three primary considerations to be taken into account in determining whether someone is fit and proper are honesty, integrity, and reputation; competence and capability; and financial soundness.

Each consideration is the subject of detailed guidance from the FSA. The guidance sets out circumstances that could lead to a person being declared not fit and proper to perform a particular function in a particular firm. A person does not fail to be fit and proper merely because his conduct falls within one or more of the matters listed in the guidance. If a matter comes to the FSA's attention and suggests that the person might not be fit and proper, the FSA will take into account how relevant and how important that matter is. Among others, factors considered are: (1) criminal offences, particularly for dishonesty, fraud, or financial crime; (2) adverse findings or settlements in relevant civil proceedings; (3) involvement in investigations or disciplinary proceedings by the FSA or other bodies and any suspension, criticism, or censure, public or private; (4) contraventions of the FSA rules or other applicable regulatory standards or rules; (5) justified complaints relating to regulated activities; (6) dismissals, including resigning when asked; and (7) whether the person has been candid and truthful in his dealings with regulators and whether he demonstrates a readiness and willingness to comply with the requirements and standards of the regulatory system and other legal, regulatory, and professional requirements and standards.

The FSA consults the Shared Intelligence database (that includes law enforcement information) for each individual who applies for approval. Further checks on persons' creditworthiness are made with commercial information providers. Additional checks are carried out externally with other regulatory bodies (both domestic and foreign). The FSA also has the right to ask an employer for an employee's disciplinary record.

The application for approved person status requires a considerable amount of information. It is the responsibility of the prospective employer to submit the application, and reckless submission of inaccurate or misleading information is a criminal offence. The full five-year employment history of the candidate must be provided, with all gaps explained. References should also be sought from previous employers, and many financial institutions

(Continued)

3

3

BOX 3.2 **The United Kingdom Regime for Controlled Persons[7]**
(*Continued*)

have developed a standard questionnaire form that usually flows directly from the questions on the application form itself. Eventually, the employment contract should (1) incorporate the Financial Services and Market Act (FSMA 2000) regulatory regime and the terms governing the conduct of approved persons by making it a term of the contract that the employee must comply with regulatory requirements; (2) contain an express statement that a breach of FSA rules and/or loss of fitness and propriety can justify summary dismissal; (3) contain an express right to suspend the employee should any breach of FSA rules be suspected. This is to ensure that the individual can be removed immediately from carrying out that controlled function or functions while the investigation takes place.

a. In 2006, there were more than 165,000 such approved persons.

BOX 3.3 **The U.S. Approach to Assessing Information Provided by Natural Persons—the OCC Management Review Guideline**

The management review guideline issued by the Office of the Comptroller of the Currency[a] (OCC) recommends that the following steps be taken in assessing information provided by senior managers in their application form:

- Require each proposed executive officer (candidate) to submit information requested in the Interagency Biographical and Financial Report, if necessary, to the board of directors for review.
- Perform a credit check of the candidate, identifying the credit bureaus or other sources used.
- Contact the candidate's references and summarize by name the comments received.
- Contact the candidate's previous employers and summarize by name and employer the nature of comments provided (for example, positive, negative, no comment).
- Prepare or obtain a summary of the candidate's duties in previous positions and discuss how that experience relates to the job description under consideration.
- Describe all terms of employment, including proposed salary, methods used to determine the amount of salary, employment contract, and other compensation.

Source: OCC, background investigations, comptroller's licensing manual, 2002.
a. The Office of the Comptroller of the Currency is one of the US banking supervisors.

environments. The adequacy of a proposed bank's AML/CFT framework should be reviewed as part of the licensing process. In Spain, bank licenses are granted by the banking supervisor (Bank of Spain) while AML /CFT supervision falls within the ambit of the Spanish FIU (SEPBLAC[8]). Contemplated AML/CFT policies need to be reviewed by the Spanish FIU and its comments considered by the banking supervisor before any license can be granted.

It is also common for the licensing authority to have a standard questionnaire/application form listing all required information that natural and legal persons have to provide as part of the licensing process. The disclosure of licensing determinations and the reasons, therefore, is a best practice for jurisdictions to follow. The public disclosure of both the standardized application and the stated reasons for granting or denying the license, including any conditions upon approval, promote transparency in the licensing process.

It is the responsibility of the applicant to provide accurate and adequate information to the licensing authority. The licensing authority should ensure that the information is accurate by such methods as (1) requiring the information to be supported by adequate evidence (for example, criminal records, reliable identification documents, financial records, or certificate of good conduct from past employers); (2) requesting third parties to verify information; and (3) using reliable publicly available information. This makes dissuasive sanctions for applicants who provide false or misleading information especially important. Such sanctions can be administrative (including barring someone from working in the industry), civil, and criminal. They should be effectively enforced and disclosed to relevant stakeholders, including domestic and foreign supervisors.

3.3 The Licensing Authority Should Have Adequate Resources to Discharge Its Duties

The licensing authority needs to have adequate human and financial resources in order to conduct a proper assessment of those wishing to establish a new bank or, as discussed below, to acquire ownership or control of a designated percentage of a bank's shares or voting rights. "Adequate human resources" means that persons with appropriate experience and authority make licensing decisions. "Adequate financial resources" means that the licensing authority has an adequate budget to pay its staff and conduct its operations.

3.4 Licensing Requirements Should Apply to Subsequent Changes in Share Ownership or Control and in Senior Management Positions

Beyond the initial licensing process, the same concerns for criminals, or otherwise unfit natural or legal persons, gaining control of significant shares or voting rights, or serving in senior management positions, can occur with sales of existing shares or voting rights and with changes in senior management positions. Core principle 4 of the BCP requires the supervisor to have the power to review and reject any proposals to transfer significant ownership or controlling interests held directly or indirectly in existing banks to other parties (for further details, see box 3.4).

BOX 3.4 **Essential Criteria (EC) Regarding the Transfer of Significant Ownership Interests**

- Laws or regulations contain clear definitions of "significant" ownership and "controlling interest." (EC1)
- There are requirements to obtain supervisory approval or provide immediate notification of proposed changes that would result in a change in ownership, including beneficial ownership, or the exercise of voting rights over a particular threshold or change in controlling interest. (EC2)
- The supervisor has the power to reject any proposal for a change in significant ownership, including beneficial ownership or controlling interest, or to prevent the exercise of voting rights with respect to such investments if they do not meet criteria comparable to those used for approving new banks. (EC3)
- The supervisor obtains from banks, through periodic reporting or on-site examinations, the names and holdings of all significant shareholders or those that exert controlling influence, including the identities of beneficial owners of shares being held by nominees or custodians and through vehicles which might be used to disguise ownership. (EC4)
- The supervisor has the power to take appropriate action to modify, reverse, or otherwise address a change of control that has taken place without the necessary notification to or approval from the supervisor. (EC5)

Source: Bank for International Settlements (BIS), Core Principles Methodology, principle 4, 2006.

Notes

1. FATF recommendation 23.
2. For instance, in France, licenses are granted by the credit institutions and investment firms committee (CECEI) which is chaired by the Governor of the Banque de France (who also chairs the French banking supervisor, the Commission bancaire) and includes the Head of Treasury, the Head of the Securities supervisor, the Head of the Deposit Guarantee Fund, two magistrates, two representatives of the banks and investment firms association, two representatives of trade unions, and two persons chosen for their competence. Cooperation arrangements exist between the AML/CFT supervisor (which is also the banking supervisor) and the licensing authority, the CECEI, which are both hosted by the Banque de France.
3. Basel Committee on Banking Supervision, 2006 Core Principles Methodology.
4. The more mature the banking system, the more likely it is that persons to be vetted will have adequate track records to demonstrate their integrity.
5. Enhanced due diligence measures should be implemented where a cash payment is made for shares. The licensing authority should be in position to ascertain the origin of such funds before granting a license (or vetting a new shareholder or an increase in an existing shareholder's stake).
6. "In France, in order to avoid any ambiguity about the identity of responsible shareholders, the [licensing authority] prefers [shareholders] to hold their equity interest in the [bank] directly. However, if for particular reasons one or more holding companies are interposed between the investors and the institution, they are asked to give an undertaking not to transfer control of the holding companies without first obtaining the [licensing authority]'s authorization." CECEI, Annual report, share ownership structure of credit institutions and principles corresponding to different types of situations, 2005.
7. This box largely draws on Freshfield, Bruckhaus, and Deringer's outline (2007) of the approved persons regime.
8. Servicio Ejecutivo de la Comisión de Prevención des Blanqueo de Capitales e Infraccionnes Monetarias (Executive Service of the Prevention of Money Laundering and Monetary Offences).

CHAPTER 4

AML/CFT Off-Site Supervision

Contents

1   Overview

In keeping with principle 20 of the Basel Core Principles for Effective Banking Supervision (BCP), Anti-money laundering and Combating the Financing of Terrorism (AML/CFT) supervision should consist of both on-site and off-site processes. While off-site supervision is part of an ongoing process, an on-site examination is a defined event with a scheduled beginning and end.[1] The supervisor, based upon the particular conditions and circumstances of the jurisdiction,[2] determines the appropriate mix of on-site and off-site supervision.

Similarly, to be effective, AML/CFT supervision should consist of both on-site and off-site processes. Off-site supervision is used to

- Conduct regular reviews and analyses of AML/CFT compliance at individual banks, using prudential reports, statistical returns, and other appropriate sources, including publicly available information;
- Follow up on matters requiring further attention, evaluate developing risks, and help identify the priorities and scope of further work; and
- Help determine the priorities and scope of on-site work.[3]

In designing an off-site supervision apparatus, the AML/CFT supervisor should emphasize a risk-based rather than a one-size-fits-all approach. With a risk-focused approach, the supervisor takes into account the quality of an individual institution's internal risk management systems and processes. Supervisors are then able to devote fewer resources to those banks they recognize as well managed, and to focus on those that are less well managed.[4]

4

2 Main Features of the Off-Site Supervision System

2.1 General Characteristics of Ongoing Supervision

AML/CFT supervision, as part of the overall ongoing supervision process, should be fundamentally based on the analysis of declared documents which, depending largely on the institution's size and activity, it submits at prescribed intervals. These are accounting and financial documents, calculations done to meet statutory standards, annual internal supervision reports, and various other books and materials.

Off-site supervisors, who, in addition, make use of documents published by banks, should maintain direct contact with the institutions, their directors, and their auditors, and should engage in the increasingly common practice of regular meetings and visits.

2.1.1 Main Features of Off-Site Prudential Supervision

The design and implementation of AML/CFT off-site supervision is largely inspired by that of prudential off-site supervision, whether AML supervision is undertaken by the prudential supervisor or not. It is therefore useful to identify some key characteristics of off-site prudential supervision (while identifying in the rest of the chapter where off-site AML/CFT supervision differs).

- *It is meant to be continuous.* At any given institution, there is ongoing monitoring by the teams in charge. The nature of the monitoring is updated on the basis of new information, which may have been provided in regular reports, or at meetings, or during regular visits.
- *It is meant to be universal.* In principle, as part of the entire banking system, all institutions, large or small, are closely monitored as part of the entire national banking system. Banks that appear to be weaker, however, will generally be more carefully monitored, will be required to submit additional analyses, will receive more numerous requests for information, and so forth.
- *It covers the totality of banking regulations.* In fact, the prudential supervisor is responsible for enforcing compliance on the part of the institutions using the prudential standards established by the regulator.
- *It has a warning and preventive role.* From the initial signs of a bank's difficulty or increased risk, documentary supervision must include any measures deemed necessary to analyze the problems and to prevent any loss.

2.1.2 Resources for Ongoing Supervision

Ongoing supervision includes access to numerous resources, but the resources actually used depend on the organization and operational methods of the particular supervision authority.

- The mass of information gathered from the entire banking system means that off-site control systems are able to cross-reference data and thus have access to large databases, including AML/CFT (statistical series, average figures by type of institution, and so forth).
- Placed at the center of the banking system, off-site supervision is alert to developments in the industry and receives all kinds of information, including complaints from competitors and allegations of possible involvement in money laundering and terrorist financing schemes. Any or all of these may indicate an increase in ML/TF risk.
- It is normal for departments in charge of ongoing supervision to work in close collaboration with the other relevant agencies involved in AML/CFT, namely the financial intelligence unit or other supervisory agencies. They can take advantage of certain databases used by those institutions.
- Supervisors, if need be, can request additional input, such as interviews with directors, to enrich their available data, and can obtain clarifications on changes of AML/CFT strategy or on the development of certain cases.

Finally, the administrative authority can ask for the initiation of on-site supervision or audit by an external auditor. The scope of this supervision will depend on the nature and seriousness of the authority's specific concerns.

4

2.1.3 Limits to Ongoing Surveillance

Off-site supervision, alone, cannot be sure of the fullness or the accuracy of the information transmitted. Unless the supervisor has the capacity to verify the fullness and accuracy of the information provided, compliance with statutory regulations, including AML/CFT, is likely to be merely superficial. This explains the key role on-site supervision also has to play (see chapter 5). Alongside these supervisory controls, other checks and balances should be in place (involving internal control bodies, external auditors, and also credit rating agencies or financial analysts).

Moreover, off-site supervision requires information which will not necessarily be derived from available publications or easily accessible from direct contacts with the institutions.

2.2 Primary Objective of Ongoing Surveillance

Off-site supervision is primarily concerned with assessing the design and implementation of banks' AML/CFT frameworks, without having access to individual information which could lead to the identification of suspicious transactions. For that reason it is sometimes not seen as an effective part of an AML/CFT program. However, it should be noted that supervision in general should be primarily concerned with ensuring that proper AML/CFT measures are in place (and thus that ML/FT can be deterred).

Off-site supervision can generate a great deal of valuable information that can be used both to identify outliers and foster compliance. AML/CFT supervision should first rely on information gathered by the banking supervisor and the FIU, with a view to understanding bank activities in particular, associated risks as well as their governance and risk management frameworks. Such information may include the following:

- Accounting and prudential data on bank activities
- Assessments undertaken by the banking supervisor (for example, on-site inspection reports, risk profile analysis, and so forth)
- Reports by internal control bodies and external auditors

Supervisors should also take a proportionate approach to assessing an institution's risks. Rather than having a fixed view of what constitutes an acceptable level of business risk or a risk management standard, supervisors should assess whether risk management systems and internal controls are commensurate with the institution's risk and business profiles. Institutions that engage in complex financial businesses must be able to demonstrate that their risk management capabilities match both their appetites for risk and their operations, while institutions that engage in less complex or less risky financial activities may find that simpler risk management processes are appropriate for their purposes.

4

3 Key Tasks to Be Performed by Off-Site Examiners

Off-site examiners should perform several activities as part of the ongoing surveillance process, with the aim of collecting as much relevant information as possible. Once the data is collected, its analysis should be undertaken with a view to understanding the AML/CFT apparatus of the banks under scrutiny.

3.1 Collection of Relevant Information

One of the biggest AML/CFT challenges for off-site supervisors is to collect relevant and detailed information on practices that will help the supervisor

- Understand the strengths and weaknesses in each bank,
- Identify shortcomings that may generate systemic risks,
- Establish a supervisory risk assessment system to prevent problems, and develop risk factors for determining a risk-based approach.

"Relevant" information is not necessarily limited to information specific to AML/CFT, and, as discussed, information on bank governance and internal control frameworks can be extremely useful. Specific AML/CFT information that the AML/CFT supervisor collects can be qualitative or quantitative. Quantitative information is useful (see box 4.1 for details), but qualitative information is the primary focus of AML/CFT supervision and demands the greater part of its resources.

4

BOX 4.1 **Collection of Quantitative AML/CFT Information: Recordkeeping and Reporting Requirements in Italy**

Italian banks must have a single IT database (Archivo Unico Informatico, AUI) containing detailed information on transactions and customers. Some data must be kept for 10 years, including the following:

- The date and reason for a transaction.
- The total amount of any transaction exceeding 12,500 euros which must be recorded using one of the 112 analytical codes provided. This allows cash transactions to be separated from others.
- The name, surname, date, and place of birth of persons carrying out transactions, including the details of identification documents presented. This applies regardless of whether the persons are acting on their own behalf or on behalf of third parties.
- In the case of legal persons, the name and registered office of the person for which the transaction is undertaken or the account, or other continuing relationship, opened.

(Continued)

4

| **BOX 4.1** | **Collection of Quantitative AML/CFT Information: Recordkeeping and Reporting Requirements in Italy (*Continued*)** |

- The fiscal code of the person or persons executing the transaction or opening the account or other continuing relationship, and the fiscal code of the person on whose behalf the transaction is to be executed or the account or other continuing relationship opened.
- In the case of credit or payment orders, the identification of the person originating the orders and the beneficiaries and intermediaries involved.

GIANOS (Generatore Indici di Anomalia per Operazioni Sospette[a]) is a software program implemented by banks in order to short-list unusual transactions and identify ML trends. The project, which began in 1993, has been operating since 1995. A committee, made up of legal, organizational, computer, and statistics specialists from banks, together with the Italian FIU,[b] determines GIANOS operating rules, its algorithms, and its decision tables (which identify unusual transactions according to confidential criteria). GIANOS determines the risk profile of each customer from a 12-month transaction track record. It pays attention to all transactions above 3,100 euros. This threshold was adopted to identify structured operations where the total amount may exceed the legal threshold of 12,500 euros.

Using GIANOS, banks analyze 30 million operations and 3.5 million customers each month. From these numbers, 200,000 operations and 40,000 customers are short-listed as unusual. Most suspicious transaction reports (STRs) filed with the FIU are initially identified by GIANOS. The process helps ensure that all bank transactions, as long as they are properly recorded in the AUI, are analyzed using standard criteria, and it helps alleviate any pressure, whether internal or external, bank staff may face not to report transactions.

The Italian FIU has developed a state-of-the-art analysis capacity based on a harmonized system of computerized data collection. It manages a central financial database (Archivo Aggregato), which incorporates data extracted each month from the banks' AUI as well as from other reporting institutions. Each month, the aggregated data average 3 million records for 30 million transactions. Customer names, however, are not included in the information provided to the FIU.

The FIU's analysis aims to identify potential ML behaviors and trends, as well as outliers that require on-site inspections. It assumes that ML behaviors cause trend alterations in banks' aggregated data. Operative guidelines implemented include the following:

- Time-series analysis of aggregated data.
- Cross-section analysis in a particular geographic context.

(Continued)

BOX 4.1 **Collection of Quantitative AML/CFT Information: Recordkeeping and Reporting Requirements in Italy (*Continued*)**

- Detection of outliers in multivariate data environments. The objective is to identify parameters or combinations of parameters that characterize ML behaviors and then to create relevant algorithms.
- Time series analysis of cash transactions in a local context.
- So-called scientific visualization.

The FIU's statistical unit takes part in the preparation of the annual on-site inspection program. It identifies outliers, such as:

- Those that do not file aggregated reports.
- Those whose reports contain information inconsistent with their activity.
- Those whose number of STRs is either unusually low (in absolute or relative terms) or whose STRs do not contain the required information.

When an on-site inspection is about to begin, the statistical unit, which employs seven analysts, provides inspectors with detailed materials on the bank such as:

- The number of transactions, including cash transactions.
- The number of cross-border transactions, records, and wire transfers per country reported during the previous 2 years.
- Some specific ratios such as incoming /outgoing transactions or cash transactions amount /total transactions amount per branch.
- Detailed information on wire transfers carried out during the previous 2 years, including the average value of transfers, identifying those realized with offshore financial centers (OFCs). These transfers include so-called triangular transactions, that is, incoming wire transfers received from an OFC and followed by an outgoing wire transfer to an OFC.
- Transactions with some countries for which ML cases were identified.

a. See chapter 1, endnote 10.
b. See chapter 1, endnote 10.

4

Specific qualitative AML/CFT information, collected either regularly or only on an ad hoc basis, includes AML/CFT compliance reports (where banks prepare such documents) and bank policies. It also includes reports from internal audits to assess banks' AML/CFT frameworks, and from external audits in cases where they have been required.

In Germany, for example, local law requires external auditors to report annually on AML systems and controls in banks. In Switzerland, there is also a legal requirement for external auditors of banks to audit AML compliance annually and report their findings to the bank and its local regulator.[5] In Australia, all reporting entities are required to complete an Annual Compliance Report at the beginning of each year.

In Spain, banks are required to set up internal procedures, such as "know your customer" admission policies and control and reporting procedures, which involve the designation of a compliance officer or money-laundering officer. These policies and procedures are reviewed annually by an independent outside expert who must complete a full written report and make it available to SEPBLAC, the Spanish FIU, for a period of six years. It is illegal for this external control to be carried out by any person who has had professional or business dealings with the bank within the previous three years.[6]

In France, in 2000, the French banking supervisor (Commission bancaire) introduced a specific AML/CFT reporting requirement that is both qualitative and quantitative and comprises four different money laundering questionnaires (Questionnaire de Lutte Contre le Blanchiment, QLB; see annex 2).[7] For each regulatory requirement, the questionnaire includes a series of multiple-choice questions (yes, no, N/A) on the enforcement of various operations to be performed with due diligence by the bank.

Each year, all banks have to submit this information, both electronically and by regular mail, to the Commission bancaire. The questionnaire must be signed by one of the two most senior managers of the bank, a requirement that helps raise AML/CFT awareness and the quality of the answers. With the electronic version, answers can be analyzed at great speed, so banks with large numbers of negative answers, which may indicate inadequate procedures, can be easily pinpointed. More attention is paid to some particularly critical questions, such as an ability to file suspicious transaction reports (STRs) or to identify customers. Conceived as a tool for off-site supervision, the questionnaires lead supervisors to a better understanding of a bank's AML/CFT internal apparatus and help identify any shortcomings.[8] The results of this computerized analysis help prioritize supervisory follow-up.

A line supervisor with good knowledge of the bank then thoroughly reviews the electronic analysis of the questionnaires. During the review, the off-site supervisor considers the specific features of each bank and, even more specifically, assesses previously provided information that had appeared abnormal. The supervisor may then be able to identify some shortcomings not picked up by the computerized analysis, such as nonapplicable answers that are not consistent with bank activity.

Where significant shortcomings appear, there will be various follow-up actions. The Commission bancaire may send letters requiring adequate measures to be taken and set a timeframe for implementation. The Commission may also organize interviews with senior management and/or compliance officers with the object of clarifying issues and, if appropriate, of requiring corrective actions. It will also

4

assess the relevance of any remedial actions already contemplated or in the process of being implemented. As well, it can initiate on-site inspections.

Although the off-site supervision department has the responsibility for the analysis of questionnaires, it cooperates closely with the on-site inspection group (the two being distinct in France). Cooperation includes having the on-site inspectors provide comments on draft letters, take part in specific meetings with banks, and review the quality of answers provided by the bank after the on-site visit. Poor or false answers are a regular feature of those AML/CFT cases that result in disciplinary sanctions.

Lastly, the FIU also can provide relevant quantitative information, including individual and/or aggregated STR activity.[9] Specific banks also can provide quantitative information, such as the number of people attending AML/CFT training, or the number of audits undertaken in the area.

3.2 Meetings with the Management of a Bank

Meetings with individual banks help a supervisor gain a proper understanding of their AML/CFT frameworks. Although only on-site inspections allow an in-depth assessment of a bank's AML/CFT framework, off-site meetings are also useful in identifying shortcomings in the frameworks' design and implementation. Such meetings help supervisors assess how familiar the senior management of a bank is with the requirements for AML/CFT, and they can then regularly update the information about AML/CFT frameworks to make sure the bank adequately addresses the ML/TF risks.

Meetings must be tailored to each bank and must take into account both its risk profile and all previous supervisory actions such as interviews, on-site inspections, and sanctions. An initial meeting might address the following issues specific to AML/CFT:

- AML/CFT policies and procedures in relation to such aspects as the role of the board of directors and senior management in their preparation and approval, their availability and regular update, the coverage of activities undertaken, specific procedures for specific activities, group dimension, where appropriate, job profiles, and new products.
- Resources dedicated to implementing AML/CFT policies and procedures: These resources should include measures taken to ensure that the AML/CFT compliance officer(s), the AML/CFT reporting officer(s), and the internal auditor(s) are adequately resourced and independent. Resources should also include the management information systems (MIS) used to screen customers' activities[10] (such as periodicity, customers' risk profiles, criteria used) and to sort out possible "unusual" transactions.
- STR decision-making process.

- Implementation of the AML/CFT framework, such as the major outcomes of the implementation of policies and procedures, resources dedicated to AML/CFT, the shortcomings identified in the AML/CFT framework and the measures contemplated or taken to address them, as well as the number of staff trained and the number of audits undertaken.
- Assessment of the bank's AML/CFT risk profile. This should be based on operations undertaken (types of activities, business relationships, and so forth), the environment in which the bank operates, and the efficiency of its framework to address these risks (the AML/CFT framework in particular).

Meetings can be organized differently, depending on the seniority of people attending (for example, directors, senior managers, compliance officers, auditors, business lines on the bank side), and/or the meeting's scope (AML/CFT-specific or with a broader agenda, for example, a yearly meeting with a bank or a meeting on a specific activity) and prior supervisory actions.

Beyond assessing a bank's AML/CFT framework, such meetings can help raise the awareness of both the board of directors and senior management by helping them first, to understand the rationale for the commitments and resources needed to fulfill AML/CFT requirements and second, to become personally committed to providing the resources. They must be willing to design and implement a risk-based approach that is not a simple "box-checking" exercise, but properly reflects the specific risks faced by their bank.

4

4 Other Responsibilities of Ongoing Supervision

4.1 Structured Analysis of AML/CFT-Relevant Information

Off-site AML/CFT supervision needs to be clearly structured. Policies and procedures must define the types and frequency of controls to be undertaken and must also specify the individual supervisors responsible for them. The extent of controls to be undertaken should be sufficient to enable the off-site supervisor to form an up-to-date judgment of each bank's AML/CFT frameworks. As well, outcomes of on-site inspections should be factored into such off-site monitoring.

Such assessments should first take into account a bank's "intrinsic" AML/CFT risk profiles, such as transparency and governance, types of activities, customers, and countries with which the bank deals. Second, the assessments should consider a bank's risk management framework. This framework, designed to mitigate such "intrinsic" risks, includes areas such as bank governance, AML/CFT policies, MIS, ML reporting officer, ML compliance function, and training. These outcomes of the supervisory process should be documented.

4.2 Coordination with On-Site Inspection Activities

Off-site supervision also has a key role to play in the preparation and follow-up of on-site examinations.

The outcomes of such work can usefully be incorporated into any existing system for supervisory risk assessment, which is generally synthetic and focuses on key shortcomings. The outcomes can be a useful resource with which to assess a bank's risk profile and to identify major shortcomings where they exist. They can help both to integrate AML/CFT into the daily work of banking supervisors and ensure that, in planning on-site inspections, due consideration is given to AML/CFT. Incorporating these outcomes reduces the risk of working in silos and helps to structure and formalize the process. They can be useful tools in following up on supervisory action, including areas where AML/CFT shortcomings are known to exist.

Off-site supervision also has a role to play in the preparation and follow-up of on-site examinations. When teams identify banks that require on-site examinations, which may be, for example, because they have not been examined for a long time, or are deemed to be especially exposed to ML/TF, or because they have shortcomings that have been identified, they give the relevant information to examiners before they go on-site. With respect to the follow-up to on-site examinations, off-site teams first analyze the on-site examination reports, and then, in some cases, they issue recommendations that banks must follow, and then follow up on the banks' implementation of those recommendations.

In Spain, the AML/CFT supervisor has developed an integrated MIS in which all information relevant to the follow-up of on-site examinations is listed. This

4

information includes examination dates, letters that were subsequently sent and received, decisions that were taken within the supervisory body, and so on. Thanks to this system, supervisors can easily access all relevant information, make sure proper approval of supervisory actions has been obtained, and verify that no significant delays exist (on the bank side as well as the supervisor side).

4.3 Determination of Risk Profile and Rating[11]

Supervisory risk assessment systems are part of the banking supervision process because they provide continuing help in assessing banks' risk profiles. Such systems can usefully provide further indications about the AML/CFT supervisory process, by providing both information on banks' risk profiles and a structured approach to undertake off-site supervision. AML/CFT is in practice frequently taken into account in such supervisory risk assessment systems, as banking supervisors are generally responsible for assessing banks' compliance with AML/CFT requirements.[12]

Supervisory risk assessment systems are commonly used in off-site banking supervision to

- Undertake systematic assessment of banks within a formalized framework.
- Identify banks and areas within banks where problems exist or are likely to emerge.
- Prioritize bank examinations for optimal allocation of supervisory resources.
- Initiate timely action by the supervisor.
- Share information among authorized parties within the supervisory body. The early identification of problems in banks is a key element of any supervisory risk assessment system.

A bank's overall assessment should be captured in a single rating, and the process leading to such a rating defined by clear policies (as shown in box 4.2). The final rating is the result of a summing up of the individual ratings given to each different risk component (usually the total is fewer than 10). Each risk component is subjected to a structured analysis of both quantitative and qualitative information, which ranges from regulatory reports to media information to internal bank documents. It is important that all key information, particularly regulatory reports, is identified and provided when required.

Ratings are meant to reflect the reasoned assessments of supervisors. Determining what the ratings are is not an exercise in compliance, where supervisors merely review ratios that have been automatically computed or formally respond to a list of detailed criteria. It is essential that supervisors have a proper understanding of a bank's risk profile. As well, these assessments must not only be objective, but also consistent across the industry. Detailed policies need to be established for that purpose. The policies must clarify, among other things, the risk components to be rated,

BOX 4.2 Example of Qualification Used by Dutch Examiners[13]	
General Qualification	**Notes**
No control or weak control (qualification 4)	The institution has absolutely no control measures in place, or the CDD management framework needs serious and immediate improvement so that risks may be identified, analyzed, or controlled. The CDD management framework is not, or is barely, geared to the institution's activities and customers.
Unsatisfactory control (qualification 3)	The institution's control measures have not been set up satisfactorily, are not effective enough, or do not serve to control the main risk areas or primary risks. The design and operation of the CDD control measures are insufficiently geared to the institution's activities and customers and are in need of significant improvement.
Satisfactory control (qualification 2)	The design and operation of the institution's control measures are in minimum compliance with requirements that can reasonably be imposed. Relevant risks are identified and analyzed, and the control of these risks is secured as part of internal business operations. The CDD management framework is adequately and satisfactorily geared to the institution's activities and customers.
Strong control (qualification 1)	The institution's control measures are of high quality in terms of design and operation. The CDD management framework safeguards sound control of the risks and is adequately geared to the institution's activities and customers.

the information to be analyzed, the rating approaches to be followed (including the definitions and criteria for ratings and the individuals ultimately responsible for approving them), and the periodicity of required follow-up actions.

Reviews of bank ratings across the industry and over an extended period help foster consistency. Consistency is especially important because ratings are not only used to assess the condition of an individual bank, but also to oversee the entire banking system. Consistency helps in the identification of outliers and in the allocation of supervisory resources. When the systems identify institutions as potentially risky, the institutions, typically, are subjected to greater supervisory surveillance and to an on-site examination before enforcement of formal actions is initiated.

Although an on-site tool, the US risk assessment system, CAMEL,[14] has had a strong influence on the way most off-site supervisory risk assessments systems are approached. CAMEL ratings are normally assigned every 12–18 months, depending on the frequency with which every bank in the United States has to be examined on-site. Ratings range from 1 to 5. In the case of problem banks (those with a CAMEL rating of 4 or 5), the ratings may be assessed more frequently because these banks are subject to more frequent on-site examination. Conversely, in the case of sound banks (those with CAMEL ratings of 1 or 2), on-site examinations may be conducted after an interval of 18 months, and the ratings would be assigned accordingly. The US does not assign ratings for AML/CFT compliance; but a bank's AML/CFT compliance program is reflected within the management rating, which encompasses, among other factors, compliance with banking laws and regulations, adequacy and compliance with internal policies, and the existence and adequacy of qualified staff and programs.

In Chile, the supervisor (Superintendencia de Bancos e Instituciones Financieras, SBIF) has also designed a CAMEL-like internal rating system in which a bank's compliance with AML/CFT regulations is viewed as a key element of its internal control. The off-site supervisor assigns different ratings, which range from "fully compliant" to "materially compliant" to "noncompliant." Once all criteria have been examined, banks are classified in categories from A to C, category A being the highest. In category B, some shortcomings have been identified, and in category C serious deficiencies have been detected.

4.4 Collaboration with Other Agencies Involved in AML/CFT

A regular assessment of major AML/CFT risks in the industry should be undertaken, in collaboration with the FIU and other relevant agencies (for further details, please see chapter 7).

4.5 Collaboration with the Banking Industry

A well-designed outreach to the industry improves the efficiency of the supervisory process. The role of supervisors is to ensure that all banks have a consistent understanding of AML/CFT requirements. This understanding is gained through examinations, through outreach to the industry, and by clearly defining supervisory expectations, such as how the supervisor expects banks to implement AML/CFT standards and how their compliance will be assessed (for further details, see box 4.3).

BOX 4.3 Guidance and Outreach to Banks in the United States

FinCEN,[a] in conjunction with the federal financial regulators, provides domestic financial institutions with various types of guidance for compliance with AML/CFT requirements, and it is all posted on FinCEN's website. FinCEN's guidance materials include:

- Letter rulings explaining BSA[b] requirements that apply to specific facts and circumstances
- Answers to frequently asked questions about BSA requirements
- Advisories and bulletins on (1) specific ML/TF schemes, (2) jurisdictions with seriously deficient AML/CFT regimes, and (3) institutions or individuals who may be engaged in fraudulent activities or be deemed to be of a high ML/TF risk

The FFIEC[c] Manual for the banking industry, published in June 2005, provides comprehensive guidance to the sector. Following its publication, the FDIC, FRB, OCC, and OTS[d] held conference calls (involving about 8,200 people) to provide an introduction and overview of the manual. Additionally, the FDIC, FRB, OCC, and the OTS conducted regional banker outreach and examiner training events, attended by about 2,800 individuals in five large metropolitan cities. One outreach event was broadcast via the Internet and was viewed by approximately 12,400 people. FinCEN and OFAC[e] participated in all these events.

The publication of the FFIEC Manual seems to have been a watershed in the understanding between the regulators and the banks, and has focused and clarified the latter's expectations of what constitutes an effective AML/CFT regime. This increased awareness can be expected to help improve the levels of compliance considerably.

Outreach programs are also in place. In these, the Federal Banking agencies, in partnership with FinCEN, conduct symposiums for banking industry representatives to discuss current issues, trends, regulatory requirements, challenges, and coordination with law enforcement. On a day-to-day basis, the Federal Banking agencies, through formal and informal methods, provide interpretive guidance to banking organizations subject to their supervision with respect to AML/CFT regulations. This guidance is promulgated through supervision and regulation (SR) letters, bulletins,

(Continued)

4

> | **BOX 4.3** | **Guidance and Outreach to Banks in the United States** |
> | --- | --- |
> | | ***(Continued)*** |
>
> advisories, and other forms of notification, all of which are readily accessible on the agency Web sites.
>
> *Source:* Abstract from the Financial Action Task Force (FATF) mutual evaluation report[f]
> a. Financial Crimes Enforcement Network (FinCEN) is a bureau within the Department of the Treasury. In addition to being the financial intelligence unit (FIU) of the US, FinCEN is responsible for the development, issuance, administration, and civil enforcement of regulations implementing the BSA; in concert with the IRS, for collecting and maintaining BSA (Bank Secrecy Act) data and providing government-wide data access service to information collected under the BSA and other data; and, in concert with the federal functional regulators, certain self-regulatory organizations and the IRS, for ensuring compliance with that regime.
> b. Bank Secrecy Act (BSA), the primary statute which establishes anti-money laundering compliance requirements
> c. The Federal Financial Institutions Examination Council
> d. U.S. banking supervisors: Federal Deposit Insurance Corporation, Federal Reserve Banks, Office of the Comptroller of the Currency, and Office of Thrift Supervision.
> e. The Office of Foreign Assets Control
> f. FATF, third mutual evaluation report on AML/CFT, United States of America, 2006. This manual was revised and updated in August 2007.

4

"Soft" instruments such as guidance, statements of principles, or feedback to the industry (though they are usually not enforceable) can be used to reach these goals. They are useful in

- Outlining the legal and regulatory framework across the banking sector
- Interpreting the requirements of the relevant law and regulations and explaining how to implement them in practice
- Indicating good practice in AML/CFT procedures
- Assisting firms to design and implement the necessary systems and controls to mitigate the risks of the firm's being used in connection with money laundering and terrorist financing

Supervisors cannot amend laws and regulations,[15] but they can communicate useful information on acceptable ways to implement them; they can particularly take into account any practical issues raised by their implementation. These might include problems arising from existing laws and regulations that do not encompass the requirements of the new banking activities, or that arise from ambiguities in laws and regulations or from practical issues. Banks or supervisors must deal with these problems until some of them can be alleviated by amending laws that are partially outdated.

Guidance is usually prepared in cooperation with the industry. In the United Kingdom, industry has the primary responsibility for drafting guidance to prevent money laundering and combat the financing of terrorism. The word "industry" here includes not only the banking sector, but also other financial industries; their aim is to build and implement a framework that is consistent. The detailed guidance the Joint Money Laundering Steering Group[16] (JMLSG) prepared, however, is then endorsed by the regulatory authority, namely, the UK Treasury. When seeing an ML/TF case,[17] the courts have to consider whether the framework has been adhered to. The Financial Services Authority (FSA), the AML/CFT supervisor in the UK, has also taken a "comply or explain" approach with regard to this guidance. Institutions, therefore, either have to apply recommendations provided by the guidance or justify that the approach they took was more effective in achieving the goals of the AML/CFT framework.

Supervisory expectations can be established in a number of ways. They can be established through dialogue with the industry, through disclosure of examination manuals and annual reports, through disclosure of sanitized cases handled by the supervisor, and through working papers or conferences (whether organized by the supervisor or by the industry). It is also a best practice to disclose the main characteristics of the supervisory framework. These include its design and method of implementation (for example, the number of examinations undertaken) and its enforcement actions. If the framework has shortcomings, or if changes have occurred in the regulatory framework, they also should be disclosed, perhaps in the annual report, or in a set of specific notes.

4

Notes

1. In the rest of the document, the terms "ongoing supervision" and "off-site supervision" have a similar meaning.
2. Essential criterion 1, principle 20, 2006 Methodology for BCP. This recommendation should not, however, be interpreted as dictating the specific mix of on-site and off-site supervision for a given bank, which is based upon factors unique to the bank.
3. Essential criterion 4, principle 20, 2006 Methodology for BCP.
4. See BCP 19, essential criterion 3: "The supervisor uses a methodology for determining and assessing on an ongoing basis the nature, importance and scope of the risks to which individual banks or banking groups are exposed. The methodology should cover, inter alia, the business focus, the risk profile and the internal control environment, and should permit relevant comparisons between banks. Supervisory work is prioritized based on the results of these assessments." See also the FATF Guidance on the risk-based approach to combating money laundering and terrorist financing, June 2007, especially the section on supervision, paragraph 2.30 onwards (http://www.fatf-gafi.org/dataoecd/43/46/38960576.pdf).
5. Deloitte, Global anti-money laundering survey 2007.
6. Royal decree 54/2005, article 16.1 and Law 19/1993, article 3.7, City of London, comparative implementation of European Union directives (II), money laundering, December 2006.
7. The first questionnaire (QLB 1) includes the names, titles, and phone numbers of people who are allowed to file STRs with TRACFIN (the French FIU); the second questionnaire (QLB 2) mentions branches and wholly-owned subsidiaries that operate in countries where they cannot (1) fulfill requirements to pay special attention to certain large and unusually complex transactions and (2) pass adequate information to the head office for AML/CFT purposes; the third questionnaire (QLB 3) contains the most detailed set of information, encompassing (1) procedures related to the different AML/CFT requirements, (2) solo and group levels, and (3) quantitative indicators such as the number and amount both of STRs filed and of large and unusual transactions identified (FATF R.11) and the number of people who received AML/CFT training. It primarily contains AML/CFT requirements set in laws and regulations but also includes some best practices for implementing them; the fourth questionnaire (QLB 4) mentions branches and wholly owned subsidiaries that operate in noncooperative countries and territories as identified by the FATF (the latter is no longer used).
8. Using an Excel software program, the document includes 100 key questions and will make it possible to assign not only a grade for each checkpoint, but also an overall grade resulting from the weighted average of all grades.
9. If permitted by law.
10. "A manual transaction monitoring system consists of a review of various reports generated by the bank's management information systems (MIS) or vendor systems. Some banks' MIS are supplemented by vendor systems designed to identify

reportable currency transactions and to maintain required funds transfer records. Many of these vendor systems include filtering models for identification of unusual activity. Examples of MIS reports include currency activity reports, funds transfer reports, monetary instrument sales reports, large item reports, significant balance change reports, and non sufficient funds (NSF) reports. The process may involve review of daily reports, reports that cover a period of time (e.g., rolling 30-day reports, monthly reports), or a combination of both types of reports. The type and frequency of reviews and resulting reports used should be commensurate with the bank's [...] AML risk profile and appropriately cover its high-risk products, services, customers, and geographic locations.

[...] Automated account-monitoring systems typically use computer programs that have been developed in-house or purchased from vendors, to identify individual transactions, patterns of unusual activity, or deviations from expected activity. These systems can capture a wide range of account activity, such as deposits, withdrawals, funds transfers, automated clearing house (ACH) transactions, and automated teller machine (ATM) transactions, directly from the bank's core data processing system. Banks that are large, operate in many locations, or have a large volume of high-risk customers typically use automated account-monitoring systems."

Source: FFIEC, BSA/AML Examination Manual, August 2007.

11. Also see chapter 2.
12. Also see chapter 2.
13. Source: De Nederlandsche Bank
14. Capital adequacy, Asset quality, Management factors, Earnings, and Liquidity.
15. Here, the word "regulation" refers to regulations issued by other competent authorities or other legislative bodies.
16. The members of JMLSG are: the Association of British Insurers (ABI), the Association of Foreign Banks (AFB), the Association of Friendly Societies (AFS), the Association of Independent Financial Advisers (AIFA), the Association of Private Client Investment Managers and Stockbrokers (APCIMS), the British Bankers' Association (BBA), the British Venture Capital Association (BVCA), the Building Societies Association (BSA), the Council of Mortgage Lenders (CML), the Electronic Money Association (EMA), the Finance & Leasing Association (FLA), the Futures and Options Association (FOA), the Investment Management Association (IMA), the London Investment Banking Association (LIBA), the PEP & ISA Managers' Association (PIMA), and the Wholesale Market Brokers' Association (WMBA).
17. "Although the JMLSG Guidance notes do not have the force of law, in that they do not contain binding legal requirements, they do have strong persuasive value. Under s.330 (8) of the PCA [Proceeds of Crime Act] 2002, the court must consider whether the defendant in a money laundering prosecution under the Act followed any relevant guidance issued and published by a supervisory authority or other appropriate body, that has been approved by the Treasury. The JMLSG Guidance notes, which were last revised in February 2006, have been approved by the Treasury." City of London, comparative implementation of EU directives (II), money laundering, December 2006.

4

The On-Site Supervisory Process[1]

Contents

CHAPTER 5

1 Overview

The on-site supervisory process aims to ensure that banks comply with all laws, regulations, and policies of the jurisdiction and have systems in place both to ensure ongoing compliance and to identify any weaknesses in the compliance system. To meet these objectives, supervisors should develop a comprehensive examination program that incorporates a review of all the legally required key anti-money laundering and combating the financing of terrorism (AML/CFT) elements. The examination should adopt a risk-based approach to optimize the use of limited resources and budgets and to focus on higher-risk areas.

The bank examination process should not only ensure compliance with legal requirements, but should also review AML/CFT bank policies and procedures, and determine whether they are working as designed, and are effectively meeting their objectives. To establish whether this is the case, the examination should always include some level of transaction testing.

An effective and successful AML/CFT on-site examination program depends on many factors, including sufficient resources and a well-trained staff of competent bank examiners who have full and complete access to all bank and customer records.

This chapter is arranged in four sections and addresses a variety of the steps required to successfully conduct a comprehensive AML/CFT bank examination. Section 5.2 discusses examination issues and approaches. Section 5.3 describes how to determine the scope of plan for staff, and generally prepare for an on-site AML/CFT examination. Section 5.4 gives an overview of the key AML/CFT elements to be reviewed during the examination, while section 5.5 shows how to develop and communicate its findings and conclusions.

5

2 Examination Issues and Approaches

An AML/CFT supervisor must first organize and develop the examination program. Before an efficient and comprehensive AML/CFT examination program can be developed, a number of issues, some of which are discussed below, must be taken into account.

2.1 Risk-Based Approach Versus Standardized Approach

A comprehensive examination would examine every bank for every AML/CFT issue every year. Unfortunately, because of limited budgets and a similarly limited number of bank examiners and other supervisory experts, that approach is not a practical one. Approaches to bank examinations may vary but, in today's world there seems to be one particularly effective and efficient way to supervise banks, and that is the risk-based approach shown in box 5.1.

This approach uses the bank's risk profile as the basis both for reviewing a bank's AML/CFT compliance program and for determining the effectiveness of its AML/CFT policies and procedures.[2] It verifies whether systems actually function as designed by using transaction testing.

By adopting a risk-based approach, bank supervisors can focus on those banks that are at high risk for money laundering and financing of terrorism (ML/FT). Larger, more complex banks involved in cross-border transactions, or those banks that focus on private banking, are examples of likely candidates for additional scrutiny.

2.2 The Inspection Cycle and Examination Notification

2.2.1 Examination Frequency

The frequency of examinations varies by jurisdiction, but many jurisdictions base it on several factors such as bank size, complexity, rating, and risk profile. A bank operating with few or no problems might be examined every 12 to 18 months, for example. Those banks with significant issues, however, or ongoing problems identified in past examinations, would be scheduled for more frequent examinations. It might be appropriate for banks experiencing some problems to have an annual examination, while banks with more serious issues might be visited every six months or even more frequently. In addition to the on-site examination, an effective banking supervisory system also includes an off-site supervisory process and regular contacts with bank management.[3]

2.2.2 On-Site AML/CFT Examination Notification

Many jurisdictions notify bank management in advance of the proposed examination and the specific date that it will begin.[4] During the notification, the management of

BOX 5.1   Example of the Risk-Based Approach in Singapore

The Monetary Authority of Singapore (MAS) adopts a risk-based approach to supervision, rather than rules that are prescriptive and one-size-fits-all. Under this framework, an institution's assessment is built on a thorough understanding of its activities, risk management processes, and operating environment. The key stages in the risk assessment process are:

- Determining the significant activities undertaken by a bank
- Assessing the inherent risks and adequacy of corresponding risk management systems and internal controls for each of these activities
- Assessing the financial strength of the institution and the adequacy of the Board and Senior Management oversight of its businesses, including AML/CFT
- Determining the overall risk rating for the bank and, consequently, the supervisory measures needed

To determine a risk profile of a bank, MAS gathers information from a number of sources, both onsite and offsite:

- Bank's regulatory returns including financial statements
- Bank's internal policies, procedures, and its self-assessed risk profile
- Internal and external audit reports
- For foreign banks, information from home country supervisors
- Past inspection reports
- Copies of bank's suspicious transaction reports (STRs) submitted to the Singapore financial intelligence unit (FIU)

Based on its risk-based approach, institutions are placed in distinct supervisory categories and are thus differentiated in terms of scope and intensity of supervision. MAS determines the frequency of on-site examinations, the types of inspection (focused on AML/CFT or AML/CFT as part of a full scope inspection), and the areas that require enhanced supervision.

5

the bank is also provided with the request letter so that bank-prepared information will be available for the examiners to analyze before or during the visit. The advantage of the prior notification and the request letter is that the bank has time to prepare all the necessary information in advance, and also to arrange for the appropriate bank staff to be available to assist the examiners. This facilitates the examination process and allows the examiners to finish in a reasonable time.

An alternative approach is an unannounced examination, where examiners enter the bank without notifying bank management in advance. This approach certainly has the element of surprise, and it may lead to the exposure of ongoing fraudulent activity that cannot be quickly concealed from examiners. The approach, nonetheless, has many disadvantages. Bank management, being unaware of the pending examination cannot be ready with all the information needed. The examination, therefore, takes longer, first, because of the time needed to assemble this information and, second, because some key bank staff may not be available to discuss examination issues with examiners at the right time.

2.3 Targeted AML/CFT On-Site Inspection Versus General On-Site Visit

2.3.1 Prudential and Stand-Alone AML /CFT Examinations

In addition to compliance issues such as AML/CFT, jurisdictions examine banks for prudential activities such as capital requirements, loan quality, investments, liquidity, and other banking activities. Some jurisdictions prefer to conduct prudential and compliance examinations together, while other jurisdictions separate the two examinations. When the AML/CFT examination is performed separately, it is conducted as a stand-alone examination. Many countries, however, conduct all or most compliance examinations as stand-alone examinations, with AML/CFT usually being an integral part of them.

The Basel Core Principles recommend that banks have a permanent compliance function to assist senior management in managing the compliance risks faced by the bank more effectively.[5] There are pros and cons for both methods. Stand-alone AML/CFT examinations are usually conducted by expert examiners having specialized skills in AML/CFT, skills that prudential examiners are unlikely to have been able to acquire. On the other hand, there are economies to a combined operation, and it is generally more costly to have separate AML/CFT and prudential examinations. Jurisdictions have to decide which approach, or variant of it, is best for them.

2.3.2 Targeted Examinations

Targeted examinations focus on specific areas within a bank's operations, and they are used when there is evidence that a particular bank has AML/CFT problems, when bank supervisors want to address specific issues such as customer due diligence (CDD), or when supervisors are looking at groups of banks in a specific geographic area, especially one that is considered high risk. In those cases, the scope of the examination would be restricted to the area of interest, and the examination staff would be experts in that area.

2.4 How Far to Go during an AML/CFT On-Site Examination

In the countries visited, there is not one single approach that defines the depth of an on-site AML/CFT examination. In some jurisdictions, the scope of AML/CFT compliance inspections is rather more limited than the Financial Action Task Force (FATF) standards recommend. Examiners only look at the procedures, and ensure,

5

for example, whether they exist, comply with the national AML/CFT law, and cover all the banks' activities. Another approach goes further and makes sure the AML/CFT internal apparatus is properly and effectively implemented. This approach, found in several countries, leads the inspection team to perform transaction testing to analyze a sample of customer's files and operations, and to examine the bank's internal audit process and methodology. The FATF Methodology for Assessing Compliance with the 40 Recommendations and the FATF 9 Special Recommendations[6] gives some indications about the expected depth of the on-site examination, noting that "inspections should include the review of policies, procedures, books and records, and should extend to sample testing.[7]" It also notes that "supervisors should have the power to compel production of or obtain access to all records, documents and information relevant to monitoring compliance. This includes all documents or information related to accounts or other business relationships, or transactions…[8]". One can infer from this that the approach that best meets the FATF's standard is the one that reviews all internal procedures, and also includes sample and transaction testing.

Jurisdictions should also consider several pending issues when they establish the depth of an on-site examination. The most controversial issue concerns unusual or suspicious transactions discovered during the examination. Examiners may discover unusual or suspicious transactions during an on-site visit, and examination procedures should be in place to guide the examiners on how to resolve these situations. The fieldwork suggests there are divergent practices to deal with this. In some countries, after reviewing the situation with senior supervisory management, the bank examiner can file an STR with the FIU[9] or with another competent authority.[10] In some other countries, without any further investigation,[11] the lack of STRs and the circumstances surrounding the absence of declarations are described in detail in the examination report. In others, the supervisory authority gives a written instruction to the bank to report the information.[12] In yet other jurisdictions, examiners, after discussions with bank management, recommend that the bank file an STR where the examiner believes one is needed. If there should be a dispute about filing an STR, examiners defer to their supervisors on how to proceed. In any event, the issue must be examined closely to determine why the bank did not file an STR. Bank procedures should be reviewed and tested to determine whether they failed to identify unusual transactions.

A second issue is whether it is appropriate for the examiners to look at the personal accounts of the bank's top management to identify possible suspicious activities in which these managers might be involved. Also, should examiners perform enhanced checks on customers the bank has flagged to the FIU? One could argue that neither of these actions fit the role of a bank examiner, but rather the role of a law enforcement officer. Again, are examiners expected to detect suspicious transactions in the books of an inspected bank in order to test the effectiveness of the bank's internal detection/monitoring device? Fieldwork shows there is no clear consensus as to whether AML/CFT on-site examinations should encompass detection of suspicious operations.

5

In light of these issues, standard inspections should include interviews; document-based analyses; examinations of books, procedures and records; as well as sample testing.

2.5 Examination of Foreign Branches

Some banks based in one jurisdiction may also have branch offices and subsidiaries in other countries, and bank supervisors should plan to examine all these branches in order to ensure that they follow the AML/CFT rules of the home country (see box 5.2). Permission from the host jurisdictions is necessary to conduct these examinations.[13] One of the most common legal bases for this arrangement is a Memorandum Of Understanding between both parties, allowing the home country to perform on-site AML/CFT compliance inspections in the host country.

2.6 Resources, Skills, and Methodology

2.6.1 AML/CFT Expert Examiners and Generalist Examiners

Another issue is whether AML/CFT examinations should be conducted by trained experts or by generalist examiners. Generalist examiners have some AML/CFT knowledge but focus most of their time on prudential regulatory matters. Some jurisdictions, where the prudential examination also covers AML/CFT, are able to use generalist examiners to conduct both the AML/CFT examination and the safety and soundness examination. There are arguments for and against this approach and, of course, one method may not be appropriate for all jurisdictions. AML/CFT has become somewhat complex, however, and may eventually require trained AML/CFT experts.

In Canada, the OFSI has adopted a specialist approach to AML/CFT assessment. The AML/CFT examiners do not form part of the prudential supervisory group, although each assessment is conducted in close cooperation with them. The advantages of this approach to OSFI are that it enables generalist supervisors to focus on prudential matters and also enables OSFI to analyze inherent ML risk separately from financial risks, because under OSFI's AML/CFT framework the two are not mutually dependent.

2.6.2 Methodology

The supervisor should develop a bank examination manual to guide examiners in conducting the examination process. As a minimum, the manual should include the following:

- An overview of ML/FT in today's global environment
- A review of international standard setters for AML/CFT and other international bodies involved in combating ML/FT
- The ML/FT situation in the jurisdiction

BOX 5.2   **On-site Examination of Foreign Banks in Hong Kong, China;**
Singapore; and Canada

Hong Kong. The Hong Kong Monetary Authority (HKMA) adopts a group-level approach in the supervision of large and complex banks, and of overseas branches and subsidiaries. Overseas branches of banks incorporated in Hong Kong are required to follow HKMA regulations and guidelines, provided they do not conflict with regulations of the host country.

In Hong Kong, every on-site examination includes an AML/CFT assessment component. Within a Tier 1, evaluation of AML/CFT is part of a full bank assessment. Tier 2 evaluations are conducted by specialist teams and focus only on AML/CFT issues. Two kinds of Tier 2 assessments may take place: (1) full AML/CFT assessments of a specific bank or (2) horizontal assessment of a single AML/CFT issue across the entire banking industry, such as CDD in private banking. Selection of banks and scope of Tier 2 examinations are determined annually, based on a bank risk profile. The profile is derived from information gathered from a number of sources, including discussions of AML/CFTspecialists with examiners responsible for banks' full scope examinations.

Singapore. In Singapore, information sharing with foreign supervisors takes several forms. Following the examination of a branch of a foreign bank in Singapore, the Monetary Authority of Singapore (MAS) sends the examination report to the bank's home country supervisor, the branch's headquarters, and the branch itself. If a foreign supervisor conducts an examination of its Singapore branch joint inspection, teams may be created, comprising MAS and foreign supervisor staff. When there is an on-site examination of a branch of a Singapore-incorporated bank, MAS coordinates with the local supervisor to provide it with a copy of the examination report.

Canada. The Office of the Supervisor of Financial Institutions (OFSI) regularly assesses whether foreign branches and subsidiaries of banks and insurance companies are subject to local risk management standards and requirements equivalent to those in place at the Head Office in Canada. OSFI also shares the results of its work in host jurisdictions with local financial regulators. There is no regulatory restriction on the ability of a foreign regulator to inspect a branch or subsidiary of a home bank in Canada; however, OSFI usually requests the foreign regulator to collaborate with it on the visit and the examination.

5

- A list of all national agencies involved in AML/CFT with a detailed explanation of the role of each agency
- A detailed review and explanation of all national laws, regulations, and policies as they apply to banks
- A list of bank sanctions and penalties for noncompliance in the jurisdiction

- Examination procedures and steps that cover every key AML/CFT component to be conducted during the on-site examination
- A discussion of how to develop and write the examination report
- An appendix covering laws, regulations, policy statements, references, and other important AML/CFT materials that can assist the examiners

5

3 Planning and Preparing for the AML/CFT On-Site Examination

Before an AML/CFT bank examination, certain steps must be undertaken. These steps are critical to the examination's success and provide needed information for efficient management of the examination.

3.1 Pre-planning Process

Before the examination team enters the bank, there should be preliminary discussions with bank management as part of the pre-planning process. In these discussions, management is asked to gather information necessary for the examination.

In order to keep the element of surprise, some jurisdictions do not notify bank management of a pending examination. In those cases, examiners will contact management and ask for information only after they have actually entered the bank.

Planning the scope and other aspects of the examination starts with gathering and analyzing the following information:

- The bank's AML/CFT risk assessment
- Prior examination reports and correspondence between the bank and supervisor
- Internal and external audits or other independent reviews
- Off-site monitoring information[14]
- Information received as a result of the supervisory request letter

3.2 The AML/CFT Risk Assessment Before the Visit[15]

As part of the planning process, and to accomplish the goals of the AML/CFT examination, the mission chief should review the AML/CFT risk analysis prepared by the bank or, if one is not available, should prepare a risk assessment based upon the factors available (see chapter 2 for further details). It is recommended, nevertheless, that all banks prepare AML/CFT risk assessments and implement their compliance programs according to the particular risks identified.

The risk assessment process should weigh a number of factors, including the identification and measurement of risk with respect to products, services, customers, and geographic locations. The completed assessment helps a bank to manage AML/CFT risk effectively and to develop appropriate internal controls for the AML/CFT compliance program.

The examiner's review of a bank's AML/CFT risk assessment should guide the planning process. This review should include a consideration of all factors pertinent to a bank's particular risk profile, and it should review the risk assessment to determine if it is commensurate with the bank's actual risk.

5

3.3 Prior Examinations and Correspondence with the Bank

Findings from past examinations and work papers and from ongoing correspondence between the bank and its supervisor are important sources of pre-planning information. Previous violations or an absence of appropriate policies and procedures, among other AML/CFT compliance deficiencies, should be flagged and followed up at the examination. Public items such as news articles are also useful sources of information about the target bank.[16]

3.4 Internal and External Audits or Other Independent Reviews

Internal and external audit reports covering AML/CFT issues and deficiencies can also yield important information in examination planning (see box 5.3). In their reviews, examiners should determine the quality and scope of the audits and how well they address the AML/CFT compliance programs. It is also important to review any correspondence between bank management and the auditors, and to identify any remedial action taken to correct possible deficiencies. In Hong Kong's supervisory practice, for example, HKMA collaborates with the bank's external auditors. HKMA may require the bank to commission an external auditor approved by HKMA to undertake a review of a specific area of operation of the bank. The scope of the review is determined by HKMA and the results of the review are used by HKMA in its supervision of the bank. In Malaysia, the Labuan Offshore Financial Service Authority (LOFSA) confirms that external auditors play an important role both in monitoring a bank's internal controls and procedures and in ascertaining its compliance with national AML regulations. LOFSA has issued guidelines to internal auditors that require AML/CFT measures and controls as a minimum standard.

3.5 Off-Site Monitoring Information

Data elements collected through available off-site monitoring systems are also an important part of the on-site process, because they might include information from outside regulatory and law enforcement agencies. Such information may include filing errors for suspicious activity reports (STRs), or large cash reporting, or the volume of STRs and large cash activity in relation to the bank's size, growth, and geographic location. These might be followed by civil money penalties or other sanctions imposed by the competent authorities, such as law enforcement subpoenas or seizures. Before the visit, in those jurisdictions where on-site and off-site supervision responsibilities are split into two departments, the on-site inspection team usually meets with off-site supervision department staff responsible for the ongoing surveillance of banks. The purpose of the meeting is to discuss issues of common concern, such as areas of higher risks, sectors or types of activities requiring deeper investigations, and failures previously detected but not yet addressed.

BOX 5.3	Example of Useful External Information

In France, Regulation 97-02 of 21 February 1997 regarding internal control institutions and investment firms (as amended by Ministerial Orders of 31 March 2005, 17 June 2005, 20 February 2007, and 2 July 2007) requires banks to prepare and transmit two types of reports to the supervisor (the General Secretariat of the Commission bancaire).

At least once a year, as set forth in article 42, reporting institutions, irrespective of the nature of risks the bank is facing, are required to draw up a report on the conditions in which internal control is conducted. For each type of risk (defined in regulation 97-07), the report shall include, among others, (1) a description of the main actions carried out in relation to internal control and the lessons drawn from these actions; (2) an inventory of investigations carried out, identifying the main lessons to be drawn, especially the main shortcomings observed and the follow-up to the corrective actions taken; and (3) a description of significant changes made in relation to internal control during the period under review. In addition to that, article 43 of regulation 97-02 stipulates that at least once a year, the reporting institutions shall draw up a report on the measurement and monitoring of their risk exposure, and their report may be included in the report required by article 42.

As laid down in article 44 of regulation 97-02, reporting institutions must submit the reports stipulated in articles 42 and 43 annually, not only to the decision-making body but also to the Commission bancaire, as required in a letter of 19 September 2007 from the Secretary General of the banking Commission to the AFECEI (Investment Firms and Credit Institutions Association). These reports are extremely useful not only from the perspective of off-site examinations but also in anticipation of on-site inspections. This is because they provide examiners, before the visit, with a good overview of potential weaknesses in the bank's internal controls, including AML/CFT, and they allow the mission chief to plan the mission accordingly.

5

As a result of these preliminary discussions, inspection teams get a better understanding of issues requiring special attention. Before the visit, the on-site inspection team also should meet with the FIU to discuss possible concerns about the target bank—lack of STRs, for example—that might indicate a weak reporting process.[17]

3.6 Request Letters

Before the AML/CFT examination, the mission chief should deliver a request letter to bank management asking for important information intended to enable the examination to be completed with minimal disruption and in good time.[18] Examiners can also request specific materials for an AML/CFT examination, either beforehand or at the beginning of the visit. The following examples of such materials include areas considered to be AML/CFT best practices and follow many of the FATF Recommendations, but are not, by any means, all-inclusive. This list should be tailored to the jurisdiction's laws, regulations, and policies, to the bank's AML/CFT risk profile, and to the scope of the planned examination.

3.6.1   The Bank's AML/CFT Compliance Program

This information is important because it assesses the effectiveness of the bank's AML/CFT compliance program, its compliance with national laws and regulations, and its effectiveness in combating ML/FT. It also describes the structure of the bank's compliance program. As well, the information helps mission chiefs determine their examination bank contacts.

- Name and title of the AML/CFT compliance officer
- Organization charts showing reporting lines
- Copies of the most recent written AML/CFT compliance program approved by the board of directors
- Copies of policies and procedures relating to all reporting and recordkeeping requirements, including suspicious transaction reporting
- Bank correspondence among its supervisors, FIU, and law enforcement authorities since the previous AML/CFT examination
- Copies of all internal procedures and policies relating to Know Your Customer (KYC) and CDD

5

3.6.2   Audit Records

Audit records provide insight into concerns and possible problems within the bank and how bank management has dealt with them. It is important to review the scope of the audit and to note whether it included a review of the bank's AML/CFT program. The mission chief should request:

- Copies of the results of any internal or external independent audits performed since the previous AML/CFT examination, including the engagement letter and management's responses
- Access to the auditor's risk assessment, audit plan and program, and work papers used in the audit or for testing

3.6.3   The Risk Assessment

The risk assessment, as discussed, is one of the key documents used to plan for the on-site examination and also to assist the mission chief in its staffing. The following documents and reports help the examiner, in developing the AML/CFT risk analysis, to understand the bank's methodology and rationale:

- Available copies of management's AML/CFT risk assessment of products, services, customers, and geographic locations
- A list of bank high-risk accounts

3.6.4 Customer Identification Program

Banks should have a written customer identification program (CIP) delineating the customer identification process and the requirements for account opening. CIPs should enable a bank to form a reasonable belief that it knows the true identity of its customers.[19] To review the CIP, the mission chief should request the following:

- List of all accounts lacking appropriate identification numbers
- File correspondence requesting identification numbers for bank customers
- Written description of the bank's CIP
- List of new accounts for all product lines
- List of any accounts opened for which verification has not been completed or any accounts opened that have exceptions to the bank approved CIP
- List of customers for whom the bank took adverse action on the basis of its CIP
- List of all documentary and nondocumentary methods the bank uses to verify a customer's identity
- Copies of contracts with financial institutions and with third parties that perform all or any part of the bank's CIP

Examiners should pay special attention to the issues of KYC and CDD. Fieldwork has shown a very weak compliance with Recommendation 5 or Know Your Customer and Customer Due Diligence, as shown in figure 5.1.

3.6.5 Suspicious Transaction Reporting

The suspicious transaction reporting (STR) reporting process is a key component of any AML/CFT compliance program.[20] Details of the bank's STR reporting system should be examined to determine whether the reporting system complies with national laws, regulations, or policies, and whether the system is working as designed. The following information assists the mission chief in making these determinations:

- STRs filed with the FIU during the review period, including supporting documentation (where access to STRs is permitted by national laws, regulations, or policies[21]).
- Analysis and documentation of any activity for which an STR was considered but not filed and for which the bank is actively considering filing an STR.
- The bank's expanded monitoring procedures applied to high-risk accounts.

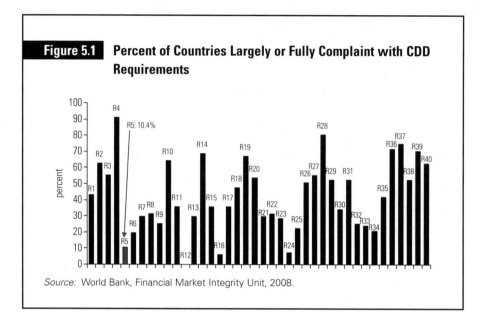

Figure 5.1 Percent of Countries Largely or Fully Complaint with CDD Requirements

Source: World Bank, Financial Market Integrity Unit, 2008.

- A determination of whether the bank uses a manual or an automated account monitoring system, or a combination of the two. If the system is vendor supplied, obtain information about the vendor.
- Copies of reports used for identification and monitoring of suspicious transactions.
- Correspondence filed with national law enforcement authorities about the disposition of accounts reported for suspicious activity.
- Copies of criminal subpoenas received by the bank since the previous examination.
- Copies of policies, procedures, and processes used to comply with all criminal subpoenas.

3.6.6 Large Cash Reporting

Some jurisdictions, as part of their ML/FT oversight, require the reporting of large currency transactions. The following information helps to determine whether the large cash reporting (LCR) process is functioning properly and whether it meets national requirements:

- Filed large cash reports (LCRs)
- Internal reports used to identify reportable currency transactions for the review period
- List of products or services that may involve currency transactions

3.6.7   Training Records

The mission chief should request appropriate training documentation,[22] including training schedules with dates, attendees, and topics, in order to confirm that the bank has adequately implemented all required training programs.

3.6.8   Sanctions and Blocked Accounts

Examiners should determine whether the bank is in compliance with laws, regulations, and policies concerning sanctions, and whether the bank's systems are effective. The information required includes

- Copies of sanctions (if any), policies, and procedures
- Copies of the bank's risk management process as it relates to sanctions
- A list of blocked or rejected transactions with individuals or entities on the United Nations or national list

In brief, the preparation for an on-site examination has five basic steps.

1. Review the bank's AML/CFT risk assessment to become aware of any high-risk situations. Based upon the risk assessment determine the scope of the examination, and select the necessary technical experts to staff it. In situations where a bank may be heavily involved in international transactions, for example, the mission chief will need to focus the examination on cross-border transactions, wire transfers, foreign correspondent account relationships, and so on, and will need to staff the examination with examiners having appropriate experience. The scope of the examination for those banks involved in private banking will be different, and there will be different experts on the examination team.

2. Review previous examinations and work papers, and note any problems or deficiencies identified. Review all correspondence between the supervisor and the bank since the last AML/CFT examination to determine any relevant ongoing issues.

3. Review all available off-site monitoring data, including publicly available materials such as news reports.

4. Closely review all internal and external independent audits, their work papers, and any correspondence between the bank and the auditors that relates directly or indirectly to AML/CFT issues.

5. Assemble and analyze all information gathered, and finalize the scope of the examination. Based upon the pre-examination information, make appropriate staffing assignments and organize and conduct the on-site examination (see box 5.4).

5

> **BOX 5.4** **Examples of Planning Procedures for On-Site Visits in Malaysia and South Korea**
>
> Bank Negara Malaysia (BNM) has adopted a risk-based approach when preparing for an on-site examination. BNM appoints relationship managers to take charge of off-site examination and to gather all available information about a specific bank. They then prepare a risk-based examination memorandum that identifies areas requiring enhanced supervision. Managers gather input from many sources including BNM departments and the bank's internal and external auditors. After the pre-examination information is analyzed, a risk-control matrix is prepared, pinpointing areas of particular risk and areas with inadequate controls that require enhanced supervision. Based on the completed risk profile, BNM examiners then determine the scope of the on-site examination and identify the appropriate staff requirements. In addition, they determine the frequency of examinations, which cannot be given less often than an examination every 12 to 18 months.
>
> In South Korea, to determine the scope, organization, and staffing of an on-site inspection, the Financial Supervisory Service (FSS) gathers information about the bank from a number of sources. These include the Korea Financial Intelligence Unit (KoFIU), law enforcement authorities, media, and bank-prepared risk profiles. Based on this information, the FSS is able to determine the scope and frequency of examinations and the size and composition of the on-site examination team.

5

4 Overview of the Key Areas to Be Assessed

Key AML/CFT on-site inspection criteria vary depending on the laws, regulations, and policies of various jurisdictions. For the purposes of this guide, however, the important elements generally follow the FATF Recommendations and other international best practices required for a comprehensive AML/CFT compliance program. An important key element is the AML/CFT compliance program, which is necessary if a bank is to control ML/FT risks effectively. Such compliance programs must be assessed by supervisors, first, for adequacy and effectiveness and, second, to establish how well they meet regulatory requirements.

4.1 AML/CFT Compliance Program[23]

All banks should have a written, board-approved AML/CFT compliance program that consists of policies, procedures, and processes and that must be reviewed by supervisors for adequacy (see box 5.5). An appropriate and functioning AML/CFT program should meet four basic requirements:

- Appointment of an AML/CFT compliance officer
- A system of internal controls to ensure that the program is working as designed
- Independent testing of the AML/CFT compliance program
- AML/CFT training for bank personnel

4.1.1 AML/CFT Compliance Officer

Meetings with the bank compliance officer (CO)[24] are key to the on-site inspection process, helping the team to reach a better understanding of the integration of AML/CFT compliance issues into the bank's overall compliance apparatus (see box 5.6). The maintenance of integrity within financial institutions depends on the role of the CO, who is the first line of defense against fraud and ML/TF.

Each bank should appoint a qualified individual to serve as an AML/CFT compliance officer subject to the approval of the bank's board of directors.[25] This officer should report to senior management or to the board of directors and should act independently and function at the management level. For the most part, COs function as independent and objective individuals, reviewing and evaluating compliance issues and concerns within the bank. They coordinate the planning and implementation of compliance programs and are responsible for designing policies and procedures for program application and implementation.

Compliance officers must be fully knowledgeable about AML/CFT requirements and all related laws and regulations because they are responsible for managing, coordinating, and monitoring the bank's compliance regime with AML/CFT laws and regulations. In addition, COs must exhibit awareness and understanding

5

BOX 5.5 **Example of a Comprehensive Supervisory Framework**

In Malaysia, BNM adopts a comprehensive supervisory framework for assessment of a bank's AML/CFT compliance. The framework consists of five core areas designed to assess the adequacy and effectiveness of reporting institutions' AML/CFT policies, procedures, systems, and controls. The core areas include the following:

- Board and management oversight
  - AML/CFT policies approved and endorsed by the board
  - Periodic reviews of AML/CFT policies by the board and senior management
  - Risk assessment on new products and services
- Policies and procedures
  - Identification of account holder, monitoring of transactions, record-keeping, and so forth
  - Detection and reporting of suspicious transactions
  - Roles and responsibilities of compliance officers
  - Board of directors-approved AML/CFT operations manual
- Human resources and training
  - Regular and ongoing training for all staff
  - Staff awareness of institution's AML/CFT measures
  - Regular review of employees' backgrounds to ensure integrity
- Management information systems
  - Timely dissemination of AML/CFT initiatives to relevant parties
  - Timely update to employees on changes to AML/CFT initiatives
- Internal Audit
  - Independent audit function to assess AML/CFT
  - Regular audits
  - Timely corrective action

---

of the ethical and moral principles consistent with the mission and values of specific banks.[26]

AML/CFT compliance officers require adequate resources to implement and manage effective AML/CFT compliance programs. They should also have access to customer identification data when they need it, as well as to other customer information and transaction records. They should understand the relevant bank's products, services, customers, and geographic service areas, and they should also understand the risks of money laundering and terrorist financing associated with those activities and geographic areas. The role of inspection teams is to make sure that COs meet all these criteria (see box 5.6 below).

Various field operations show that many jurisdictions have successfully implemented strict AML/CFT compliance programs. The Hong Kong Monetary Authority

> **BOX 5.6** **Examples of Key Issues to Consider during Compliance Officer Interviews**
>
> - Are duties for CO, managers, and internal auditors clearly delineated?
> - Describe the reporting line. Does the CO report to the bank's management directly?
> - What is the scope of duties of the CO, including AML/CFT (where applicable)?
> - Is there a compliance hotline employees may use to report problems and concerns relating to ML/TF without fear of retaliation?
> - Does the CO monitor the AML/CFT compliance plan for periodic updates, when needed?
> - Does CO coordinate and conduct inquiries and/or investigations on AML/CFT when deemed necessary?
> - How many resources have been dedicated to the AML/CFT compliance program?
> - Does the CO delegate responsibilities for conducting appropriate AML/CFT compliance investigations (for example, legal or internal audit) to ensure proper follow up?

(HKMA), in its Supplement to the Guideline on Prevention of Money Laundering, requires banks to appoint compliance officers, who play an active role in the identification and reporting suspicious transactions. They are responsible for regularly checking that banks have policies and procedures ensuring compliance with legal and regulatory requirement and for testing such compliance. Compliance officers must be of sufficient status within the organization and have adequate resources to perform their functions. Apart from compliance officers, however, internal audits periodically carry out independent evaluations of banks' AML/CFT policies and procedures.

In Malaysia, the Association of Merchant Banks has developed an AML/CFT program that requires banks to maintain a compliance program and also to cooperate with the FIU and relevant enforcement agencies. The program recommends that banks implement internal programs to guard against and detect ML/FT offences; conduct independent audit functions to ensure compliance; and perform integrity checks that include personal, employment, and financial history.

In the offshore financial center of Labuan (Malaysia), compliance officers are subject to strict standards. The offshore regulator, LOFSA, pays particular attention to compliance officers' profiles, gathering information on their qualifications, including their previous employment, their total work experience at the bank, the time spent in their present position, training courses they have attended, and their experience in AML and financial crime prevention.

5

4.1.2 Internal Controls

Each bank should establish and maintain internal procedures, policies, and controls to prevent ML and FT in the institution. At a minimum, the internal control structure should include, among other reporting obligations, customer policies requiring due diligence, record retention, and the detection of unusual and suspicious transactions.

Internal controls are defined as those of the bank's policies, procedures, and processes that limit and control risks, and that achieve compliance with AML/CFT laws and regulations. Their level of sophistication should be commensurate with the size, structure, risks, and complexity of the bank, with large complex banks being more likely to implement departmental internal controls for AML/CFT compliance. Departmental internal controls typically address risks and compliance requirements unique to a department or to a particular line of business, and are part of a comprehensive AML/CFT compliance program (see box 5.7).

BOX 5.7 **Relationship between a Bank's Internal Controls and Its AML/CFT Compliance Program**

Inspection teams should look at all the following internal control elements to determine the adequacy of a specific bank's internal control system:

- Identify banking operations (products, services, customers, and geographic locations) more vulnerable to abuse by money launderers and criminals; provide for periodic updates to the bank's risk profile and provide for an AML/CFT compliance program tailored to manage risks.
- Inform the board of directors, or a committee thereof, and senior management of compliance initiatives, identified compliance deficiencies, and corrective action taken. Notify directors and senior management of suspicious transaction reports (STRs) filed.
- Help to meet all regulatory recordkeeping and reporting requirements, provide recommendations for AML/CFT compliance, and issue updates when regulations are changed.
- Implement risk-based customer due diligence policies, procedures, and processes.
- Identify reportable transactions and accurately file all required reports, including STRs and large currency transaction reports.
- Provide sufficient controls and monitoring systems for timely detection and reporting of suspicious activity.
- Provide for adequate supervision of employees who handle currency transactions, complete reports, monitor for suspicious activity, or engage in any other activity covered by AML/CFT implementing regulations.

5

4.1.3 Independent Testing

Banks should maintain an adequately resourced and independent audit function to test compliance with their AML/CFT procedures, policies, and controls (see box 5.8). Independent testing can generally be carried out by an internal audit department, outside auditors, consultants, or other qualified independent parties. The persons conducting the AML/CFT testing should report directly to an audit committee made up primarily or completely of outside directors.[27]

Audits should be risk based and should evaluate the quality of risk management for banking operations, departments, and subsidiaries. Risk-based audit programs vary with the bank's size, complexity, scope of activities, risk profile, quality of control functions, geographic diversity, and use of technology.

4.1.4 Training

Banks should establish ongoing employee training programs to ensure that all personnel whose duties demand knowledge of AML/CFT requirements receive appropriate training. For these employees, basic training must include knowledge of current ML/FT techniques, methods, and trends, as well as AML/CFT laws and

---

BOX 5.8   Examples of Independent Testing for AML/CFT

The examiner's role is to ensure that the internal audit has accomplished all of the following steps:

- Evaluate the overall integrity and effectiveness of the AML/CFT compliance program, including policies, procedures, and processes.
- Review the appropriateness of the bank's risk assessment, given the bank's risk profile (products, services, customers, and geographic locations).
- Conduct an internal audit with transaction testing to verify the bank's adherence to AML/CFT recordkeeping and reporting requirements.
- Evaluate management's efforts to resolve any violations and deficiencies noted in previous audits and regulatory examinations and management's progress in addressing any outstanding supervisory actions.
- Review staff training for adequacy, accuracy, and completeness.
- Review the effectiveness of the suspicious activity monitoring systems used for AML/CFT compliance.
- Assess the overall process for identifying and reporting suspicious activity, including reviewing filed or prepared STRs to determine the accuracy, timeliness, completeness, and effectiveness of the bank's policy.

regulations that affect the bank. Procedures requiring due diligence for customers and the institution's reporting requirements for suspicious transactions should receive particular attention.

Training requirements should have a different focus for new staff, front-line staff, compliance staff, or staff dealing with new customers as shown in box 5.9. New staff should be educated in the importance of KYC/CDD policies and the basic requirements at the bank. Front-line staff members who deal directly with the public should be trained to verify the identity of new customers, to exercise due diligence in handling accounts of existing customers on an ongoing basis, and to detect patterns of suspicious activity. Regular refresher training should be provided to ensure that staff are reminded of their responsibilities and are kept informed of new developments. It is crucial that all relevant staff members fully understand the need for KYC/CDD policies and implement them consistently.[28]

Banks should always document their training programs. Documentation regarding training and testing materials, the dates of training sessions, and attendance records should be maintained by the bank and be available for examiner and auditor review.

4.2 Other Key Areas to be Assessed During AML/CFT Inspections[29]

Because of differing requirements in laws, regulations, and supervisory policies, key examination criteria may differ from country to country. Some of the major AML/CFT programs, elements, and issues for review follow.

5

BOX 5.9 Examples of Staff Requiring AML/CFT Training

- Cashiers – may be able to identify suspicious deposits or withdrawals
- Account opening staff – the first line of defense against ML/FT
- Compliance and audit staff – they need to be aware of the broad range of AML/CFT controls
- Foreign exchange desk – may be able to identify suspicious foreign currency transactions
- Investment department – investments have been used to launder funds
- Insurance department – insurance products have also been a vehicle to launder money
- Senior management – must know the risks to the institution of money laundering schemes
- Board of Directors – without a general understanding of AML/CFT directors cannot carry out their responsibilities

4.2.1 *Customer Due Diligence and Recordkeeping Programs*

One of the first tasks for examiners is to determine how effectively the bank is meeting its obligations with respect to customer due diligence and recordkeeping. International standards require extensive recordkeeping. The examiners, therefore, must obtain and examine the bank's record retention schedule and its procedural guidelines and must test to verify compliance with the jurisdiction's requirements.

On-site examiners should pay attention to the following issues:

- *Use of anonymous accounts.* Banks should not keep anonymous accounts or accounts in fictitious names. Where there are numbered accounts, banks should ensure that the customer is properly identified and that the identification records are available to compliance management, auditors, and examiners.[30]
- *Customer due diligence measures (CDD).* CDD procedures should allow the bank to predict with relative certainty the types of transactions in which a customer is likely to engage, and they should help the bank to determine when such transactions might be suspect.
- *Customer identification programs (CIP).* Banks should have a written customer identification program delineating the procedures both for identifying customers and for opening accounts. The program's design should enable a bank to be reasonably confident of the true identity of the customer.
- *Performance of enhanced due diligence measures for higher-risk customers.* Many banks bring enhanced due diligence to bear on higher-risk categories of customers, business relationships, and transactions, all of which can increase the risk of ML and FT. They should be subject to more care at the opening of accounts and reviewed more frequently throughout the term of their relationship with the bank. Supervisors should check whether higher-risk customers are effectively identified and subject to enhanced scrutiny.
- *Bank policies and CDD requirements regarding relationships with politically exposed persons (PEPs).* PEPs can be another category of high risk. The policies of many banks include risk management systems that determine whether a potential customer is a PEP. Additional management safeguards are often brought into play, such as the need for senior management approval of PEP transactions, and for continuing enhanced monitoring of these relationships.
- *Cross-border correspondent banking relationships.* Cross-border correspondent banking relationships may be judged a higher-risk activity requiring that the normal due diligence procedures be enhanced. Banks should obtain sufficient information about a respondent bank to understand the nature of the business and its reputation and the quality of supervision the correspondent is subject to.
- *Bank policies and procedures addressing new technologies.* If risks are to be minimized, special care is needed in non-face-to-face business relationships such as those acquired over the Internet, and banks require policies and

5

procedures that address them. Examiners should carefully analyze how customers are identified, most especially when the bank has relied on an external information source.

- *Bank relationships with other reporting entities.* Banks engaged in relationships with investment and insurance companies should have policies and procedures to ensure that these companies are in compliance with AML/CFT requirements. To be sure of adequate coverage, the banks and these entities should reach formal agreements specifying who is responsible for what application of due diligence and for what type of monitoring.

- *Record retention policies.* Banks should maintain records for auditors, examiners, and other competent authorities to review. While international practice requires that records be retained for five years, some jurisdictions require them to be retained for longer periods.

- *Unusual transactions.* It is important to review bank policies and procedures that address either complex, unusually large transactions, or unusual patterns of transactions having no apparent or visible economic or lawful purpose.

4.2.2 Reporting of Suspicious Transactions

- *Reporting of suspicious transactions.* Examiners should review bank policies and procedures regarding the reporting of suspicious transactions to the FIU or other competent authority.

- *Policies regarding any "tipping off" prohibitions.* As stipulated by the FATF, financial institutions and their directors, officers, and employees should be prohibited from warning ("tipping off") their customers when information relating to them is reported to competent authorities. Examiners should pay attention to these policies.

4.2.3 Other Measures to Deter Money Laundering and Terrorist Financing

Examiners should perform the following tasks in the course of their on-site examination:

- *Review policies for reporting large cash transactions.* If laws or regulations require reporting of large cash transactions, review the bank's reporting policies.

- *Review enhanced due diligence policies.* Review bank policies and practices for those customers and activities that present a higher risk of ML/FT.

- *Foreign branches and subsidiaries of the bank.* Review the bank's policies regarding foreign branch and subsidiary operations. The policies should ensure that foreign branches and subsidiaries conform to the AML/CFT requirements of the home country. When the host country does not permit the application of home country rules, the supervisors in the home country must be notified.

- *Funds transfers.* Funds transfers may be a high-risk area for ML/FT. To assess whether the bank is following prudent banking practices and is in compliance with the record-keeping requirements of the jurisdiction, bank examiners need access to records of funds transfers, including incoming, intermediary, and outgoing transfers. To this end, the inspection team should review the policies and procedures that address foreign and domestic wire transfer documentation and recordkeeping. In that respect, some transactions testing is also highly desirable.
- *Foreign correspondent accounts and transactions with shell banks.* These accounts and transactions may also present a high risk of ML/FT. Banks allowing use of payable-through-accounts[31] in foreign correspondent accounts should take special precautions for managing the resulting risk. Banks are prohibited from establishing, maintaining, administering, or managing a correspondent account for a foreign shell bank[32].
- *Currency-shipment activity.* To address risk in currency-shipment activity, the mission chief should examine the volume of currency shipped between branches, the central bank, and or correspondent banks, which can be an indicator of suspicious activity. These records should be readily available, and the bank should also provide any records that reflect currency shipped to, and received from, the central bank and/or correspondent banks.
- *Searching and reporting to authorities on listed terrorist names.* Field work has shown that in some jurisdictions, the AML supervisor reviews, as part of the onsite AML/CFT visit, the procedures for searching for, and reporting on, listed terrorist names. Canada, for example, uses OSFI as the chief communications conduit for notifying the financial sector of the listing of Designated Persons as determined by the UN Security Council, as well as for domestic listings. OSFI's AML unit reviews the systems in place to ensure that terrorist names are checked against the Canadian government lists and also requires more frequent searching if financial institutions conduct the searching less frequently than weekly.

4.3 Core Risk Areas Requiring Enhanced Due Diligence

While any account or bank activity can be used for the purpose of ML/FT, some accounts or activities are more susceptible than others and should be supervised more stringently. To achieve this, banks should establish specific policies requiring enhanced due diligence measures reasonably designed for high-risk customers,[33] and procedures, controls and systems designed to help the bank to detect and report instances of ML/TF.

The following customers and businesses are among those that may require enhanced supervision. Based upon its own AML/CFT risk profile, however, each bank should develop its own list of higher-risk areas.

- Correspondent accounts (foreign and domestic)
- Payable-through accounts
- Nonresident customers
- Legal persons or arrangements
- Private banking customers
- Companies with nominee shareholders or bearer shares
- Politically Exposed Persons
- High-net-worth customers
- Cash intensive businesses
- Use of intermediaries
- Casinos
- Remittance businesses
- Arms dealers
- Wire transfers
- Foreign exchange dealers
- Bank foreign exchange operations
- Safe deposit boxes
- Monetary instruments
- Nonbank financial institutions
- Offshore companies
- Customers from countries with weak AML/CFT regimes

Depending on the requirements of a particular jurisdiction and the results of an AML/CFT risk assessment of a particular bank, there may be many other areas that an AML/CFT inspection should review. In addition, there are even more complex elements to be examined in the case of more complex banks that deal in brokered deposits, operate private banking departments, operate trust departments, sell insurance products, and are involved in trade finance activities.[34]

Regarding the areas requiring enhanced due diligence, the issue of politically exposed persons should be given particular attention from a supervisory stand point.

A relatively new area of AML concern that was introduced into the 2003 version of the FATF Recommendations and that subsequently found its way into the UN Convention against Corruption, concerns the issue of Politically Exposed Persons (PEPs), those vested with significant public power, which makes them vulnerable to corruption. Basically, the rule is that financial institutions should undertake enhanced due diligence when dealing with PEPs and their family members and close associates.[35]

The FATF defines PEPs as: "individuals who are or have been entrusted with prominent public functions in a foreign country, for example Heads of State or of government, senior politicians, senior government, judicial or military officials, senior executives of state-owned corporations, important political party officials." The UN Convention widens the circle considerably by not limiting itself to foreign

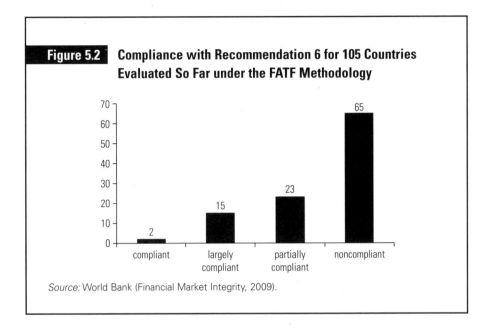

Figure 5.2 **Compliance with Recommendation 6 for 105 Countries Evaluated So Far under the FATF Methodology**

Source: World Bank (Financial Market Integrity, 2009).

individuals. The FATF standard defines the minimum level of enhanced due diligence to be implemented on such clients (in particular, additional requirements for identification of PEPs, senior management approval of the opening of the business relationship, reasonable measures to establish the source of wealth, enhanced on-going monitoring of the business relationship).

As is evident from figure 5.2, compliance with Recommendation 6 is very low across the board, with the vast majority of countries rated either partially compliant (22%) or, more likely, noncompliant (62%), and with developing countries performing slightly worse (92% partially compliant or noncompliant) than developed countries (72% partially compliant or noncompliant).

Even if the evaluated country has a rule or regulation that addresses the issue of PEPs, implementation remains challenging. One key difficulty is the identification of PEPs—even if the 3rd European Directive provides (among others) a useful reference to operationalise the FATF requirement. Guidance on PEPs tends to be high level, with authorities cautious about being too specific in such guidance for fear that it may exclude categories or persons that should be subject to a higher level of due diligence. The content of the enhanced due diligence, and how to do it in practice, remains also too elusive. In the absence of such guidance, compliance per bank will vary widely, with most banks designing their own interpretations of what the obligation entails.

The absence of a clear regulatory framework similarly renders the obligation very difficult to supervise since there are no firm benchmarks against which to determine whether someone qualifies as a PEP. In fact it provides an illustrative example of the challenges attached to the transition from a rule-based to a risk-based

5

system in which one allows more freedom to the supervised entities. Apart from a review of the type of information gathered from the client by the bank when initiating a business relationship what view will the supervisory body take of the further action that a financial institution is to undertake? To what extent is the supervisor expected to conduct its own due diligence and collect information independently? Is it supposed to review the thousands of hits following a Google search on a particular person?

The lack of a clear unequivocal definition of what constitutes a PEP—while understandable—implies that this area of due diligence has received too little attention and remains underdeveloped. Many banks now do searches on their clients on commercial databases and add print-outs of these searches to their client files so they can show the supervisor what action they have taken to comply with PEP requirements. In the absence of a clearer consensus, however, this will remain an area of some confusion, allowing some to do only the bare minimum.

Several countries have taken steps in implementing the FATF PEPs requirements—even if the legal instruments (guidance) elicited has not always allowed those countries to meet the threshold of Recommendation 6. The World Bank plans to undertake in the coming months a review of the current practices, including an analysis of the tools currently available for the private sector to identify PEPs. It also plans to identify "best practices" and challenges in the enhanced due diligence currently undertaken by banks—as well as "best practices" in the supervision of the compliance with PEPs requirements.

5

5   Preparing the Examination Report

Having completed the on-site portion of the examination, the examiners must then prepare the examination report, which describes the findings of the on- and off-site supervisory analyses. The information should be presented to the bank both in writing and through discussions with management. The supervisor should also meet periodically with senior management and the board to discuss the results of supervisory examinations, external audits, and the progress that has been made to correct any deficiencies.[36]

The report contains the conclusions of the examination team and should include comments, and also a supervisory response, based upon the findings. The examiners should provide a general conclusion about the adequacy of the bank's AML/CFT compliance program and should identify both those procedures that have been carried out and any violations and deficiencies. Having formulated their conclusions, the examiners should recommend corrective action.

5.1   Developing Conclusions

When developing conclusions for the examination report, the examiners should accumulate all pertinent findings from the actual AML/CFT examination procedures and determine whether

- The AML/CFT compliance program is effectively monitored and overseen in relation to the bank's risk profile
- The board of directors and senior management are aware of AML/CFT regulatory requirements, effectively oversee AML/CFT compliance, and make commitments to implement any necessary corrective action
- AML/CFT policies, procedures, and processes are adequate to ensure compliance with applicable laws and regulations and appropriately address high-risk operations involving products, services, customers, and geographic locations
- Internal controls ensure compliance with national laws and regulations and provide sufficient management of risk, especially for high-risk operations involving products, services, customers, and geographic locations
- Independent testing is appropriate to establish compliance with required laws, regulations, and regulatory policies
- AML/CFT compliance officers are competent and have the necessary resources and authority to carry out their responsibilities
- Personnel are sufficiently trained to adhere to legal, regulatory, and policy requirements

5

Examiners should also determine the underlying cause of deficiencies in policy, procedure, or process. These deficiencies may be the result of a number of factors, including, but not limited to, a situation in which

- Management has not assessed, or has not accurately assessed, the bank's AML/CFT apparatus;
- Management is unwilling to create or enhance policies, procedures, and processes;
- Management or employees disregard established policies, procedures, and processes;
- Management or employees are unaware of or misunderstand regulatory requirements, policies, procedures, or processes; and
- Changes in internal policies, procedures, and processes are poorly communicated.

Examiners must also determine whether deficiencies or violations have been previously identified by management or through an audit, or whether they have been identified only as a result of the current examination. Once all deficiencies are identified and the evidence gathered, on-site examiners should develop the AML/CFT compliance findings and conclusions and should discuss them with the supervisor. The role of on-site examiners, however, is not limited to the detection of shortcomings within the bank's internal AML/CFT apparatus. One duty is to specify what actions are appropriate to correct deficiencies or violations. Among other things, these may require the bank to conduct more detailed risk assessments or to take appropriate corrective action. At the end of the process, the findings should be discussed with bank management with the aim of obtaining a commitment to make improvements or to take corrective action where needed. These discussions, and management's commitments, should be documented in the final report of the examination.

5.2 Preparing the AML/CFT Comments for the Examination Report

Several tasks have to be undertaken at this stage. The on-site examiners should formulate conclusions about the adequacy of the bank's AML/CFT compliance program and should discuss its effectiveness with the bank, indicating whether it meets all the regulatory requirements.

Examiners should ensure that work papers are prepared in sufficient detail to support the issues presented in the report. Written comments should cover areas pertinent to the findings, all of which should be shown in the report, including the degree of commitment shown by the board of directors and senior management to AML/CFT compliance. It is important for examiners to judge both whether management has a strong AML/CFT compliance program and whether the program is fully supported by the board of directors. They must also determine whether the board of directors and senior management are kept fully informed of AML/CFT compliance efforts, together with audit reports, details of compliance failures, and the status of corrective action.

The report must also state in detail whether the bank's policies, procedures, and processes for STR filings, large currency transactions (if required), and wire funds transfer meet the regulatory requirements. As part of the on-site process, examiners must also have recorded any violations of law or regulations and must have assessed their severity. Where appropriate, these violations are described in the examination report, and the examiners must discuss possible enforcement actions with supervisory management and legal staff (see box 5.10 for further details).

BOX 5.10   Structure of a Model Report

The inspector should be guided by three major concerns:

- Compliance with legal and regulatory provisions
- Adequacy of organizational resources and monitoring support, especially information technology (IT) support
- Performance of the in-house AML/CFT program

Recommended format:

- Introduce the bank (organization, commercial activity, branches, and so forth).
- Describe how it is organized and its internal AML rules (client screening process, KYC, and recordkeeping).
- Present and assess the surveillance and unusual-transaction detection system.
- Give a description and appraisal of the internal monitoring mechanism.
- Assess the performance and accuracy of the STR process.

Important tips to keep in mind:

- Each remark must be substantiated by precise facts.
- Any unusual transactions detected and not reported to the FIU must be described in precise detail and will be used by the relevant authority (central bank, banking commission, FIU) to justify any penalties applied.
- Keep copies of any breaches observed (copies of files, alerts, STRs, and so on).

5

Notes

1. In developing this handbook, the World Bank team visited several jurisdictions to identify various bank supervisory processes, procedures, and best practices. Most jurisdictions considered their AML/CFT supervisory handbooks confidential and were unable to share them with the World Bank team. However, the US handbook is a public document and was available for review. Recommendations and suggestions in this chapter were obtained from various jurisdictions visited in the study tour, the US AML examination manual, the Basel Committee on Banking Supervision Core Principles for Effective Banking Supervision, and from other AML/CFT organizations.

2. See the Basel Committee on Banking Supervision Core Principles Methodology, principle 19, Supervisory approach.

3. See Basel Core Principle 20 (http://www.bis.org/publ/bcbs129.pdf).

4. In Spain, banks are informed one month before a mission begins and must provide the SEPBLAC (the Spanish Financial Intelligence Unit also responsible for AML/CFT compliance investigation) with requested information 15 days before the mission starts.

5. See the Basel Committee on Banking Supervision Core Principles Methodology, principle 17, Internal control and audit.

6. FATF, February 27, 2004, updated as of June 2006.

7. See criteria 29.2 of the Methodology.

8. See criteria 29.3 of the Methodology.

9. In Algeria, for example.

10. The Basel Committee on Banking Supervision Core Principles Methodology, in essential criterion 11 under principle 18 (Abuse of financial services), states: "The supervisor is able to inform the financial intelligence unit and, if applicable, other designated authority of any suspicious transaction. In addition, it is able, directly or indirectly, to share with relevant judicial authorities information related to suspected or actual criminal activities."

11. That is the case in France, for example.

12. In Thailand.

13. Basel Committee on Banking Supervision , *Consolidated KYC Risk Management*, October 2004, §20, points out that "In a cross-border context, home country supervisors should face no impediments in verifying a branch or subsidiary's compliance with group-wide KYC policies and procedures during on-site inspections." However, "the host country supervisor retains responsibility for the supervision of compliance with local KYC regulations (which would include an evaluation of the appropriateness of the procedures)." See also BCBS, *The Supervision of Cross-Border Banking*, 1996 (http://www.bis.org/publ/bcbs27.htm) and the core principles 24 and 25.

14. See chapter 4 for details.

15. See the Basel Committee on Banking Supervision Core Principles for Effective Banking Supervision at http://www.bis.org/publ/bcbs129.htm and the US Federal Financial Institutions Examination Council publication Bank Secrecy Act Anti-Money Laundering

Examination Manual at http://www.occ.treas.gov/handbook/1-BSA-AMLwhole.pdf for more background information on risk management.

16. In Spain, SEPBLAC receives all banks' AML procedures. It identifies those institutions with the highest risk operations, in terms of products and countries, and assesses the quality of their procedures. In Belgium, all banks must submit a compliance report to the Banking, Finance, and Intelligence Commission (CBFA) annually. In Italy, authorities use a variety of information to scope their examinations and identify those banks to be inspected. That information is drawn from: (1) STRs and aggregated returns compiled and sorted out by the statistical unit of the Italian FIU (for example, amount of cash and cross-border transactions for a set period, wire transfers per country, transfers to and from offshore financial centers, comparisons between a bank's activity and its peer group's activity, and so forth) and (2) discussions on banks' risk profiles held among off- and on-site divisions, the Bank of Italy, and the FIU (formerly the UIC, Ufficio Italiano dei Cambi).

17. For further offsite monitoring information, see chapter 4.

18. As indicated above, some countries may prefer not to inform the bank in advance.

19. See the Basel Committee on Banking Supervision General Guide to Account Opening and Customer Identification (February 2003) at http://www.bis.org/publ/bcbs85annex.htm, the Basel Committee on Banking Supervision paper, Customer due diligence for banks, at http://www.bis.org/publ/bcbs85.htm and FATF recommendation 5 at http://www.fatf-gafi.org/document/28/0,2340,en_32250379_32236930_33658140_1_1_1_1,00.html#40recs.

20. See the Basel Committee on Banking Supervision, Core Principles Methodology, principle 18, Abuse of financial services, at http://www.bis.org/publ/bcbs61.htm and FATF recommendation 13.

21. Evidence from fieldwork shows that in some jurisdictions strict legal secrecy provisions preclude bank examiners from having access to special administrative regions (SARs), which are accessible only to the FIU.

22. See Section 5.4.1.4.

23. For more information on compliance program requirements and best practices see the FATF methodology recommendation 15 at http://www.fatf-gafi.org/dataoecd/45/15/34864111.pdf and the Basel Committee on Banking Supervision Core Principles Methodology principle 18, Abuse of financial services, at http://www.bis.org/publ/bcbs 130.pdf.

24. See Basel Committee, Customer Due Diligence, §56, as well as the paper on Compliance and the Compliance Function in Banks, April 2005.

25. In some banks, especially the small ones, the CO takes care of all compliance issues, including AML/CFT. Besides, when the size of the bank does not justify entrusting the CO's responsibility to a specially appointed person, the person responsible for permanent control shall coordinate all arrangements contributing to performance of compliance control assignments, including AML/CFT.

26. See, for example, Securities and Exchange Commission of Pakistan, AML Unit, A Project Under Technical Assistance of the World Bank, Brief series, Vol. IV, 2004.

5

27. See Basel Committee, Enhancing Corporate Governance for Banking Organizations, February 2006, §22 and 23. "To achieve sufficient objectivity and independence, the audit committee should be comprised, at a minimum, of a majority of board members who are independent and who have a firm understanding of the role of the audit committee in the bank's risk management and governance. The audit committee often consists solely of non-executive directors. Where executives normally attend audit committee meetings, to promote frank discussion it may be beneficial for the non-executive members of the audit committee to meet separately."

28. See BCBS Customer Due Diligence paper (§58).

29. See the FATF 40+9 Recommendations at http://www.fatf-gafi.org/document/28/0,2340,en_32250379_32236930_33658140_1_1_1_1,00.html#40recs and http://www.fatf-gafi.org/document/9/0,2340,en_32250379_32236920_34032073_1_1_1_1,00.html

30. In this case, examiners should ask for the list of numbered accounts and the relating names of customers, including all supporting documents, including copies of the IDs.

31. *Payable-through accounts* refers to correspondent accounts that are used directly by third parties to transact business on their own behalf.

32. According to the FATF, "Shell bank" means a bank incorporated in a jurisdiction in which it has no physical presence and which is unaffiliated with a regulated financial group.

33. For more information, see FATF recommendation 5 and the Basel Committee on Banking Supervision Core Principles Methodology at principle 18, Abuse of financial services.

34. Section 5.4, therefore, is not intended to address all conceivable key areas that might need assessment in an AML/CFT examination.

35. PEPs can be defined as "Individuals who are or have been entrusted with prominent public functions in a foreign country." This category typically includes (i) Heads of state or of government, (ii) senior politicians, (iii) senior government, (iv) judicial or military officials, (v) senior executives of state owned corporations and (vi) important political party officials. Business relationships with family members or close associates of PEPs involve reputational risks similar to those with PEPs themselves. The definition is not intended to cover middle-ranking or more junior individuals in the foregoing categories.

36. See the Basel Committee on Banking Supervision Core Principles Methodology principle 20, Supervisory techniques, and the US Federal Financial Institutions Examination Council publication, Bank Secrecy Act Anti-Money Laundering Examination Manual.

Sanctions and Corrective Measures to Be Taken by Competent Authorities

Contents

CHAPTER 6

1 Overview

The establishment of a robust system of sanctions, whether criminal, civil, or administrative, is, as the Financial Action Task Force (FATF) recommendations make clear, critical to making sure banks play their vital role in the detection and deterrence of money laundering and terrorist financing. Without such a system to back it up, even the most comprehensive array of anti-money laundering and combating the financing of terrorism (AML/CFT) regulations and policies will not function effectively. Banks must recognize that failure to implement appropriate AML/CFT compliance procedures will bring legal and financial liabilities that can damage their reputations as well as their profitability.

As shown in figure 6.1, lessons learned from assessment reports drafted by the FATF, FSRBs, and IFIs show that most countries have sanction regimes but the effectiveness of their implementation varies widely. In developing or emerging countries, jurisdictions have little experience in applying sanctions or other enforcement measures, and the lack of experience in this regard hampers the effectiveness of their AML/CFT regimes.

This chapter outlines the possible sanctions and corrective measures that competent authorities can adopt. It describes and discusses the importance of establishing effective, proportionate, and dissuasive sanctioning systems for AML/CFT in accordance with international standards. Section 6.2 stresses the usefulness of a corrective and sanctioning regime. Section 6.3 sets boundaries on the scope of sanctions to be applied, while section 6.4 gives a snapshot of sanctions that have been handed down in several jurisdictions. It also discusses the controversial issue of publishing rulings given to noncompliant banks. Lastly, section 6.5 outlines the basic requirements for processing corrective measures and sanctions.

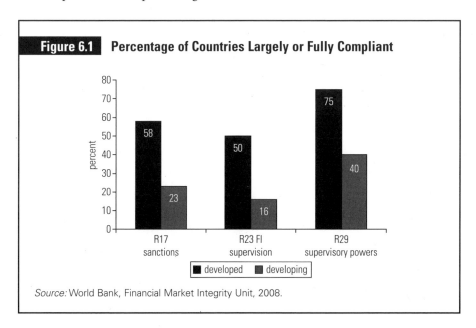

Figure 6.1 Percentage of Countries Largely or Fully Compliant

Source: World Bank, Financial Market Integrity Unit, 2008.

2 General

The following section describes and discusses the importance of establishing effective, proportionate, and dissuasive AML/CFT sanctioning systems in accordance with international standards. It is important to note that this chapter is limited to a discussion of sanctions countries may consider applying in order to enforce compliance with Know Your Customer (KYC) and Customer Due Diligence (CDD) obligations and other related preventive measures as set out in FATF recommendations 5, 6, 7, 8, 9, 10, 11, 13, 15, 18, 21, and 22 and special recommendations IV, VI, and VII (for further details, see Annex 9). This chapter does not deal with sanctions that countries should adopt for money laundering or terrorist financing offenses as set out in recommendations 1 and 2 and special recommendation II.

2.1 Preliminary Discussion

The issue of sanctions is addressed in different FATF recommendations. Rec. 1 and special recommendation II require countries to criminalize money laundering and terrorist financing. Rec. 2 covers criminal liabilities of individuals as well as criminal, civil, or administrative proceedings with respect to legal persons in countries in which such forms of liability are available. As indicated in rec. 2, legal persons should be subject to effective, proportionate, and dissuasive sanctions. Rec. 17 stipulates that countries should ensure that effective, proportionate, and dissuasive sanctions, whether criminal, civil, or administrative, are available to deal with natural or legal persons covered by FATF recommendations that fail to comply with AML/CFT requirements. Under rec. 29, supervisors should be authorized to impose adequate administrative sanctions for failure to comply with requirements to combat ML and TF. One can infer from the combination of rec. 2, 17, and 29 that sanctions to be applied under rec. 1 refer directly to ML or TF offenses while sanctions under rec. 17 and 29 are applied to punish breaching of AML/CFT requirements (basically KYC, CDD, internal monitoring, and reporting obligations). As a result, the following discussion will not cover rec. 1 and SRII because they refer to an active involvement in a criminal activity, which is not the scheme of sanctions this chapter addresses.

2.2 Importance of a Suitable Sanctioning Regime

A strong system of sanctions is critical to combating money laundering and terrorist financing activities. Even the most well designed AML/CFT laws and regulations will be ineffective if they do not include sanctions to punish non-compliant financial institutions. Specifically, sanctions support the broad goals of AML/CFT by

6

- Deterring banks and other financial institutions that might otherwise be willing to support criminal activities;
- Helping to dismantle illegal activities through encouraging subject entities to perform enhanced due diligence and monitoring; and
- Promoting a sound and accountable banking system.

On the other hand, it is worth mentioning that countries which belong either to the FATF or to FATF-style regional bodies are committed to applying AML/CFT international standards. As part of their respective mandates, both the FATF and the Financial Action Task Force Style Regional Bodies (FSRBs) are responsible for assessing members' compliance with the international AML/CFT standards, using a uniform methodology that was adopted by the FATF in February 2004 and endorsed by the executive boards of the International Monetary Fund (IMF) and the World Bank (WB) in March 2004. Members of both the IMF and the WB are also assessed on AML/CFT as part of the Financial Sector Assessment Program. In determining the level of compliance for each FATF Recommendation, the assessors (whether from the FATF, FSRBs, the IMF, or the WB) should not only assess formal compliance with the FATF Recommendations, but should also assess compliance regarding whether the recommendations have been fully and properly implemented and whether the implementation is effective. This requires an assessment not only of whether the necessary implementing measures are in force and effect,[1] but also whether the results obtained, for example, the number of money laundering (ML) convictions, the number of sanctions imposed on banks, or the number of suspicious transaction reports (STRs) filed, show that the system is effective.

In other words, the scope of sanctions available in a country being assessed and the manner in which sanctions are applied are key criteria assessors need to consider to assess the effectiveness of the sanctioning regime. The lack of sanctions or an inadequate enforcement policy should lead assessors to the conclusion that the country does not conform to international requirements. As a result, according to the methodology mentioned above, the country will be given either a Partially Compliant or a Noncompliant rating for recommendations 17 and 29, depending of the number of essential criteria that have not been met.

Understandably, different jurisdictions adopt differing sanctioning regimes according to their particular legal traditions, constitutional requirements, and systems of government. Although each country is free to determine its own regulatory, supervisory, and enforcement system, one consistent principle is that all countries, whether developing or developed, should adopt a minimum set of measures to sanction banks that fail to comply with their AML/CFT obligations, and that this set of measures should meet FATF requirements as set out in recommendations 17 and 29.

6

2.3 Preconditions for a Suitable Sanctioning and Remedial Apparatus

In establishing an effective sanctioning and remedial apparatus, it is necessary for jurisdictions to meet several preconditions.

First, each country should designate an authority with the power to apply appropriate sanctions where necessary.[2] Different authorities may be authorized to apply sanctions. In some countries, both the bank supervisor and the FIU are legally vested with the authority to impose sanctions on defaulting institutions, as, for example the USA. In others, such as Spain, it is the financial intelligence unit (SEPBLAC) only, and not the supervisor, that has the power to enforce AML/CFT requirements, while in yet others, such as France, it is the supervisor (Commission bancaire) that has the sanctioning power over banks.

Second, the sanctioning power granted to competent authorities should have a firm legal foundation[3]. There should be no doubt whatsoever as to the legal basis of a supervisor's authority. In some jurisdictions this basis is found in the banking laws, while in others, the AML/CFT legislation itself contains the specific sanctioning provisions. At the same time, whether the ruling is issued by the supervisor or by some other competent body, those institutions found to be noncompliant must have the right to lodge an appeal.[4]

Third, the sanctions themselves should rest on a strong legislative or regulatory basis, as should the requirement to disclose sanctions publicly[5]. They might be contained within specific enforceable provisions that are part of laws or supporting regulations that set out the AML/CFT requirements, or they might be part of the more general powers of sanction given to competent authorities to enable them to enforce their supervisory or monitoring role appropriately.

Lastly, in keeping with Basel Core Principles (BCP) principle 1, it is also paramount that supervisors have operational independence to enforce their decisions.[6] The irrevocability of the supervisor board members' mandate helps to assure such independence, as does the adoption of a regime of legal protection that prevents supervisors from being exposed to any kind of external interference or from being sued for acts performed in good faith in the exercise of their duties. It is, of course, essential to the professionalism and impartiality of the decision-making process that the persons in charge of taking remedial measures and sanctions have excellent backgrounds and skills, and possess high ethical standards. In France, for example, sanctions imposed on liable institutions for AML/CFT failure are rendered by a committee comprising two independent magistrates from the highest national courts.[7]

6

3 Summary of Possible Rulings and Remedial Measures

This section outlines the scope of sanctions competent authorities may impose on financial institutions that have failed to comply with AML/CFT obligations.

3.1 General Framework

In accordance with international standards, the scope of sanctions countries impose on noncompliant financial institutions should be as broad as possible. FATF recommendation 17 requires countries to ensure that effective, proportionate, and dissuasive sanctions, whether criminal, civil, or administrative, are available to deal with natural or legal persons who fail to comply with anti-money laundering or terrorist financing requirements. Further, FATF recommendation 29 states that supervisors should be authorized to compel financial institutions to produce any information relevant to monitoring such compliance, and to impose appropriate administrative sanctions when institutions fail to comply with such requirements.

BCP principle 23 recommends that banking supervisors have adequate supervisory measures at their disposal in order to bring about timely corrective action in those cases when either banks fail to meet prudential and compliance requirements (such as AML/CFT obligations) or there have been regulatory violations.

The FATF recommendations give no further specific indication of the exact nature of sanctions that may be imposed by competent authorities. The FATF Methodology for Assessing Compliance with the FATF 40 Recommendations and the FATF 9 Special Recommendations does, however, provide some elaboration, particularly in the Essential Criteria relating to recommendation 17. Other useful indications of possible remedial measures and sanctions can also be found in BCP principles 1 and 23 (although these principles do not relate explicitly to AML/CFT) and in BCP principle 18, essential criterion 7, in the BCP Methodology.

3.2 Scope and Types of AML/CFT-Related Sanctions

3.2.1 Sanctions Should be Effective and Dissuasive

Countries should ensure that effective, proportionate, and dissuasive criminal, civil, or administrative sanctions are available to deal with natural or legal persons covered by the FATF Recommendations, when they fail to comply with national AML/CFT requirements.[8] The FATF methodology, however, does not define the concepts of effectiveness, proportionality, and dissuasiveness. It can be inferred that an effective regime is one in which sanctions are actively applied by relevant authorities and are then effectively implemented. A fine, for example, should be collected by the competent authority (usually the minister of finance or the treasury). Dissuasiveness is more difficult to define because it refers to a combination of factors that comprise effectiveness, proportionality (discussed below), and the nature of

6

sanctions. For example, a small fine or a mere reminder to a bank would not be considered a dissuasive sanction for serious breaches.

FATF recommendations 17 and 29 do not imply a need to establish a regime encompassing all three types of sanctions (criminal, civil, and administrative). A sanctioning regime based only on criminal measures, however, might not suffice, because it does not fulfill the requirement of proportionality. The application of a criminal sanction like imprisonment for failure to comply with KYC obligations would, for example, be disproportionate to the nature of the breach, and, as a result, probably would not be invoked by the competent authorities. In practice, several countries have established a wide range of civil, administrative, and criminal sanctions that can be combined (see section 6.4 below).

3.2.2   Sanctions Should be Proportionate to the Seriousness of a Situation

As indicated in the FATF methodology,[9] the range of sanctions available should be broad and proportionate to the severity of a situation. Similarly, according to the Basel Core Principles, a good and suitable regime is one that allows supervisors to make a graduated response depending on the nature of the problems or the failure. Should the problem detected be relatively minor, all that is warranted might be an informal action such as a simple oral or written communication to bank management. In other instances, more formal action may be necessary, and the severity of the sanction imposed will depend upon the seriousness of the violation. In view of the FATF requirement of dissuasiveness, a mere reprimand for failing to implement KYC requirements or to report STRs to the FIU would not be sufficient. Likewise, the principle of proportionality requires that the penalty reflect the multiple and thus aggravated nature of the violation: multiple and repetitive failures must carry higher penalties than a single failure. The variety of sanctions available is also critical, as shown below.

3.2.3   Range of Sanctions Should be Broad

As mentioned in the FATF methodology, the scope of sanctions for AML/CFT failure should include the power to impose disciplinary and financial sanctions.[10] The FATF methodology[11] gives some concrete examples of the types of sanctions a country may choose to adopt in order to comply with FATF requirements. These should include the following:

- Written warnings (in a separate letter or within an audit report)
- Orders to comply with specific instructions (possibly accompanied with daily fines for noncompliance)
- Regular reports required from the institution on the measures it is taking
- Fines for noncompliance
- Imposition of conservatorship, or a suspension or withdrawal of license
- Imposition of criminal penalties where appropriate

Likewise, the BCP Methodology, at BCP 23, essential criterion 4, sets out some specific sanctioning and other remedial measures supervisors can employ (although, as noted above, these are not explicitly directed at cases of AML/CFT noncompliance). Measures relevant to AML/CFT failures might include:

- Restricting the current activities of the bank
- Withholding approval of new activities or acquisitions
- Replacing or restricting the powers of managers, board directors, or controlling owners
- Revoking or recommending the revocation of the banking license

In serious cases, supervisors should have the authority to impose conservatorship on a bank that is failing to meet essential AML/CFT requirements.

In the most extreme cases, when a bank and its senior management have been involved in deliberate money laundering or terrorist financing activities, the supervisor should have the authority to close down the bank and have its license revoked. The supervisor should also be empowered to refer the matter to the relevant criminal and judicial authorities. Although the administrative and criminal processes are separate and distinct, a criminal conviction registered against a bank for money laundering or terrorist financing would clearly be cause for a supervisor to re-evaluate the bank's directors and senior management in relation to "fit and proper" criteria.[12]

3.2.4 Sanctions Should be Applied to Senior Management as Well as to Banks

According to the FATF methodology,[13] where there has been a failure to comply with or properly implement AML/CFT requirements, sanctions may be applied not only to the legal persons that are financial institutions or businesses, but also to their directors and senior management.

Clearly, a bank, as a legal person, should not be the only culprit called to account for failure to comply with AML/CFT obligations. Directors and senior management should be and, to an increasing extent, are also being held accountable. In some countries, stockholders of publicly traded financial institutions have brought lawsuits against members of the boards of directors and have succeeded in recovering monetary damages from the individual members of the boards. The Basel Committee on Banking Supervision recently updated its Core Principles to place greater responsibility for managing risk on senior management. As indicated in the Core Principles methodology, "*the supervisor applies penalties and sanctions not only to the bank but, when and if necessary, also to management and/or the Board, or individuals therein.*"[14] Similarly, the Wolfsberg[15] Group's AML Principles have shifted the focus of responsibility to top executives, as have the United Kingdom's Financial Services Authority, along with the Joint Money Laundering Steering Group.[16]

6

Supervisors, therefore, should be vested with the power to impose sanctions on those individuals holding management positions within the bank. As indicated in the FATF methodology,[17] sanctions should include, but not be limited to, (1) barring individuals from employment within that sector, or (2) replacing or restricting the powers of managers, directors, or controlling owners.

BCP 23 similarly states that when a bank has committed severe violations, the supervisory authority should have the power to address management problems, including the authority to have controlling owners, directors, and managers replaced, or to have their powers restricted, and even, where appropriate, to bar individuals from the business of banking.

There is no indication in the Basel Core Principles whether bank employees not holding management or senior positions within the bank should be subject to sanctions for breaching AML/CFT requirements. The FATF recommendations, as well, are largely silent on this question (although recommendation 14b states that financial institutions, their directors, officers, and employees should be prohibited by law from disclosing the fact that an STR or related information is being reported to the FIU, thus implying the possibility of an employee being sanctioned). On the other hand, in the US, any partner, director, officer, or employee who fails to comply with any record-keeping requirement for a financial institution can receive a penalty of up to $US 1,000.[18] In the UK and in South Korea, employees can also be subject to sanctions as shown in boxes 6.1 and 6.2.

6

| BOX 6.1 | **Example of Sanctions Applied to an Employee in the UK[19]** |

In the UK, the Financial Services Authority (FSA) fined Sindicatum Holdings Limited (SHL) £49,000, and its money laundering reporting officer (MLRO) £17,500, for not having adequate anti-money laundering systems and controls in place for verifying and recording clients' identities. This was the first time the FSA fined a money laundering reporting officer. The FSA found failings in a number of the firm's activities, including

- Failure to implement adequate procedures for verifying the identity of its clients,
- Failure to verify adequately the identity of a significant number of its clients,
- Failure to keep adequate records with regard to the verification of the identity of its clients, and
- The money laundering reporting officer's failure to take reasonable steps to implement adequate procedures for controlling money laundering risk.

BOX 6.2 **Types and Examples of Possible Sanctions in South Korea**

In South Korea, sanctions, including reduction of salary, may also be applied to bank staff. The KoFIU (The Korean Financial Intelligence Unit) may impose penalties on banks for failing to comply with AML regulations. Other supervisory agencies, including the Financial Supervisory Service (FSS), may impose other types of sanctions, which, in certain cases, might be combined with penalties. The types and examples of sanctions that may be imposed by the FSS include

- On bank executives:
  - Recommendation of discharge from office
  - Suspension from duties
  - Notification of reprimand
  - Cautionary warning

- On bank staff:
  - Disciplinary dismissal
  - Suspension from office
  - Reduction of salary
  - Reprimand

- On institutions:
  - Cancellation of business license
  - Business suspension
  - Lock-out of business branch
  - Cautionary warning
  - Demand to publicize a violation of law

6

4 Examples of Enforcement and Sanctions Applied in Several Countries

The following is an overview of sanctions applied by different jurisdictions to banks and/or other financial institutions that have failed to meet their AML/CFT obligations.

4.1 General

The sanction imposed in a given case varies according to each country's legal and constitutional regime and upon the particular circumstances of the case. No single model of sanctions, therefore, can be generally applied. Some jurisdictions use a large array of measures that range from reprimands to license withdrawals. Others emphasize administrative sanctions and tend to shy away from financial penalties. As for the sanctioning process itself, national practices are extremely diverse. In certain jurisdictions, the supervisors and the ministry of finance share the responsibility for implementing AML/CFT sanctions. In Portugal, for instance, the bank supervisor is responsible for instituting the proceedings for administrative offences. It is the minister of finance, however, that applies fines and ancillary sanctions[20] for noncompliance with the obligations of Law 11/2004 and Law 5/2002, while the bank supervisor applies the sanctions for breaches of Central Bank Notices and Instructions.[21]

4.2 Examples of Civil Money Penalties

In France the *Commission bancaire*, which is responsible for monitoring banks and other financial institutions, has, over the last several years, imposed a number of civil penalties on banks for noncompliance with national AML/CFT regulations (see box 6.3). These civil penalties are available under Article L.613.21 of the Financial and

6

BOX 6.3 **Samples of Civil Money Penalties Imposed by the French Banking Commission**

Subject to the relevant legislative and regulatory obligations, the *Commission bancaire* monitors compliance by credit institutions, investment firms (other than portfolio management companies), and finance companies. It is empowered to issue warnings, recommendations, requests for temporary exemptions, injunctions, and sanctions. It has handed down several decisions invoking civil monetary penalties. An example is the decision in 2004

(Continued)

> **BOX 6.3** **Samples of Civil Money Penalties Imposed by the French Banking Commission (*Continued*)**
>
> against CALYON bank (see annex 8 for further details). This financial institution was fined[a] €1 million for failing, first, to require identification of customers when entering into business relations with them, second, to establish ongoing due diligence, and, third, to instruct its branches and overseas subsidiaries on the need to collect information related to any complex and unusual operations, or any operations that lacked economic justification. Another bank, CRCAM Centre-Est, was fined €200,000 for failing to establish proper procedures relating both to "know your customer" (KYC) and to suspicious transaction reports (STRs). Further, where STRs had been filed, their usefulness had been compromised because of serious deficiencies in their content. The fine was also based on internal control failures and inadequate staff training on the AML/CFT requirements as set forth in the French Financial and Monetary Code and in Regulation 2002-01 of 18 April 2002.[b]
>
> a. Financial and Monetary Code, art. L. 563-3, See *Décisions Juridictionnelles de la Commission bancaire,* décision 8, October 11, 2004.
> b. See *Décisions Juridictionnelles de la Commission bancaire,* décision 7, June 2007.

Monetary Code. Banks convicted of breaching AML/CFT requirements may be subject to several sanctions, which may include a civil fine up to the amount of the minimum capital requirement applicable to the credit institution. In England, the FSA has also fined several banks for breaching money-laundering rules (see box 6.4). In the United States, penalties may be assessed by different competent supervisory authorities and be cumulative (see box 6.5).

In the United States, while examination authority for compliance with the Bank Secrecy Act (BSA)[22] has been delegated to the federal banking agencies, the same does not apply to enforcement powers, which, under the BSA, remain with the Financial Crimes Enforcement Network (FinCEN).[23] The banking agencies, however, have their own enforcement powers, and these cover violations of "any law or regulation" (including the BSA). FinCEN, under the BSA and its implementing regulations, may bring an enforcement action for violations of reporting, recordkeeping, or other BSA requirements. Civil money penalties may be assessed, for example, for failing to have an adequate AML program in place, or for record-keeping violations, or for failing to file a currency transaction report (CTR) or for failing to file an STR.

Under the US system, civil money penalties for willful violations of the BSA range from $25,000 for each violation (or for each day that an entity fails to have an adequate AML program in place) up to the actual amount (not exceeding $100,000)

6

> ### BOX 6.4 Samples of Civil Money Penalties Imposed by the British FSA
>
> The Financial Services Authority (FSA) fined The Royal Bank of Scotland plc (RBS) £750,000 for breaches of its Money Laundering Rules.[a] The FSA's investigation showed that there were weaknesses in RBS's anti-money laundering controls right across its retail network. It had found that RBS, in an unacceptable number of new accounts opened across its retail network in early 2002, had failed either to obtain sufficient KYC documentation to establish customer identity or to retain such documentation once obtained. The documentation was frequently insufficient to show that the clients were who they had claimed to be and, in some cases, RBS was unable to supply either copies or details of the documents (such as a valid passport, a driving license, a recent utility bill) used to verify identity. Inadequate verifications of identity might be when the bank has verified only clients' names but not their addresses, or when documents obtained by the bank were simply not capable of determining identities. The FSA also fined the Bank of Scotland plc (BoS) £1,250,000 for failing to keep proper records of customer identification[b] as required by the FSA's Money Laundering Rules. The FSA's investigation confirmed not only weaknesses in BoS recordkeeping systems, but also in the controls throughout its retail, corporate, and business banking divisions. According to FSA, in over half the samples of accounts tested in late 2002, BoS had failed to retain either a copy of customer identification evidence or a record of where this evidence could be obtained. These failings were exacerbated by BoS's inability to determine the areas in which the breakdown in its recordkeeping systems had occurred.
>
> a. FSA/PN/123/2002.
> b. FSA/PN/001/2004, January 15, 2004.

6

> ### BOX 6.5 Examples of Civil Sanctions Rendered in the United States
>
> The Financial Crimes Enforcement Network (FinCEN) and the Board of Governors of the Federal Reserve System imposed a $10 million civil money penalty against AmSouth Bank of Birmingham (Alabama) for its violations of the Bank Secrecy Act. FinCEN and the Federal Reserve Board based their assessment on the failure of the banking organization to establish an adequate anti-money laundering program, as well as its failure to file accurate, complete, and timely suspicious transaction reports (STRs).
>
> *(Continued)*

BOX 6.5 **Examples of Civil Sanctions Rendered in the United States**
(*Continued*)

The agencies found that there were systemic defects in the bank's program of internal controls and employee training, and its independent reviews had resulted in failures to identify, analyze, and report suspicious activities occurring at the bank.[a]

On December 2005, ABN AMRO bank N.V. was required to pay $80 million in penalties to US federal and state regulators. The Board of Governors of the Federal Reserve System, Financial Crimes Enforcement Network, Office of Foreign Assets Control, NY State Banking Dept., and the Illinois Dept. of Financial and Professional Regulation assessed these penalties based on their findings both of unsafe and unsound practices and of systemic defects in ABN AMRO's internal controls designed to ensure compliance with US anti-money laundering laws and regulations. As a result of these defects, there had been failures in identifying, analyzing, and reporting suspicious activities, and the findings showed that ABN AMRO had participated in transactions that violated US sanctions laws.[b]

a. The Federal Reserve Board, joint press release, Board of Governors of the Federal Reserve System, Financial Crimes Enforcement network, "Civil money penalty against AmSouth Bank of Birmingham," October 12, 2004.
b. Federal Reserve Board, joint press release, December 19, 2005.

---

involved in each violation. Additionally, civil money penalties not less than twice the amount of the transaction (but not exceeding $1,000,000) may be imposed on institutions violating the BSA's special international anti-money laundering provisions.

4.3 Examples of Criminal Penalties

In the US system, in addition to civil money penalties, the regulators can impose criminal penalties for violations of AML/CFT laws. Indeed, pursuant to the Bank Secrecy Act (BSA), persons convicted of violating the BSA may be subject to up to 5 years' imprisonment and a criminal fine of up to $ US 250,000. Persons convicted of engaging in a pattern of illegal activity involving more than $US 100,000 in a 12-month period may be subject to up to 10 years' imprisonment and a criminal fine of up to $US 500,000 (for further details, see box 6.6).[24] In Sweden, criminal sanctions are available should a person subject to the AML or CFT Act fail to fulfill the requirement to examine suspicious transactions and to submit a STR to the FIU, and when there is a breach of the prohibition of disclosure.[25]

6

BOX 6.6 **Samples of Criminal Sanctions Rendered in the United States**

The first criminal prosecution against a bank for money laundering was brought in 2002 in the case of the Broadway National Bank (BNB). The BNB was issued a $4 million criminal fine, first, for failing to maintain a legally-required anti-money laundering program, second, for failing to make legally-required reports concerning approximately $123 million in suspicious bulk cash and structured cash deposits and, third, for helping customers to structure transactions valued at approximately $76 million to evade currency reporting requirements.[a] Subsequent convictions were also registered against Banco Popular de Puerto Rico in 2003 and AmSouth Bank and Riggs Bank, N.A., in 2004.

The charges against Banco Popular de Puerto Rico and the deferred prosecution agreement filed in 2003 arose out of transactions conducted by and through the bank between June 1995 and June 2000. During this time, several unusual or suspicious transactions were conducted in connection with certain accounts at Banco Popular. Although the bank filed suspicious transaction reports (STRs) on these accounts, the reports were inappropriately timed or, in some cases, inaccurate. The bank forfeited $21.6 million to the United States on charges of failing to report suspicious financial activity.[b]

In May 2004, the US Federal Reserve fined Riggs Bank $25 million for failing to implement effective programs against money laundering and for not reporting suspicious transactions executed on behalf of former Chilean dictator Gen. Augusto Pinochet and of such governments as Saudi Arabia and Equatorial Guinea. The Office of the Comptroller of the Currency and the Federal Reserve Board also put the bank under close management scrutiny, which is the severest penalty short of closing the institution.[c]

a. US Customs and Border Protection, "Manhattan Bank pleads guilty to US criminal charges...", November 27, 2002 (http://www.cbp.gov/xp/cgov/newsroom/news_releases/archives/legacy/2002/112002/11272002.xml)]
b. Department of Justice, www.USDOJ.gov, January 16, 2003, "Banco Popular de Puerto Rico enters into deferred prosecution agreement with US"
c. In effect, the bank's reputation was ruined and, because of a combination of market forces and supervisory encouragement, its owners were forced to sell it. Illustrating the speed and depth of disintegration, in July 2004, PNC Financial Services Group agreed to buy Riggs National Corp. for $779 million.

4.4   Examples of Other Sanctions

In addition to the civil and criminal penalties described above, competent authorities may take further measures should the breach be particularly serious. They can, for instance, combine fines with administrative and/or other disciplinary measures (see box 6.7). The most severe disciplinary sanction a competent body may impose

BOX 6.7 Example of Combined Sanctions in France

Under Article 613-21 of the Financial and Monetary Code, the French banking commission, the *Commission bancaire*, is authorized to impose a combination of sanctions. As a result, the *Commission* now issues fines in connection with its disciplinary decisions more frequently than it did, (74 percent of cases in 2004, compared with 17 percent in 2001). This combination of sanctions seems to be a particularly effective deterrent, especially if the decision is made public (for further details, see section 6.4.5). In 2006 for example, in addition to a reprimand, the Banque Privée Européenne was fined €100,000[a] for failing to report suspicious transactions to the FIU and for failing to perform ongoing surveillance. This was also the case for BLC Bank France SA, which was fined €200,000 in conjunction with a reprimand for breaching national internal control requirements for customer identification and suspicious transaction reporting.[b]

The *Commission bancaire* may also, instead of or in addition to those sanctions, prohibit or limit the payment of dividends to shareholders (or interest to partner shareholders) in the credit institution or investment firm.

Also, under Article L. 562-7 of the Financial and Monetary Code, the *Commission bancaire* informs the public prosecutor when, owing either to a serious lack of vigilance or to a shortcoming in the organization of its internal control procedures, a financial organization fails to report its suspicions or, alternatively, breaches its obligations with respect to the prevention of money laundering. The *Commission bancaire* took such action against eight credit institutions in 2005 and four in 2006. The *Commission bancaire* also informs the public prosecutor, under Article 40 of the Criminal Procedure Code, about probable criminal acts. This article is applicable to any acts that may constitute money laundering. Pursuant to these two articles, the *Commission bancaire* forwarded 11 cases to the public prosecutor in 2005, 9 in 2006,[c] and 4 in 2007.

Finally, Article L. 511-38 of the Financial and Monetary Code states that the *Commission bancaire* must give its prior opinion on the proposed appointment or renewal of appointment of auditors to credit institutions, investment firms, and finance companies under its supervision. The article stipulates that statutory auditors must demonstrate the highest guarantee of independence from the credit institutions, investment firms, and finance companies they audit. When the *Commission bancaire* considers that statutory auditors lack the independence, experience, and competence required to perform their duties properly, or when infringements of the Financial and Monetary Code are brought to

(Continued)

6

> ### BOX 6.7   Example of Combined Sanctions in France (*Continued*)
>
> its attention, it has access to certain additional powers endowed by Article L. 613-9. Although this situation has not yet arisen, it is possible to infer that the *Commission bancaire* could impose a kind of "collateral" sanction by opposing the renewal of appointment of external auditors who have failed to detect serious AML/CFT breaches in the course of their duties.
>
> a. Bulletin Officiel de la Banque de France, No. 88, April 2006, Décision juridictionnelle de la Commission bancaire No. 2, March 10, 2006.
> b. See *Décision juridictionnelle publiée par la Commission bancaire au cours du quatrième trimestre 2005*, décision No. 1, October 19, 2005.
> c. Annual Reports of the *Commission bancaire*, 2005, page 133, and 2006, page 161.

is the withdrawal of a license, which effectively terminates the activity of a financial institution. In the United States, this type of sanction is triggered when the bank has committed serious offenses such as the laundering of monetary instruments or willful violation of certain provisions of the BSA. In France, the *Commission bancaire* has, in the past, withdrawn several licenses for serious violations of national AML/CFT legislation. In 2003, for instance, a financial institution was struck off the list of investment firms for serious breaches of AML/CFT provisions.[26] In 2002, three limited companies engaged in money exchange activities were barred from operating as *bureaux de change* because of serious failures in their procedures for AML/CFT internal surveillance and for reporting STRs.[27]

It is important to note that such measures must be applied independently of any sanctions that competent courts may impose. The supervisory agency must be vested with the authority to file an application with a prosecutor when there are reasonable grounds to believe the bank and/or its executives participated in money laundering or terrorist financing activities. In the case of such a serious offense, the supervisor must have direct access to the prosecutor and be able to have the case prosecuted as a criminal matter, notwithstanding the supervisor's ability to impose specific administrative and/or civil sanctions.

4.5   Publication of Sanctions

The question of whether imposed sanctions should be made a matter of public knowledge is not addressed either in the FATF recommendations or in the Basel Core Principles for Effective Banking Supervision. It is currently the responsibility of each country to determine, in light of its own legal and constitutional regime, and other circumstances, if sanctions are to be published in annual reports or in official government gazettes. There are pros and cons to public disclosure, and each country should always balance the "cost-benefits" ratio of publishing, including in reference to making public the names of the offending banks.

In some countries, such as the USA, the UK, France, and Belgium, publication of sanctions is one aspect of the sanctioning process and may have several beneficial effects. If they are publicly disclosed, for example, sanctions appear to be more of a deterrent. In other words, banks become more cautious and more inclined to comply fully with AML/CFT requirements if they know that failures to comply may be aired in public. Publication, therefore, promotes stricter adherence to AML/CFT regulations within the banking community as a whole. Furthermore, publication of sanctions can be seen as an additional instrument that a competent authority may use as leverage. To some extent, the possibility of either making a ruling publicly available, or of keeping it confidential, enhances the supervisor's authority and credibility by reinforcing its power. In France, for example, the publication of sanctions and disclosure of a delinquent bank's identity is not automatic, except when it comes to AML/CFT (see box 6.8 for further details).

Disclosing the names of delinquent banks can also be seen as a means to reinforce supervision regionally or internationally. If the name of the bank is disclosed

---

BOX 6.8 **Publication of Judicial Decisions in France**

The *Commission bancaire* has a long-established tradition of publishing judicial decisions in an official gazette. Rulings, whether or not they relate to AML/CFT, can be made public depending on the seriousness of the failure. According to art. 613-21 of the Financial and Monetary code, the publication of these decisions, which may include fines and/or disciplinary sanctions, is not automatic. In practice, however, it would seem that, in cases of an AML/CFT violation, the *Commission bancaire* usually makes the rulings public. The decisions are publicly displayed at the main entrance of its premises and are also compiled in an annual report.[a]

The annual report contains all judicial decisions handed down by the Supervisor. It provides detailed information, which includes, but is not limited to, the name of the bank, the type(s) of sanctions(s), the amount of the fine, if applicable. In addition, the report presents in detail the precise grounds justifying the sanction, including the most critical failures detected during the on-site inspection, and the legal provisions that were violated (see annex 8).

a. See http://www.banque-france.fr/fr/publications/catalogue/et_4q.htm.

in its home country, supervisors in other countries in which it operates may decide to take prompt action and trigger on-site inspections of its branches. If a parent bank is not compliant, there are reasonable grounds to believe that its subsidiaries and branches abroad will not correctly apply its AML/CFT policy.

Conversely, there may be several disadvantages to disclosing the name of any financial entity in an official gazette for violating AML/CFT regulations. It can tarnish the image and reputation of a bank[28] or, indeed, the banking industry as a whole, and thus undermine public and investor confidence in a country's financial system. For that reason, in some emerging countries where the financial sector has been seriously weakened by a financial crisis in the past, competent authorities are extremely reluctant to disclose names of banks for breaching AML/CFT regulations (or other prudential requirements). The 2009 financial turmoil might make things even worse and the decision even more difficult to take. Indeed, for entities in a weak financial situation, the "name and shame" process may create a new stress and so impede their recovery. They may not be able to access the interbank market for their own refinancing, and foreign banks may decide to terminate their correspondent banking relationships with them. Some countries also believe the public disclosure of AML/CFT failure, in addition to the other administrative, civil, and/or financial penalties imposed on a bank, is in effect a "double penalty," because it sanctions the bank twice for the same violation (see the case of the Netherlands in chapter 7).

Given these factors, field work has shown that some jurisdictions favor a more balanced approach, where decisions to disclose sanctions are made on a case-by-case basis, depending on the seriousness and the frequency of occurrence of the failures. Other countries make it a general practice not to publish sanctions, or they may content themselves with publishing very general information, which refers to the overall situation in the industry (for example, number of sanctions imposed and major areas of noncompliance).

Whatever their choices about the disclosure of specific sanctions, competent authorities must be certain of their reasons for publishing or not and, if possible, develop and follow a relevant formalized policy.

4.6 Examples of Possible Remedial Actions

In some jurisdictions, sanctions are imposed as a last resort, usually after a warning has been issued to give a noncompliant bank the opportunity to take remedial measures. When this approach is followed, the warning should be written and should take the form of specific instructions that the bank must implement. The bank will then be required to provide a formal reply describing the remedial action that it has taken.

In practice, authorities may consider many options as possible remedial measures. They can, for instance, require the institution to provide regular reports describing its measures to address its most critical AML/CFT shortcomings. Supervisors may also require that the bank's compliance, suspicious activity monitoring, and its reporting programs be improved. The bank could be ordered to review prior transactions to ensure that all STRs have been filed and/or to improve its compliance regime by enhancing internal controls and management oversight.

The downgrading of the bank's rating in those jurisdictions where the supervisor uses an internal rating system to measure the level of compliance with prudential regulations should lead the bank to take corrective actions. In Hong Kong, China, for example, Hong Kong Monetary Authority (HKMA) may downgrade a bank's CAMEL (Capital Adequacy, Asset quality, Management factors, Earnings, and Liquidity) rating if it fails to comply with prudential or compliance requirements such as AML/CFT. Because the rating plays a role in determining the level of deposit protection premium, such a measure has substantial implications for the bank's financial statement.

In some countries, such measures may be accompanied by complementary sanctions. Where, for example, failures resulting in sanctions against the bank indicate professional misconduct on the part of its external auditors, monitoring authorities may also impose sanctions on the auditors. In France, in cases where there has been a serious breach of AML/CFT regulations, the mandate of external auditors who have certified the relevant institutional accounts is not renewed and new auditors are appointed.

6

5 General Overview of the Basic Requirements for Effective Sanction Proceedings

This section provides an overview of the principal steps that supervisors or competent authorities should consider taking where there has been a serious breach of AML/CFT regulations and, before any type of sanctions are undertaken, whether these are disciplinary or administrative. It also describes the basic stages for processing sanctions. In the absence of specific international standards on this matter, these guidelines are based on what are considered best practices; they are not being advanced as a "one-size-fits-all" solution. Note that this guide does not address those violations of the AML/CFT law punishable by criminal sanctions because they are a matter for the judiciary.

5.1 General

Neither the FATF recommendations nor the Basel Core Principles discuss the issue of the actual proceedings that impose AML/CFT sanctions. Each jurisdiction, according to its own legal framework and constitutional regime, is responsible for establishing its own procedures. In some countries, as mentioned earlier, the proceedings for preparing and issuing AML/CFT sanctions are established by a single authority, which is vested with the power both to monitor AML/CFT compliance and to enforce sanctions. This, for instance, is the case in Norway, where the *Kredittilsynet,* the Financial Supervisory Authority (FSA), is empowered to supervise AML/CFT, as well as to sanction noncompliant banks.[29] Similarly, in Sweden, the supervisory authority (*Finansinspektionen*) deals with all AML/CFT supervision related issues, including sanctions,[30] and in France, the *Commission bancaire* is responsible for both areas.

There is an alternative arrangement in which the responsibility for implementing sanctions for AML/CFT is shared between two competent authorities. In Portugal, for example, this duty is entrusted to the Ministry of Finance and the banking supervisor, the Bank of Portugal (BOP). The Minister of Finance applies fines and ancillary sanctions (for example, the prohibition from assuming the management of legal persons) for noncompliance of the duties of Law 11/2004 and Law 5/2002, while the BOP institutes and applies administrative sanctions for breaches of its Notices and Instructions.[31] In Italy, the Bank of Italy has the direct authority to sanction financial institutions for deficiencies in internal organization and control, but where there has been failure to report suspicious activities to the relevant authority,[32] it recommends the imposition of administrative sanctions to the Ministry of Finance.

There is a third type of arrangement in which sanctioning responsibilities are divided between the supervisor and the FIU. In Thailand, for instance, the Ministry of Finance has vested the central bank (Bank of Thailand (BOT)) with the oversight power over AML/CFT compliance in banks, while the FIU, the Anti-Money Laundering Office (AMLO), has been granted the enforcement power. When BOT examiners find a breach of provisions of the Thai AML/CFT law, therefore, they must inform AMLO, which, based on the BOT findings, will determine whether the bank is liable to any sanction under national law.

Thus, while there is no single model, it is important as a general principle for each jurisdiction to establish clear policies and procedures before taking any action against a bank failing to meet its legal and regulatory AML/CFT obligations. This systematic approach is key to ensuring an effective enforcement regime as well as to safeguard the rights of defendants.

5.2   Main Steps to be Followed

5.2.1   Notification of the Outcomes

In general, sanctions are triggered by an on-site visit that has identified serious deficiencies in the bank's internal AML/CFT regime. In many countries, the draft inspection report has to be discussed with the management of the bank before the on-site inspection process is finalized. Following the discussion, the report is sent to the relevant department of the supervisory body for analysis and action. It is important to note that the inspection team should not, at this stage, recommend sanctions even if the failures detected in the course of the visit are particularly serious. In many jurisdictions, in fact, the inspection team's role is limited only to the identification of weaknesses. Each observation made by the inspection team, however, must be substantiated by precise facts so the relevant authority is able to understand the seriousness of the breach clearly and determine appropriate sanctions.

It is a common practice for the off-site supervision department (possibly an FIU) responsible for compliance supervision to send a follow-up letter to the bank. This important document usually summarizes the main conclusions of the on-site inspection report, highlights the strengths and weaknesses of the internal organization, such as the internal control and monitoring system and the risk management mechanism, and describes in detail the most serious deficiencies detected during the on-site inspection. It also provides comments and guidance on what needs to be improved and describes the prompt action that should be taken to address all main deficiencies.

Requested actions may consist of

- A program to complete identification of existing customers,
- A program to determine customer profiles and assess transactions in relation to risk exposure,
- An assessment of the main areas of risk,
- Completion of AML/CFT policies and procedures,

- Further instructions concerning transactions identified by the inspector as potential areas of deficiency in STR reporting,
- Appointment of FIU correspondents or AML/CFT reporting officer, and
- Additional training programs.

The bank is asked to provide comments both on the inspection findings and on the supervisor's instructions in the follow-up letter. This letter is sent to the bank's senior manager, usually the CEO, and copies are also provided to the board of directors, since they have overall responsibility for the institution. In some jurisdictions, as in France, for example, a copy of the follow-up letter is also sent for information to the external auditors, who should be made aware of any deficiencies in the bank's internal organization (for further details on sanction proceedings, see box 6.9).

BOX 6.9 **Sanction Proceedings in France following an On-Site Inspection**

1. The *Commission bancaire* prepares the inspection report.
   - The inspector and the bank hold informal discussions on the draft report, to rectify possible inaccuracies or misunderstandings before the report is finalized.
   - The final report is officially transmitted to the bank's executive management, which is invited to provide comments on the main findings of the report.
   - The inspector assesses the validity of the responses to the bank's comments and addresses each of them.
2. Services in charge of off-site supervision review the report to determine appropriate action.
   - When the findings are not deemed too serious, the General Secretary of the *Commission bancaire* issues a follow-up letter asking the bank to take corrective measures within a specific time. The bank's executive management is asked to inform the board of directors about the findings and to provide their feedback and commitment to undertaking appropriate remedial actions.
   - When the findings show serious shortcomings, the file is presented to the board of the *Commission bancaire* for a thorough review, which could lead to disciplinary action (see below).
3. Disciplinary procedure is as follows:
   - When the *Commission bancaire* intends to impose a disciplinary sanction, it initiates proceedings by sending a letter to the bank indicating the facts and observations that could form the basis of the

(Continued)

BOX 6.9 **Sanction Proceedings in France following an On-Site Inspection (*Continued*)**

sanction. The bank is asked to comment and an interview is held with the representatives of the bank and their counsel. The *Commission bancaire* decides, but not in the presence of the general secretariat, whether the case should be sanctioned and, if so, whether the decision should be made public. This is generally the case, however, when the facts are related to money laundering.

- Although defendants frequently raise procedural issues, the courts generally confirm most decisions, especially when the facts relate to money laundering.

Source: Bank of France, Secrétariat Général de la Commission bancaire.

5.2.2 Follow-up Procedures

It is important that the supervisor closely follow up the inspectors' recommendations to ensure that the bank corrects all the identified deficiencies. To this end, the supervisor must make systematic checks and hold frequent meetings with bank representatives to ascertain the concrete measures adopted and the degree of progress made towards compliance. It is critical that supervisors show vigilance in their oversight of the problems by periodically checking the bank's progress in complying with the recommended measures. The supervisor can, for example, give the institution specific orders to comply with instructions, and can order regular reports from the institution that describe the measures it is taking to address the deficiencies in the AML/CFT internal apparatus. A review meeting will follow and, if necessary, there will be a new round of on-site inspections. If the problems escalate, or if bank management ignores more informal requests from supervisors to take corrective action,[33] there should be a progressive escalation of action or remedial measures.

In Malaysia, for instance, following an off- and on-site examination, Bank Negara Malaysia (BNM) provides banks with extensive feedback, as well as recommendations that address key AML/CFT deficiencies. Several meetings are organized with the bank's board of directors, the board's audit committee, and the bank's senior management. Following a consultative process, the banks establish remediation programs subject to a stringent follow-up process by BNM. Banks must report their progress in addressing their deficiencies on a quarterly basis. If the information provided to BNM is not sufficient, further information is requested and, eventually, if necessary, there will be a follow-up on-site examination.

In Singapore, the Monetary Authority of Singapore (MAS) examination report consists of two key parts. The first is a general description of AML/CFT risks and the measures taken by the bank to address them. The second part is a table that includes descriptions of qualitative findings/deficiencies identified by MAS in the bank's AML/CFT practices and a remediation plan agreed upon by the bank and the supervisor. The plan is subject to a stringent follow-up process to ensure the taking of adequate actions.

5.2.3 Hearing

When imposing sanctions, supervisors or competent authorities normally follow strict rules, especially with respect to the right to a defense. These rules are key to a fair and expeditious processing of the case. In a scheduled hearing, the competent authorities will review the inspection outcomes, as well as the specific legal and regulatory provisions that have been violated, and the possible sanctions the failures might generate. Normally, the bank has the right to object and to defend itself. At the end of the hearing, the competent authority, based upon the seriousness of the breaches, deliberates and determines the final sanctions, which are usually delivered to the bank in writing and may be subject to publication (see box 6.10).

BOX 6.10 The Hearing Process in France

The *Commission bancaire* (CB) cannot impose a disciplinary sanction on a bank without holding a hearing. A Notification Letter, detailing all the facts supporting the proposed sanctions, is prepared by the General Secretariat of the CB and is sent to the senior management of the bank, which has one month to provide comments. A copy is also sent to the bank's board, and both the French FIU (Tracfin) and the external auditors are informed of the procedure. The bank then sends the memorandum (*mémoire en défense*) to the General Secretariat of the *Commission bancaire*, upon receipt of which, the legal department of the CB conducts a review and, if necessary, sends a new document to the bank's management, in which it confirms or amends the position of the CB General Secretariat (*mémoire en réplique*). The legal department of the CB then sets the date of its hearing and notifies the bank in writing that the case will be considered an administrative jurisdiction pursuant to Art. 613-23 of the Monetary and Financial Code.

This hearing is chaired by the Head of the CB (who is actually the Governor of the Bank of France), assisted by the other members of the commission, two of whom are judges. During the hearing, the bank is permitted to make opening and closing statements, to raise objections, and to offer additional documents in evidence. The defendant is not

(Continued)

BOX 6.10 **The Hearing Process in France (*Continued*)**

required to retain a lawyer or any other representative. In practice, how-ever, most of the banks are represented by a lawyer, or by a member of a professional organization. On rare occasions, the mission chief who wrote the original report may be asked to clarify some complex issues.

The decision is not made immediately after the hearing. Members of the CB deliberate and discuss the case in camera. Usually, the final deci-sion is rendered within one month of the hearing and the bank is notified in writing. When the CB decides to make the decision public, the decision is posted in a public place (in the Commission bancaire premises), on the website of the CB, and in the CB Annual Gazette.

Source: Banque de France/Secrétariat Général de la Commission bancaire.

5.2.4 *Issuance of Sanction and Notification*

In the most serious cases, when a bank fails to comply with core AML/CFT obliga-tions (for example, failure to report suspicious transactions to the FIU), the super-visor may decide to proceed directly to the next stage by launching disciplinary proceedings, which may entail sanctions such as fines and other civil penalties (see section 6.4) and/or other types of measures, such as cautionary warnings or notifi-cations of reprimand. Where it appears that the findings may lead to sanctions, the content of the notification letter should be very detailed and follow strict require-ments. Each breach should be concisely and accurately described and supported by concrete facts so the competent authority can establish the linkage between the fail-ure and the appropriate sanction. Once all these elements have been provided to the bank, the competent authority will normally ask the bank's management to reply and provide comments.

The determination of the proper sanction is a very difficult decision to make. In some countries, as shown above, the range of sanctions available to enforce AML/CFT laws is wide, extending from reprimands to civil penalties through to criminal penalties, and the sanctioning authority must make a judicious choice among these. Sometimes, in the most extreme cases, authorities may consider withdrawing the bank's license and closing down the bank. Even in cases where a financial institution is found to have actively participated in an ML scheme, how-ever, the wisest decision may not necessarily be to close it down. The interests of law enforcement authorities may sometimes differ from those of the supervisory authorities, in that the former may value the deterrent effect of closing down an institution while the latter are concerned with maintaining financial stability and

6

not provoking a costly run on the bank. A compromise is often found by removing or discharging officers of the institution and imposing a large fine, while at the same time rehabilitating the institution with new owners and management under the watchful eye of the supervisor.[34] Such was the case in the U.S. with Broadway National Bank.

5.2.5 Appeal

The system of sanctions must be consistent with legal guarantees of an accused person's right to a defense. The bank must be able to make its observations known to the supervisor and it must also have the right to lodge an appeal before a competent jurisdiction. The appeal system itself depends on a given country's constitutional arrangements. In the US, for example, there are three levels of jurisdiction that deal with appeals. These are the Federal District Court in the area where the bank is located, the Federal Circuit Court, and, in the last resort, the US Supreme Court. In France, the Council of State is the only authority empowered to examine appeals against the Commission bancaire's rulings. In Sweden, appeals can be made to the County Administrative Board, the Administrative Court of Appeal, and finally the Supreme Administrative Court, depending on the sanction chosen by the inspection authority (*Finansinspektionen*).[35]

6

Notes

1. Full and proper implementation requires that all the necessary laws, regulations, guidelines, and so forth are in force and effect, and that any necessary institutional framework is in place.

2. See criteria 17.2 and 29.4, FATF methodology, version 2008. See also BCP 23 on corrective and remedial powers of supervisors.

3. Basel Core Principle 1, see Basel Core Principle methodology, October 2006, criteria 1(4)

4. See section 6.5.2.5 in this book.

5. See Section 6.4.5 in this book.

6. See Basel Core Principle methodology, October 2006, criteria 1(5)

7. Court of Cassation and State Council

8. See Essential Criterion 17.1, FATF methodology, version 2004.

9. See criterion 17.4, FATF methodology, version 2004.

10. See criterion 17.4, FATF methodology, version 2004.

11. See criterion 17.4, FATF methodology, version 2004.

12. See BCP Methodology, CP 3, EC 8, and CP 17, EC 4.

13. See criteria 17.3 and 29.4, FATF methodology, version 2004.

14. Basel Committee on banking supervision, Core Principle methodology, October 2006, pinciple 23, essential criterion 6.

15. The Wolfsberg Group is an association of eleven global banks, which aims to develop financial services industry standards and related products for Know Your Customer, Anti-Money Laundering, and Counter Terrorist Financing policies. The Group came together in 2000, at the Château Wolfsberg in northeastern Switzerland to work on drafting anti-money laundering guidelines for private banking. The Wolfsberg Anti-Money Laundering Principles for Private Banking were subsequently published in October 2000 (and revised in May 2002). See http://www.wolfsberg-principles.com/

16. See Third Annual European Conference and Exhibition, The Moneylaundering.com and Money Laundering Alert, Berlin, Germany, October 30-November 1, 2006.

17. See criterion 17.4, FATF methodology, version 2004.

18. See Internal Revenue Service, United States Department of the Treasury, Bank Secrecy Act, chapter 26, section 7, BSA penalties.

19. William Amos, head of retail enforcement at the FSA, said: "*It is vital to the integrity of the UK's financial markets that regulated firms are not used by criminals to launder money. Senior management must implement and follow procedures that meet our requirements so that the risks their firms face are properly managed...This fine is a warning to firms and individuals about the importance of complying with our rules in this area and we will not hesitate to clamp down on failures, where necessary.*" In deciding the penalty for Sindicatum Holdings Limited (SHL), the FSA took into account the limited financial resources of the firm and its ability to pay the fine. Had it not been for these factors the penalty would have been significantly larger. *Source:* FSA/PN/125/2008 29 October 2008.

20. For example, the prohibition from assuming the management of legal persons

6

21. See FATF Mutual Assessment Report for Portugal, October 2006, paragraph 34, page 8.

22. Under the Bank Secrecy Act, banks are required to have anti-money laundering programs that enable them to identify and report suspicious financial transactions to the US Department of the Treasury. Among other things, banks are required to develop internal procedures and controls, designate a compliance officer, maintain an ongoing employee-training program, and provide an independent audit function.

23. See FATF Mutual Evaluation report of the United States, June 23, 2006, paragraphs 797 and 798, page 180.

24. See FATF Mutual Evaluation report of the United States, June 23, 2006, paragraph 802, page 181.

25. See FATF third Mutual Evaluation report of Sweden, February 17, 2006, page 101.

26. See *Décision juridictionnelle de la Commission bancaire* of February 25, 2003, Etna Finance Securities.

27. See *Décisions juridictionnelles de la Commission bancaire* No. 3, SARL Royale Affaires, January 14, 2002; No. 6, SARL Change de Montmartre, February 26, 2002, and No. 7, SARL Compagnie Française de Change, March 28, 2002.

28. Riggs Bank in the United States is a case in point, where violations of AML/CFT regulations and the Bank Secrecy Act not only resulted in one of the highest recorded fines for ML/FT, but also in severe loss of reputation that eventually led to the bank's collapse. Following the sanctions in 2004, Riggs was acquired by PNC Bank and its name was no longer used. For more information, see: United States Senate Minority Staff Of the Permanent Subcommittee On Investigation, *Money Laundering and Foreign Corruption: Enforcement And Effectiveness Of the Patriot Act Case Study Involving Riggs Bank*, Washington DC, July 15, 2004.

29. See FATF Third Mutual Assessment Report of Norway, June 10, 2005, page 99.

30. See FATF Third Mutual Assessment Report of Sweden, February 17, 2006, page 98.

31. See FATF, Summary of the Third Mutual Assessment Report of Portugal, October 2006, page 7.

32. See Mutual Evaluation report of Italy, prepared by the IMF, February 28, 2006.

33. See Basel Core Principles, section V, principle 22.

34. See Institute for International Economics, "Chasing dirty money," Washington, DC, 2004.

35. FATF mutual assessment report of Sweden, Feb. 17, 2006, No.437, p. 102.

6

CHAPTER 7

National and International Cooperation

Contents

1 Overview

For the AML/CFT regime to be effective, a seamless flow of information between national and international agencies is of paramount importance. Recommendation 4 of the FATF states that rules and regulations should allow information to be shared, both domestically and internationally, between competent authorities and financial institutions. In addition, recommendation 31 states that "policy makers, the FIU, law enforcement, and supervisors and other competent authorities should have effective mechanisms in place which enable them to cooperate, and where appropriate, coordinate domestically with each other concerning the development and implementation of policies and activities to combat money laundering and terrorist financing."

Nationally and internationally, bank supervisors cooperate with other anti-money laundering and combating the financing of terrorism (AML/CFT) agencies and institutions, both at the policy and operational level. Nationally, supervisors should cooperate with other AML authorities to formulate policy, and to draft higher and lower domestic legislation. The findings of supervisory operations may assist other agencies in executing their AML/CFT function and, vice versa, financial intelligence unit (FIU) or law enforcement information may assist supervisors in performing their role. Internationally, national representatives, including supervisors, meet to agree on strategic priorities, to share expertise and to find ways to exchange information in a better and more effective way.

This chapter addresses national and international cooperation respectively.

7

2 The Importance of Cooperation

Arguably the most important element in any effective AML/CFT regime is the ability and willingness on the part of all stakeholders to cooperate at national and international levels. Cooperation in the widest sense of its meaning, that is, any form of interaction between stakeholders, permeates the international AML/CFT standards. The core function of the preventive regime is to gather and, where necessary, pass on or make information available to others. Operational cooperation is primarily understood as referring to the transfer of information between AML/CFT stakeholders. Cooperation at the policy level refers to AML/CFT stakeholders jointly setting policies or drafting legislation (nationally) or setting standards (internationally).

For the supervisor, the relevant FATF recommendations are R23, R25, R31, and R40. R25 addresses the need to provide guidance to reporting entities, and R31, the need for domestic cooperation "among policy makers, the FIU, law enforcement and supervisors," who are required to "co-ordinate domestically with each other concerning the development and implementation of policies." Recommendation 40 addresses the need for supervisors to cooperate across borders, by sharing AML/CFT information on banks that operate in more than one jurisdiction. Where the supervisor also has a licensing role, the other relevant recommendation is R23, which concerns the "fit and proper" tests for those who hold either significant ownerships or controlling stakes in financial institutions. Although not explicitly stated in the standard, in practice, preventing criminals or their associates "from holding ... a significant or controlling interest or ... management function" will invariably involve a check of criminal antecedents. Verification of answers cannot be done without recourse to criminal records and thus involves the cooperation of other authorities who have access to them.

As far as the *ability* to cooperate is concerned, rules and procedures can achieve a great deal. They can endow authorities with certain powers to share information, and they can take away obstacles to sharing information by lifting secrecy or confidentiality provisions. They can also establish appropriate cooperation procedures, establish committees, appoint coordinators, and so on. As far as the *willingness* to cooperate is concerned, however, a legal framework or a memorandum of understanding (MOU) can achieve little. It matters little how detailed the arrangements are to facilitate cooperation, assuming no unduly restrictive constitutional or other impediments exist. These arrangements will remain pure theory if, in fact, authorities are not willing to cooperate with one another. This points to the essential limitation in any discussion about cooperation, whether domestic or international. Suffice it to say that no AML/CFT system has ever been successful where willingness to cooperate was absent.

The following sections discuss various frameworks, both domestic and international, within which cooperation can be achieved.

7

3 National Cooperation

The purpose of AML/CFT cooperation at the operational level is to share information, intelligence, and evidence to prevent, investigate, and prosecute ML and FT
offenses. The cooperation refers to interaction between all agencies and institutions
within the AML/CFT regime, including different parts of the financial sector, FIUs,
official records and registries[1], law enforcement agencies[2], financial sector supervisors, the prosecutorial and judicial systems, as well as other informal or formal
organizations.[3] Supervisors are encouraged to go beyond their domestic environments and seek cooperation at the international level (see section 7.4). In Canada,
for example, the federal Department of Finance is responsible for the Canadian
AML regime overall. It chairs an interdepartmental working committee of other
government departments (such as Public Safety, Foreign Affairs, and Justice) and
agencies (such as the Office of the Supervisor of Financial Institutions [OSFI], the
Financial Transaction and Reports Analysis Centre of Canada [FINTRAC], the
Royal Canadian Mounted Police, the Canada Revenue Agency (income tax), and the
Canada Border Services Agency, which meet regularly to discuss policy and opera-
tional issues.

3.1 Operational

In general, the main object of domestic operational AML/CFT cooperation is to
share information, intelligence, and evidence designed to prevent, investigate, and
prosecute ML and FT offenses. The cooperation then refers to all agencies and institutions in the AML/CFT regime as shown in figure 7.1. This section considers two
flows of information—information gathered by the supervisor that may assist other
AML/CFT agencies and information originating from other stakeholders that may
further a supervisory objective.

3.1.1 Cooperation with the FIU

To inform the supervisor's risk analysis of the banking sector (and thus assist the
supervisor in determining its inspection schedule) the FIU may prove a valuable
source of information. The reports the FIU receives from reporting entities may
provide useful indications of their adherence to customer due diligence (CDD) and
other obligations. If, for instance, information on beneficial ownership is consistently lacking in reports filed by a certain institution, that omission would indicate
that the institution had significant shortcomings in meeting its CDD obligations. In
Jersey, the FIU gives exact reports on suspicious transaction reports (STRs) submitted by reporting institutions, and this feeds directly into the bank supervisor's risk
model, which ultimately determines their on-site inspection program.

7

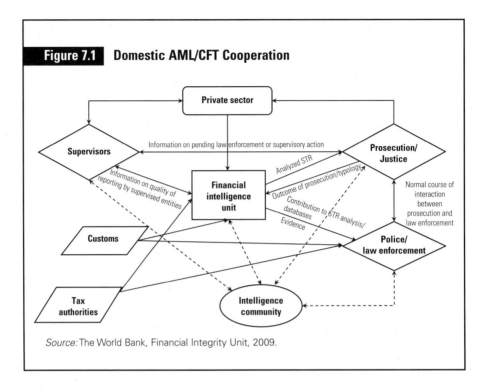

Figure 7.1 Domestic AML/CFT Cooperation

Private sector

Supervisors

Information on pending law enforcement or supervisory action

Prosecution/ Justice

Information on quality of reporting by supervised entities

Financial intelligence unit

Analyzed STR

Outcome of prosecution/typology

Contribution to STR analysis/ databases

Evidence

Normal course of interaction between prosecution and law enforcement

Customs

Police/ law enforcement

Tax authorities

Intelligence community

Source: The World Bank, Financial Integrity Unit, 2009.

It is not just the quality of an STR that is relevant, however. Other information on reporting behavior can be useful as well. Comparing the number of reports submitted by a particular bank to that of a similar bank can also indicate whether each bank is correctly fulfilling its reporting obligations. There may be cause for supervisory concern if bank A submits only a fraction of the number of reports submitted by a bank B, located in the same area, serving the same customer base, and offering the same services. Bank A might be underreporting or bank B might be reporting too much. Either way, this is valuable information to the supervisor. This information is not only relevant for sector risk profiling and determining the inspection schedule; it can also be used more straightforwardly as one element supporting an administrative sanction, such as a warning or a fine.

Because the FIU can provide information on the above issues, jurisdictions have sought to open up the channels of information between supervisors and the FIU. How this is to be done depends upon local circumstances and the national data-protection legislation. It may be possible to open these channels without providing a legal basis to allow it, but it may be that the confidentiality of FIU data also extends to information on the reporting behavior of the reporting entity. In most cases the confidentiality of data applies only to that information contained in an STR that is specifically customer related. If that is the case, the conclusions derived from a deficient or missing STR are not covered by those rules, and the FIU is free to submit such information to the supervisor. Some countries take the view, though, that *any* information derived from an STR is covered by confidentiality rules. In that case an explicit legal basis is required to enable this information to flow between the FIU and the supervisor.

In Spain and Italy, for example, FIUs and banking supervisors share their inspection reports where appropriate. In Italy, the Bank of Italy (BoI) and the FIU are considering establishing an information exchange program. This would allow the institutions to share some information from the FIU (for example, detailed aggregated returns, which the FIU receives from banks to identify outliers) and would ensure they adequately coordinate their programs, for example, in regard to deploying BoI and FIU inspection teams to visit the same bank. Also, the FIV and other agencies cooperate actively with the Ministry of Economy and Finance on enforcement matters (see box 7.1). Collaboration between the institutions may also take the form of staffing joint on-site supervision teams, in which each team member brings a unique perspective as well as skills that may allow ML/FT risks to be more effectively identified. In France, for example, members of the bank, securities, and insurance supervision agencies may all be part of on-site supervision teams. The reporting of substantial AML/CFT deficiencies that follows an off- or on-site examination of a financial conglomerate may be of interest to different supervisory agencies, or to different departments of an integrated supervision agency, or lastly, jointly exercised sanctioning processes of liable financial institutions. In Canada, the FIU (which

---

BOX 7.1 **The Role of Italy's FIU in Administrative Proceedings Aimed at Sanctioning Infractions of Reporting Obligations**

Pursuant to Italian AML/CFT legislation, apart from any complicity in the criminal offence, failure to report suspicious transactions is subject to penalties that can range between 5 percent and 50 percent of the values of the transactions involved. Because of its extensive knowledge of the reporting system, the FIU has been tasked to provide the Ministry of Economy and Finance, which is the institution formally responsible for the issuing of (pecuniary) sanctions, with a detailed opinion on infringements of the reporting obligation. To this end, all competent supervisory authorities (Guardia di Finanza, the Judicial police, the Bank of Italy, and so forth) forward their written opinions on a particular matter both to the Ministry and to the FIU (formerly the UIC, Ufficio Italiano dei Cambi). The General Affairs and Administrative Violations Unit of the AML Department is tasked with the assessment of these reports from objective and subjective points of view in order to formulate a technical opinion for submission to the ministry. Up to June 2006, the FIU had filed more than 130 opinions to the ministry.

7

is formally responsible for enforcing the AML legislation) and OSFI have an MOU under which OSFI shares with FINTRAC all information gained from its AML assessment program. FINTRAC shares with OSFI information on STR and large cash/electronic funds transfer filings and sector statistics on filing trends and effectiveness. Regular meetings are held between the two agencies to discuss trends and emerging issues, as well as the specific results of assessments of individual entities.

Conversely, there may also be a need for a flow of information the other way round, from the supervisor to the FIU. On-site inspections conducted by the supervisor may bring to light unreported suspicious activity. To remedy this, countries may provide the supervisor with the right to ensure that the FIU is informed, either by making a report directly or by having the reporting institution file a belated STR. Again, depending on the role of the supervisor in a given jurisdiction, it may be possible to make a simple agreement between the two institutions. On the other hand, where general confidentiality provisions prohibit sharing of information gathered in the execution of supervisory responsibilities, a specific legislative exemption may be required.

Finally, in countries in which the FIU is the supervisory body responsible for AML/CFT, it is necessary to ensure coordination between the prudential supervisor and the FIU, which would clearly consider information encountered on deficient internal controls in the course of a prudential inspection to be important. Similarly, such information gathered by the FIU would be important to the prudential supervisor.

3.1.2   Cooperation with Law Enforcement Authorities

The supervisor might, of course, uncover much more serious evidence during an on-site visit—not simply evidence of an overlooked transaction, but of the bank's involvement in criminal behavior, whether that behavior was the result of active involvement or of gross negligence. In that case, the supervisor may wish to inform law enforcement authorities to consider further action.[4] The supervisor may, in fact, have no choice, and be obliged to report any evidence of wrongdoing. Because such a situation deals with criminal conduct, any information the supervisor gathers should not be covered by any supervisory confidentiality provisions. To put matters beyond doubt, however, legislators may choose to include an explicit provision to this effect in the law.

There is, in any event, a need for dialogue and structural cooperation between supervisory and law enforcement authorities. In the above example, it could be the case that a law enforcement agency was already investigating the bank in question. If the supervisor decided to take independent action without any dialogue or coordination, the entire criminal investigation could be disrupted. If the supervisory action included the imposition of administrative sanctions, these sanctions could preclude criminal sanctions from being applied (see box 7.2). Similarly, a prosecutor who took law enforcement action without consulting the supervisor might cause a run on the

7

BOX 7.2 Supervisor–Prosecutor–Law Enforcement Cooperation

In the Netherlands, the AML supervisors meet regularly with the prosecutor's office and the investigative authorities for financial economic crime. This meeting is known as the Tri-Partite Meeting (*Tripartiete Overleg or TPO*). The need for the TPO is both practical and legal. Because Dutch law determines that the imposition of an administrative fine is a punishment, such an imposition triggers the principle of double jeopardy. In consequence, it is not possible to impose both an administrative fine and a criminal sanction for the same offence. Any enforcement action taken by the supervisor regarding a particular infringement of AML/CFT obligations therefore precludes action being taken by the law enforcement authorities, and vice versa. The TPO's primary purpose, then, is to decide what route to take, because the single choice of either the administrative or the criminal route is binding. This is known as the *una via* principle.

Although there are no clear-cut rules for deciding whether the prosecutor or the supervisor will take action in any given case, there are some underlying considerations. The primary intention of administrative action is to ensure the compliance of the relevant institution, while criminal action is seen as the ultimate remedy. In other words, the assumption is that the state will first take administrative action and resort to criminal action only when administrative action has proved ineffective. This occurs in cases of recidivism and of deliberate money laundering and, very occasionally, on other grounds, when a supervisor can demonstrate that criminal sanctions are the only appropriate remedy for certain conduct. Recidivism cases are those in which administrative action has demonstrably failed to bring about the desired effect of compliance. The institution or person at fault either continues to operate *contra legem* or does not take any measures to prevent AML legislation infringement. When a legal entity is involved, the investigation and prosecution should target not only the entity, but also the natural person who is actually responsible for the criminal conduct. Sanctions other than monetary penalties may be applied, because they are unlikely to have the desired effect when substantial administrative fines have already failed. In such cases, suspended jail sentences or other sanctions have to be considered. In cases of deliberate money laundering, where there are concrete indications that AML legislation is being deliberately violated to facilitate or perpetrate money laundering, supervisory action will serve no purpose and criminal investigation and prosecution is, therefore, the only option.

In principle the TPO meets once a quarter, but there is a procedure for dealing with emergency situations. The TPO only addresses the infringement of AML legislation and possible cases of money laundering.

Participants can register cases with the TPO secretary using a standard form. The registration should include case content, full identification information, evidence of wrongdoing, possible problems, the relevance for TPO participation, the nature of the desired action and, where relevant, sensitivity, recidivism history of the suspect, that is, any earlier administrative action taken or threatened, and other important circumstances.

7

bank, putting the bank in danger of collapse, or might cause unintended consequences that could possibly affect the stability of the banking system. The prosecutor's concern, that of punishing criminal behavior, should be balanced against those of the supervisor, namely, safeguarding the integrity and stability of the domestic banking system.

Countries may opt for cooperation/coordination to take place on an ad hoc basis, but a memorandum of understanding, or a covenant, can formalize such coordination. Similarly, it is possible to formalize mutual considerations on whether to proceed via the administrative or the criminal route or a combination of both. Points of discussion[5] may include, among others:

- Whether the authorities want to punish the institution or prefer to make it comply
- How much money is involved in the offense
- Concurrence with other criminal behavior
- Whether similar conduct has occurred before
- Time delays involved in criminal action
- Possible repercussions of the criminal action

Finally, the degree to which supervisory instruments can complement the tools of law enforcement should be pointed out. Where, for example, a prosecutorial agency cannot find sufficient evidence to bring a case, it may wish to pass the case to the supervisor. Even where there is insufficient evidence for establishing the existence of a criminal offense of money laundering, the inquiry might have shown breaches of AML/CFT requirements, such as customer identification, monitoring, or reporting, that could be sanctioned by the supervisor.

3.2 Cooperation at the Policy Level

3.2.1 With all AML Stakeholders

If day-to-day operational contact among all institutions that play a role in the AML/CFT system is essential to the proper functioning of the system, periodic consultation among high-level representatives of those institutions is equally indispensable if their continuing commitment is to be guaranteed. Through discussions and by becoming aware of the capabilities and objectives of the other actors in the AML/CFT system, these high-level representatives can ensure that duplications and gaps are avoided. It is to achieve these goals that FATF R31 recommends that "policy makers, the FIU, law enforcement and supervisors … coordinate domestically with each other concerning the development and implementation of policies and activities to combat ML/FT."

These high-level meetings generally comprise representatives from relevant ministries, law enforcement authorities (both investigative and prosecutorial), all financial supervisors, the FIU, sometimes also the tax authorities, and industry and professional bodies (see boxes 7.3 and 7.4). Apart from resolving potential difficulties in implementation and otherwise paving the way for cooperation at an operational level, these bodies may also have a role, either formal or informal, in preparing and reviewing draft legislation. This input and commentary from the most important stakeholders, at the highest level, may well facilitate a smooth passage of pending draft legislation. Should reporting entities be involved in this body, the meetings may also serve to replace a consultation process, at least to provide feedback that can then be placed in the consultation draft to pre-empt some of the comments.

3.2.2 With Other Supervisors

Where supervisors, in order to implement formal legislation, have been granted the power to issue lower supervisory regulations, they must coordinate their efforts with those of other supervisors to determine how those regulations are drafted and implemented. Equality before the law implies equal treatment in similar circumstances, and this equality is to be reflected, not only in the regulations, but also in individual cases. All other things being equal, a security institution's incidental failure to report should not be penalized by a US$100,000 fine when a bank would receive a mere warning from the banking supervisor for a similar failure. Although

---

BOX 7.3 **National Policy Cooperation in the U.S.**

The Bank Secrecy Act Advisory Group (BSAAG) comprises representatives from the Department of the Treasury, FinCEN (the Financial Crimes Enforcement Network—the US FIU), the Department of Justice, the Office of National Drug Control Policy, various law enforcement agencies, financial regulatory agencies (including self-regulatory organizations [SROs] and state regulatory agencies), and financial services industry representatives subject to Bank Secrecy Act regulations (including trade groups and practitioners). The BSAAG receives, for consideration and comment, information from the Secretary of the Treasury or his designee(s) concerning the administration and enforcement of the BSA and associated reporting requirements and concerning law enforcement's use of such data. It also informs the participating private sector representatives how law enforcement agencies make use of the filed reports. On the basis of this dialogue, the BSAAG advises the Secretary of the Treasury on ways in which the reporting requirements could be modified to enhance the ability of law enforcement agencies to use the information, and/or to reduce the burden on reporting entities.

7

BOX 7.4 **A Model of Cooperation: The Financial Expertise Centre in the Netherlands**

In order to fight financial economic crime more effectively and to safeguard the integrity of the financial system, Dutch authorities established the Financial Expertise Centre (FEC) in December 1998. This is a collaborative effort among all authorities involved in the supervision, regulation, or investigation of the financial sector, under the management of the Ministries of Finance and Justice.

The FEC participants are the Dutch Central Bank, the Netherlands Financial Markets Authority, the Netherlands Tax and Customs Administration, the Public Prosecutions Office, the Fiscal Intelligence and Investigation Department, the Netherlands FIU, the National Police Services, and the Amsterdam-Amstelland Regional Police Force. The AIVD (Dutch General Information and Security Service) also takes part on an ad hoc basis. Supervision, monitoring, criminal investigations and prosecutions, and intelligence are thus all brought together.

The FEC carries out joint studies in financial economic crime areas, including the financing of terrorism. In particular, its focus is on identifying possible criminal elements in the regulated financial sector and on finding early warning signs that indicate terrorist financing and loss of integrity in regulated institutions, and evidence of offenses already committed. The idea is that, working in unison, participants can identify and detect facts and trends they would not have been able to find out working in isolation. The FEC then decides how to deal with these offenses, using administrative and/or criminal law. Generally, FEC projects result in administrative action, legal or policy advice, fiscal penalties, or criminal prosecution.

Since its establishment, the FEC has made a clear contribution to the participants' performance of their duties. Several projects have been conducted. The project on criminal networks resulted in three investigations involving a total of 58 financial institutions (4 of which were considered complicit with the criminal networks). The project on underground banking resulted in the confiscation of drugs, firearms, 2.5 million euros, and the imposition of four prison sentences. In addition, projects on nonprofit organizations and terrorism financing, on the use of FIU information, and on securities institutions have all been completed. Projects are being conducted on the use of "straw men," on real estate, and on money exchange offices, resulting in three criminal investigations: a money laundering investigation involving 36 million euros; the identification of criminal staff in money exchange offices and a bank; and on securities deposits.

Source: WB staff interviews, 2007.

7

a binding rule at a higher level already goes some way toward securing equality, supervisors must ensure that equality is maintained at the most detailed level, and that similar infringements committed by entities supervised by different supervisors receive similar penalties.

3.2.3 With the FIU

Given the expertise of FIUs in the realm of AML/CFT, and the fact that, in the domestic domain, they are at the front line of discovering new trends and methods, there is a valid reason for supervisors to receive training from them. Such training can help them determine the areas of higher risk in their on-site/off-site inspections and target the information they need from the institution. It may be that the mere provision of relevant information is sufficient, rather than actual training, depending upon the exact circumstances. The FIU can also provide basic training to those supervisors who are new to the area of AML/CFT and who need a standard introduction. Conversely, of course, the FIU may itself carry out some supervisory tasks, and may need training in how to carry out on-site inspections. In Belgium, for instance, it is the banking supervisor that helps and trains the FIU in how to conduct on-site supervision.

3.2.4 With Reporting Entities

According to recommendation 25, "competent authorities" should establish guidelines and should also provide feedback to reporting institutions. While provision of feedback would typically be executed by the FIU, it may be the supervisor who establishes the guidelines that help the supervised entity to fulfill its AML/CFT obligations. It is, after all, the supervisor who subsequently monitors these obligations.[6]

Recommendation 25 of the FATF, among other standards and practices on the same subject, states that the guidelines should "assist financial institutions and DNFBP[7] to implement and comply with their respective AML/CFT requirements."[8] Guidelines typically clarify the means to implement AML/CFT policies, including CDD processes, AML/CFT risk assessments, beneficial ownership structures, recordkeeping, reporting of suspicious transactions, and maintaining an adequate level and mix of expertise through staff training. Depending on specific local circumstances, the guidelines may vary from jurisdiction to jurisdiction. In Jersey, guidelines to clarify AML/CFT requirements are prepared by the Jersey Financial Services Commission (JFSC) with the assistance of a steering group representing the financial industry. The guidelines give special importance to corporate governance issues (board responsibilities, ML/TF compliance officer's missions, and so forth) and to cultural barriers to the implementation of an effective AML framework. The guidelines are extensively discussed with the industry. In Italy, the Bank

7

of Italy issued the "Decalogo," a regulation which gives practical guidelines on ways to implement internal control and unusual transactions indicators requirements.

From an international perspective, the issuing of guidelines reaffirms that the jurisdiction is committed both to the development of effective legal instruments and to the enhancement of banks' AML/CFT practices. The effect is to improve the country's credibility and its climate for doing business.

Guidelines and ongoing collaboration between the public and the private sectors not only build trust (see box 7.5), but are also important components of an effective AML/CFT regime. Responsiveness to ML/FT risks can be improved when authorities understand the local conditions and circumstances, and when they apply adequate regulation, which the private sector is able to grasp and implement effectively.[9] An AML/CFT regime is unlikely to be effective if there is mistrust between the public and private sectors, or if the regime is operating without the private sector's full participation.

Guidance is typically regarded as soft law because it is not directly enforceable, but when a supervised entity continually disregards guidance, that disregard may be a factor in decisions on possible future action. Guidance is generic, however, and is different from the recommendations or instructions a supervisor may issue following an inspection, which typically are both binding and enforceable, and which are always directed at an individual institution. Guidance concerns an entire group of supervised entities and may relate to every aspect of the AML/CFT preventive

---

BOX 7.5   Building Mutual Trust and Confidence in Hong Kong

The Hong Kong Monetary Authority (HKMA) builds trust with the private sector through regular meetings and discussions. Specifically, HKMA

- Develops guidelines on the implementation of regulations in the private sector and consults the private sector in the development process,
- Engages in ongoing dialogue with the private sector, and
- Participates in industry working groups on specific AML related topics, such as private banking and politically exposed persons (PEPs).

To address specific concerns, HKMA posts letters to the banking industry on its Web site. In HKMA off-site examination teams, each bank is assigned a case officer who is responsible for maintaining ongoing communication with the bank, including following up on banks' remediation of deficiencies identified in the course of on-site examinations.

Source: WB Staff Interviews with HKMA, 2006.

system. It does not impose new obligations on entities, but it does seek to illustrate how certain obligations, already imposed, may be fulfilled in practice.

Finally, the banking supervisor often functions as the distribution point for lists published periodically by the United Nations Security Council Committee pursuant to Security Council Resolution 1267, the Al-Qaida/Taliban Sanctions Committee. The lists designate natural and legal persons thought to be associated with these terrorist groups, and all countries are obliged to freeze all funds belonging to or controlled by them. To this end, a central authority, typically the central bank or the banking supervisor, distributes the lists among its national financial institutions to ensure that, if any institutions hold such funds, the funds are frozen.

Supervisors also play an important role in organizing AML/CFT training, which is also part of the cooperation process. Depending on the country the supervisor may provide training directly to the financial institutions (usually on a train-the-trainers basis) or otherwise may encourage other institutions, such as the national bankers' association or compliance officers' association, to provide it. In Korea, for example, the FIU (KoFIU), in cooperation with the Korean Financial Supervisory Service (FSS), is the agency that provides AML education and training to banks. The KoFIU organizes workshops on a semiannual basis, where people from the FSS, together with bank internal auditors and chief compliance officers, gather to discuss compliance matters, including issues related to AML/CFT. The purpose of these meetings (together with a good training program) is to help banks enhance their compliance with AML standards, and so reduce ML risk. The discussions include general guidelines on AML, such as the typologies of unusual transactions detected in the course of on-site examinations, and the responsibilities banks have for AML, for information-sharing, and for bank secrecy regulations. The workshops aim to shape banks' AML policies and to create/update training plans. To that end KoFIU has developed a training curriculum that banks can use to train their own staff.[10]

Given the difficulties in identifying beneficial ownership structures of bank customers in Hong Kong, the Hong Kong Monetary Authority (HKMA) has issued special guidelines on this issue. These require banks to verify the identities of owners of client companies (including beneficial owners), and, in cases when business has been introduced through third parties, the banks are also required to evaluate the "fit and proper" criteria for all intermediaries.

7

4 International Cooperation

4.1 General

International meetings of equivalent AML authorities from different countries provide a forum to set international standards and develop best practices, rather like national meetings between AML authorities that serve to set domestic policy and legislation. With the development of the financial industry, and the growth and consolidation of banking groups active in more than one jurisdiction, cooperation between banking supervisors from different jurisdictions is both more frequent and more institutionalized. There are a number of fora which serve to promote such cooperation and sharing of expertise.

Some well-established AML/CFT international fora include the Financial Action Task Force (FATF), FATF-Style Regional Bodies (FSRBs),[11] the Egmont Group (for FIUs in charge of bank AML/CFT supervision),[12] and, for supervisors, the Basel Committee on Banking Supervision.

The Basel Committee on Banking Supervision (BCBS) works to strengthen banking supervisory frameworks, to promote the advancement of risk management in the banking industry, and to help improve financial reporting standards. The BCBS produces publications on capital adequacy accounting and auditing; banking problems; cross-border issues; core principles for effective banking supervision, credit risk, and securitization; market risk; operational risk, transparency and disclosure; and, of course, money laundering and terrorist financing.

The committee does not possess any formal supranational supervisory authority, and its conclusions do not have legal force. Rather, it formulates broad supervisory standards and guidelines, and recommends statements of best practice, in the expectation that individual authorities will take steps to implement them through detailed arrangements, statutory or otherwise, that are best suited to their own national systems. In this way, the committee encourages convergence toward common approaches and common standards but does not attempt detailed harmonization of member countries' supervisory techniques.[13]

4.2 Cooperation among Supervisors

The BCBS issued its "Core Principles for Effective Banking Supervision" (BCP) in 1997, and a revised version in 2006.[14] An essential element of banking supervision, as principle 24 points out, is that supervisors should supervise a banking group on a consolidated basis, that is, that they should adequately monitor all aspects of the group's business conducted worldwide. The principle emphasizes that banking risks, including reputational risk, are not limited to national boundaries. It is only possible to obtain the full and complete information required to evaluate the risk run by the supervised institution if the home supervisor, that is the institution supervising the international bank's main operations/head office has access to data on all the bank's operations, both at home and abroad. Conversely, the host supervisor, that is, the government agency supervising at least some of the international bank's foreign branches or subsidiaries, might require access to information from the head office. The standards on international cooperation, then, concern access to information by both the home and host supervisors, and the conditions in which information is provided.

BCP 25 deals more specifically with home-host supervisory relationships. In dealing with material cross-border operations of its banks, a supervisor should identify all other relevant supervisors and should establish informal or formal arrangements (such as memoranda of understanding) with them for appropriate information sharing. The information would concern the financial condition and performance of such operations in the home or host country, and would be shared on a confidential basis. Where agreements are reached on formal cooperation arrangements, the relevant banks and banking groups should be informed.

A home supervisor should provide a host supervisor with information about

- The bank or banking group, so as to allow a proper perspective of the activities conducted within the host country's borders,
- The specific operations in the host country, and
- Significant problems arising in the head office or elsewhere, where appropriate, if these might have a material effect on the safety and soundness of subsidiaries or branches in the host countries concerned.

A host supervisor should provide a home supervisor with information about

- Material or persistent noncompliance with relevant supervisory requirements,
- Adverse or potentially adverse developments in the local operations of a bank regulated by the home supervisor,
- Adverse assessments of qualitative aspects of a bank's operation, such as risk management and controls at the offices in the host country, and
- Any material remedial action taken about the operations of a bank regulated by the home supervisor.

In most circumstances, it will be necessary to exchange at least a minimum level of information between the home and host supervisors, but its frequency and scope will vary depending on its importance. To this end, the host supervisor will inform the home supervisor when the operations of the banking group are material to the financial sector of its country. Conversely, the home supervisor will inform the host supervisor when the operations of the host country's banking groups are material to those of the home country. Foreign banks should be subject to prudential, inspection, and regulatory reporting requirements similar to those for domestic banks.

7

The host supervisor, before issuing a license, should establish that the home supervisor has made no objection or has provided a statement of having no objection. The host supervisor, for the licensing process, as well as for ongoing supervision of cross-border banking operations in its country, should assess whether the home supervisor practices global consolidated supervision.

Home country supervisors, in order to assess the group's safety and soundness, and its compliance with Know Your Customer (KYC) requirements, should have on-site access to a bank's local offices and subsidiaries. Before making visits to local offices and subsidiaries of banking groups, however, home supervisors should inform host supervisors. In that particular circumstance, usually, host supervisors participate, as observers, in on-site visits led by home supervisors. As well, supervisors intending to take consequential action based on information received from another supervisor, should, to the extent possible, first consult with that supervisor.

4.3 Supervisors Cooperation on AML/CFT

The BCBS's CDD paper, "Customer due diligence for banks" (October 2001) relates more specifically to AML/CFT, and sets out standards and provides guidance for the development of appropriate practices. The BCBS has been promulgating these standards worldwide to the banking industry and to supervisors. In February 2003, the BCBS released a general guide to good practice in account opening and customer identification. In October 2004 these papers were complemented by a paper on "Consolidated KYC Risk Management," which set out principles for an effective groupwide approach.

The standards in the BCBS's CDD paper relate both to the AML/CFT rules that must be observed and to the supervisory practices that oversee and enforce those rules. The supervisory standards also address the supervision of banks active in more than one jurisdiction.

During on-site inspections, the home country supervisor or auditors should face no impediments in their task of verifying the unit's compliance with KYC policies and procedures. When reviewing customer files and conducting random sampling of accounts, these supervisors should not be impeded by local bank secrecy laws and should require access to sampled individual customer account information to form a proper evaluation both of the application of KYC standards and of risk management practices. There should, of course, be safeguards to ensure that individual account information is used exclusively for lawful supervisory purposes and that the recipient can protect it in a satisfactory manner. Where the KYC policies of a parent bank are imposed by its home authority and conflict with what is permitted in a cross-border office, the home supervisor should confirm with the host supervisor whether genuine legal impediments exist. If insurmountable impediments exist, and if no satisfactory alternative can be found, the home supervisor should make it clear that the bank may itself decide to close down the operation

7

in question or may be required to do so by its home supervisor. In the final analysis, any arrangements for on-site examinations should include a mechanism permitting an assessment that the home supervisor finds satisfactory.[15]

Other than the Basel Committee, there are several regional organizations and committees that also provide a forum for discussing issues of international supervisory cooperation.[16] FATF recommendation 40 deals with, among other things, supervisory cooperation. It makes clear that any information exchanged should be used only for the supervisory purpose for which it is sought, and the information should not be passed on to other authorities without permission from the supervisor that supplied it. The information should, however, be shared both upon request *and* pro-actively because the supplying supervisor believes the information might be valuable to the other supervisor. It should also be made available in a manner that is rapid, constructive, and effective. Supervisors should be able to conduct inquiries on behalf of other supervisors and, if permitted under domestic law, to conduct investigations upon request (see box 7.6 for further details).

BOX 7.6   Scope of Supervisory Cooperation in the EU

For supervisors based in the European Union, the Committee of European Banking Supervisors (CEBS) issued its "Guidelines for co-operation between consolidating supervisors and host supervisors" in 2006. The scope of cooperation/information exchange is determined by the specific entity's significance or systemic relevance to the supervisor. The CEBS guidelines note the following:

(1) The extent of cooperation and information sharing will be influenced by the significance or systemic relevance of the entities, both within the group and in their local market(s). The consolidating supervisor and the host supervisors may have different views on the degree of significance or systemic relevance of the various entities and on the risks stemming from these entities for the group. Significance and systemic relevance remain relative concepts to be assessed by the consolidating and host supervisors on a case by case basis, and determined by the consolidating supervisor for the purposes of the supervision on a consolidated basis. In making their assessment, supervisors should consider, at a minimum, the complexity, potential impact, and size of the entity.

(2) The assessment of significance may consider a broad set of factors, taken into account separately or in combination. For assessing significance, a nonexhaustive list of factors is listed below. Supervisors are invited to consider a wider range of criteria whenever appropriate.

(Continued)

7

> **BOX 7.6**   Scope of Supervisory Cooperation in the EU (*Continued*)
>
> (3) The consolidating supervisor and the host supervisors may each have a different focus in their supervision of a given entity. It is therefore important for them to communicate to each other their assessment of the entity's significance and the rationale for that assessment, and to take each others' assessments into account in structuring their cooperation. A periodic review of the assessment is recommended.
>
> For the full text of the guidelines see www.c-ebs.org/pdfs/GL09.pdf.

> **BOX 7.7**   Hong Kong's Collaboration with Foreign Supervisors
>
> Hong Kong has established MOUs with foreign supervisors, and HKMA maintains up-to-date information about those jurisdictions in which Hong Kong banks operate. Conversely, authorities supervising foreign branches of Hong Kong banks are granted access to HKMA. Foreign supervisors may also obtain HKMA inspection reports of foreign bank branches located in Hong Kong.
>
> The HKMA also plays an active role in the Executives' Meeting of East Asia Pacific (EMEAP) Central Banks, which is a cooperative organization of central banks and monetary authorities whose primary objective is to strengthen cooperation among its 11 members from the East Asia and Pacific region. Three working groups have been established, the first on payment systems, the second on financial market development, and the third on banking supervision. The HKMA has, in the past, chaired the Working Group on Banking Supervision and has participated as a member in the other two working groups.
>
> In addition to its connection with EMEAP, HKMA also maintains strong relationships with FSRBs and with US supervisory agencies. Recently, the HK and US authorities launched a knowledge exchange program, within which HKMA staff visited FinCEN and the OCC and took part in on-site examinations of US banks.
>
> *Source:* WB staff interviews with HKMA, 2006.

7

The standards cited above recommend that the relevant parties create a memorandum of understanding (MOU) or other written agreement to facilitate cooperation between supervisors (see box 7.7). Typically these documents are bilateral between one supervisor and another, but platforms are now being established within the regional organizations mentioned above to allow for multilateral cooperation among supervisors.[17]

Bilateral arrangements will vary according to the envisaged scope of information exchange. The more frequent and intense the cross-border banking activity, the more detailed will be the MOU or other document.

Other than exchanging information, supervisors may also exchange staff. The Committee of European Banking Supervisors (CEBS) is providing a Web-based information platform for CEBS members and observers who are willing to organize temporary staff exchanges. The Association of Banks of the Americas organizes internships for professionals who have less than three years' experience in banking supervision. The aim is to improve participants' skills by exposing them to more technically developed environments.

7

Notes

1. These may include records and registries of law enforcement agencies, identity/passport, supervisors, tax authorities, customs authorities, land registration, vehicle records, company registry, commercial databases, and others.

2. These may include police, specialist police units (for example, drugs, terrorism), criminal records, anti-corruption agencies, customs, internal/external security/intelligence agencies, supervisors, tax inspectors, and others.

3. A dialogue should also be established between the government and nonfinancial businesses and professions, for example, lawyers, accountants, and real estate agents. For example, in Korea, chief compliance officers in the banking industry have formed an informal knowledge sharing network, and they meet to discuss compliance with AML/CFT and other legislation on a monthly basis.

4. Basel Core Principles Methodology, CP 18, EC 11.

5. Similar considerations (but at a different level) may also be relevant to the supervisor's deciding whether to take the more severe action of imposing an administrative fine or to content itself with simply sending a letter or issuing a warning.

6. In this regard, it is noteworthy that R25 is included in the section of the recommendations that is entitled: Supervision and Regulation.

7. DNFBP: designated nonfinancial businesses and professions.

8. Guidelines are useful to bring clarity to AML/CFT legislation and national and international standards, particularly those that have been newly implemented. In June 2004, for example, the HKMA disseminated a *Supplement to the Guideline on Prevention of Money Laundering* and interpretative notes reflecting the revised 40 FATF recommendations. In the process of preparing the Supplement, the HKMA engaged in a consultative process with the banking industry to discuss views of common concern and practical implications of introducing new guidelines. In this regard, HKMA organized workshops on specific AML/CFT issues like CDD for private banking, correspondent banking, including offshore centers, PEPs, third party introducers, and cross-border transactions.

9. World Bank and IMF, 2004.

10. At KB Bank, a comprehensive employee training program builds on the KoFIU guidelines, among others. It includes AML education at the KB Learning Center, branch self-learning, an on line course for all employees, KB satellite broadcasting education, assembly AML education for internal control managers, and notifications on unusual types of transactions. In 2005, for example, 23 notifications were distributed.

11. The regional FATF-style bodies have similar form and functions to those of the FATF, though on a regional basis. Some FATF members are also members of these bodies. For FSRBs, see Financial Action Task Force on Money Laundering in South America (GAFISUD, http://www.gafisud.org), Caribbean Financial Action Task Force (CFATF, http://www.cfatf.org/), Eurasian Group (EAG, http://www.eurasiangroup.org/), Eastern and Southern Africa Anti-Money Laundering Group (ESAAMLG, http://www.esaamlg.org/), Intergovernmental Action Group against Money-Laundering

7

in Africa (GIABA, http://www.giabasn.org/), and Middle East and North Africa Financial Action Task Force (MENAFATF, http://www.giabasn.org/).

12. In 1995, for example, a group of FIUs at the Egmont Arenberg Palace in Brussels decided to establish an informal group for the stimulation of international cooperation, now known as the Egmont Group. See: http://www.egmontgroup.org/.

13. See BCBS, *History of the Basel Committee and its Membership*, January 2007.

14. For a full text of the Basel Core Principles see http://www.bis.org/publ/bcbs129.pdf. See http://www.bis.org/publ/bcbs130.pdf for the Methodology for assessing the BCP.

15. For a full discussion see the Basel CDD paper, paragraphs 63 and further at http://www.bis.org/publ/bcbs85.pdf?noframes=1. In addition to the papers mentioned, the Basel Committee also published a paper called "Sharing of financial records in connection with the fight against terrorist financing" (April 2002), which is basically a summary of a meeting of G10 supervisors and legal experts in Basel in December 2001.

16. They are the following: The Association of Financial Supervisors of Pacific Countries, the Arab Committee on Banking Supervision, the Association of Supervisors of Banks of the Americas (ASBA) (www.asbaweb.org), the Caribbean Group of Banking Supervisors, the EMEAP Working Group on Banking Supervision (www.emeap.org), the Group of Banking Supervisors from Central and Eastern European Countries, the Committee of European Banking Supervisors (www.c-ebs.org), the Banking Supervision Committee of the European System of Central Banks, the Group of French-speaking Banking Supervisors, the Gulf Cooperation Council Banking Supervisors' Committee, the Islamic Financial Services Board (www.ifsb.org), the Offshore Group of Banking Supervisors (www.ogbs.net), the Regional Supervisory Group of Central Asia and Transcaucasia, the SADC Subcommittee of Bank Supervisors, the SEANZA Forum of Banking Supervisors, and the Committee of Banking Supervisors in West and Central Africa.

17. In this respect, reference can be made to the setting up of so-called "colleges" of supervisors under the umbrella of the Committee of European Banking Supervisors (for detailed information see http://www.c-ebs.org/press/documents/CEBS%202007%2017%20rev%202%20(template%20for%20written%20agreements)%20final%202.pdf)

7

Annexes

Annex 1: Designing an Effective AML/CFT Framework That Supports Initiatives to Broaden and Deepen Financial Access by the Poor

The world community recognizes the positive economic impact of broad access to financial services.[1] An inclusive financial system provides appropriate financial services to as many as possible, especially the poor and the socially vulnerable, who have lacked access to such products and services in the past.

Governments committed to financial inclusion must ensure that their AML/CFT frameworks are effective and meet international standards, but should also ensure that the AML/CFT controls do not undermine access unnecessarily. AML/CFT controls are inherently exclusive because they are aimed at identifying and deterring potential criminal abuse of the financial system. However, if the controls are not designed with care, they may also exclude honest clients who are socially vulnerable.

The AML/CFT laws may, for instance, require potential clients to verify their particulars by means of official documentation that is not easily available to the poor. Such a requirement not only undermines financial inclusion but also undermines the AML/CFT system. The effectiveness of the AML/CFT system depends on its reach: the greater the number of persons and transactions that fall outside the reach of the system, the less it is able to identify suspicious transactions in the economy at large.[2] AML/CFT is therefore strengthened when the system responds sensitively to the need for financial inclusion.[3]

AML/CFT controls are often costly and should therefore be required, and imposed, to the extent necessary. Overly conservative controls may create unnecessary cost barriers for poor clients and may also undermine competition in the market: controls can raise the administrative costs of small service providers to such an extent that they are forced out of the market. This in turn will restrict the offering of financial services, thereby undermining financial inclusion.

The risk-based approach of the Financial Action Task Force (FATF) and the flexibility of many of its recommendations provide a framework for the development of an effective AML/CFT system that supports financial inclusion.[4]

A 1.1 The Design of Appropriate Policy

An alignment is required between a country's AML/CFT policy and its policy on financial inclusion. This alignment occurs best when particular matters are consciously addressed in policy. Where the FATF recommendations allow flexibility and tailoring, the country should strive to attune its AML/CFT measures to the domestic environment, especially domestic money laundering and financing of terrorism (ML/FT) risks. A recent study identified a number of guidelines that may assist a country in the formulation of its policy in this regard. These guidelines are summarized in box A1.1.

When it formulates its policy, a country should consider the factors to be used to determine whether products or services pose a higher or lower risk of ML/FT abuse. Such factors often include the value of the transaction; the nature of the transaction; and the nature, identity, and nationality of the parties to the transaction. Restrictions that address the relevant factors can be imposed to limit potential ML/FT risk posed by a specific product. See the example in box A1.2.

Monetary limits can be used to restrict money-laundering risks but they have not been endorsed by the FATF as appropriate to control terrorist financing risk. Money laundering generally involves larger amounts, while terrorist activities can be funded by modest sums. Monetary limits on their own are therefore not effective at controlling terrorist financing risks. However, few controls are effective when employed on their own. Control mechanisms that combine a number of controls are more effective. The same would apply to the use of monetary limits in respect of terror financing risk.

Recent experiences in respect of transformational mobile phone banking, as described in Annex 2, illustrate a service-based approach in this regard. Lessons that can be drawn from South African experiences with low risk products are set out in Annex 3.

BOX A.1.1 **Developing an Effective AML/CFT System That Supports Financial Inclusion: Policy Guidelines**

1. Develop a policy
   Before an AML/CFT regime is enacted, or even if already enacted, the domestic financial sector policy maker or regulator should consider the interaction between imposing AML/CFT controls and financial inclusion. Policy makers should guard against adopting templates or regulations imposed in other jurisdictions without first considering the appropriateness and potential impact of those regulations in their own jurisdictions.

2. Follow a consultative and flexible approach
   Getting the balance between effective AML/CFT controls and financial inclusion right will require regulators to consult on an ongoing basis with the key interest groups. These include financial institutions, both registered and unregistered, law enforcement agencies, and other national agencies, notably those responsible for the national identification infrastructure.

3. Assess and define the risk
   The financial sector policy maker, relevant regulators, and law enforcement and intelligence agencies must assess the domestic ML and FT risks, drawing upon information provided by the agencies concerned as well as formal and informal financial and other relevant institutions. The identified risks must be mapped to financial subsectors, institutions, transactions, client categories, or other relevant characteristics (for example, geographic area) to produce a risk framework and resultant priorities for regulation and control.

4. Identify excluded and vulnerable groups
   Identify the levels of financial exclusion, as well as the main causes for such exclusion, in order to scope the potential impact of AML/CFT controls on financial inclusion. Excluded groups refer to all persons who do not use financial services provided by financial institutions registered with the relevant supervisors of financial services, and typically include the poor and informal and undocumented migrants.

5. Assess the domestic resource envelope
   The imposition of AML/CFT controls that cannot be implemented within the domestic resource envelope tends to increase financial exclusion without contributing to effective AML/CFT risk management. Key national resources to assess include (1) the capacity of financial services providers (for example, their systems), (2) the capacity of the financial sector regulator/supervisor (including the FIU, if one is already established), and (3) the coverage, integrity, and accessibility of the national or other identification systems.

(Continued)

BOX A.1.1 **Developing an Effective AML/CFT System That Supports Financial Inclusion: Policy Guidelines (*Continued*)**

6. Reduced control for lower-risk transactions
   Where the risk of money laundering (as opposed to the risk of the financing of terrorism, for which no risk-scaling model has yet emerged) is lower, reduced controls can be applied to facilitate financial inclusion. These adjustments aim to mitigate or reduce inability or difficulty for clients in providing documentary evidence to verify identity or residential address; compliance costs for financial institutions flowing from systems requirements; and CDD and record-keeping obligations (notably a requirement to keep physical records, especially for one-off transactions).

7. Risk-based sequencing of AML controls
   Where countries do not have the capacity to implement full and effective AML/CFT controls on all relevant transactions and institutions all at once, a sequencing approach can be followed. The level of controls imposed must be scaled to the capacity of the regulator and the institutions involved. Sequencing and scaling must be coupled with a framework to manage an increase in the required capacity to ensure that international standards are reached.

8. Promote market-based reforms facilitating formalization
   The twin objectives of effective AML/CFT controls and financial inclusion can be greatly enhanced by market incentives that (1) formalize informal or unregistered providers of financial services and/or (2) migrate users of informal financial services to formal or registered providers. Although such reforms are not strictly part of AML/CFT regulation, their short-term impact on both objectives may be more significant than the actual AML/CFT regulation, and should be favorably considered by regulators seeking to implement AML/CFT controls.

9. Develop the national identification infrastructure
   If a country's national identification infrastructure and other private databases lack coverage, integrity, or are not easily and cost-effectively accessible to financial institutions for verification purposes, the state should address the deficiencies.

Quoted from Bester, H., D. Chamberlain L. de Koker, C. Hougaard, R. Short, A. Smith, and R. Walker. *Implementing FATF standards in developing countries and financial inclusion: Findings and guidelines* FIRST Initiative (2008).

A 1.2 The Importance of Appropriate Supervision

In a country where financial inclusion is not a government priority, the supervisor tends to focus fairly narrowly on the AML/CFT controls of the regulated institutions. Institutions that maintain conservative controls can normally expect a positive report. However, in a country that also supports financial inclusion, the supervisor will consider the appropriateness of the controls in relation to the risk posed by the range of products and services. Conservative controls are required for higher-risk products and services but are not necessarily appropriate for lower-risk products. Such controls may contribute to addressing the low level of ML/FT risk those products pose, but they may have a serious negative impact on access to those products. If the controls undermine financial access, they will also restrict the AML/CFT footprint, thereby undermining the broader AML/CFT objectives.

If a supervisor believes a regulated institution has implemented overly cautious controls on a particular product, it is important to communicate with the institution to understand the reason for the controls. A regulated institution should protect itself against criminal abuse. A supervisor should, therefore, be careful to interfere and press for diluted controls if the institution believes they are inappropriate. However, it may transpire that controls were designed without a proper analysis or appreciation of the risks or the impact of the controls. If this is the case, the supervisor can engage the institution about the general quality of its risk assessment and risk management processes. If inappropriate controls were adopted as a result of ignorance, guidance may be provided to institutions to support the development and adoption of appropriate controls. If, however, the supervisor concludes that inappropriate AML/CFT controls are being employed to exclude low-income clients, regulatory intervention may be required.

The supervisory process should also be used to assess the crime risk of the lower-risk products. Controls are normally designed on the basis of assumptions made about the risks products and services will pose. It is important to test these assumptions after the controls have been implemented.[5] The supervisor should consider whether the controls counter the risk in a cost-effective and pragmatic manner. Key factors to consider would include the following:

- Why the bank regards the product or service as low risk
- The nature and extent of the controls imposed
- The ability of the controls to mitigate the risk posed by the product or service
- Whether more cost-effective controls could be employed by the bank
- Whether the general public is able to meet the requirements of the controls with relative ease

The examiner should request statistics regarding identity fraud, theft, money laundering, and terror financing that occurred with the higher- and lower-risk products of

---

BOX A.1.2 **KYC Procedures in South Africa**

South Africa wished to facilitate the offering of basic financial services to the poor. It therefore disposed of the requirement to obtain and verify residential address particulars with respect to basic financial products. These products were subjected to the following controls and limits to lessen any ML/FT risk that may be introduced by the reduced requirements:[a]

1. *Type of customer:* the products are available only to natural persons and not to companies and other legal persons.
2. *Nationality of the customer:* the customers must be South African citizens or residents.
3. *Domestic transactions:* cross-border transfers may not be made, save for point-of-sale payments or cash withdrawals in the Rand Common Monetary Area.
4. *Monetary limits:* there is a daily limit as well as a monthly limit on withdrawals, transfers, and payments. If the product is an account, a limit is placed on the balance that may be maintained in the account. The latter limit is reinforced by restricting the customer to not more than two such accounts at the same institution.

a. De Koker, *Money laundering and terror financing risk management of low risk financial products and services in South Africa.* FinMark Trust 2008.

---

a regulated institution. These statistics, if they are available, which in practice is rarely the case, should be analyzed to determine whether they validate the risk assumptions that were made. Realistically, low-risk products can be expected to show a measure of criminal abuse. However, the abuse should be limited, and the level of abuse should be substantially less than the abuse suffered by the higher-risk products. If the statistics do not validate the assumptions, the relevant regulations and the design of the controls of the institutions will need to be revisited.

Notes

1. Demirgüç-Kunt, A., T. Beck, and P. Honohan. *Finance for all? Policies and pitfalls in expanding access.* The World Bank (2008). http://econ.worldbank.org/WBSITE/EXTERNAL/EXTDEC/EXTRESEARCH/EXTPRRS/EXTFINFORALL/0,,menuPK:4099731~pagePK:64168092~piPK:64168088~theSitePK:4099598,00.html.

2. De Koker, L. "Money laundering control and suppression of financing of terrorism: Some thoughts on the impact of customer due diligence measures on financial exclusion." 2006 (1) *Journal of Financial Crime* 26 43-44.

3. Bester, H., D. Chamberlain, L. de Koker, C. Hougaard, R. Short, A. Smith, and R. Walker. *Implementing FATF standards in developing countries and financial inclusion: Findings and guidelines* FIRST Initiative (2008).

4. Isern, J., D. Porteous, R. Hernandez-Coss, and C. Egwuagu. *AML/CFT regulation: Implications for financial service providers that serve low-income people.* CGAP Focus Note 29 (2005). http://www.microfinancegateway.org/content/article/detail/27418

5. De Koker, L. *Money laundering and terror financing risk management of low risk financial products and services in South Africa.* FinMark Trust (2008).

Annex 2: Managing ML/FT Risks of Low-Risk Products: The Example of Branchless Banking

Many banks have offered mobile phone banking services for some time. These services generally supported the use of bank accounts that were opened in the traditional manner, after contact with a representative of a bank. However, recently a number of countries allowed limited financial services, especially banking services, where accounts are opened and activated via a mobile phone, without personal contact with the bank or a representative of the bank.[1] Porteous classifies the former as "additive" mobile banking, and mobile phone banking account origination that can extend financial services to the unbanked as "transformational" mobile banking.[2]

Transformational mobile financial services present a powerful channel to broaden financial access, especially in countries with large territories and sparse populations that cannot support traditional branch-based banking.[3] It can therefore be used to increase the footprint of a country's AML/CFT system and to formalize transactions currently concluded informally in cash. However, several features of mobile phone banking can also lead to criminal abuse. A World Bank paper[4] identified the following potential vulnerabilities:

- *Anonymity:* the risk of not knowing a customer's actual identity
- *Elusiveness:* the ability to disguise mobile transaction totals, origins, and destinations
- *Rapidity:* the speed with which illicit transactions can occur
- *Poor regulatory and supervisory oversight:* the risk that the lack of clarity about the role and responsibilities of telecommmunications and financial regulators diminishes the quality of oversight

The paper advises a service-based rather than a provider-based approach when assessing actual money laundering and terror financing risks for mobile financial services. The lines differentiating financial providers in the banking, telecom, credit card, and mobile commerce sectors have become blurred. With the crossover of mobile phone and payment systems operators into the financial services sector, potential risks more likely depend on the characteristics and complexity of service provided than on the service provider. A service-based approach offers greater flexibility to identify and diminish actual ML/TF risks, and is more favorable to creating an equal playing field for all providers of all types.

In order to analyze money laundering and terrorist financing risks and suggest effective risk mitigation practices, the paper advises that the four major types of mobile financial services need to be analyzed separately. The four core services of mobile financial services are the following:

- *Mobile financial information:* enabling customers to view their personal account data and general financial information *without* conducting transactions.
- *Mobile bank and securities accounts:* enabling bank and securities account holders to conduct transactions.
- *Mobile payments:* enabling *non*bank and securities account holders to make payments with mobile phones.
- *Mobile money:* enabling users to store value on their mobile phone, or mobile phone account, in the form of electronic currency that can be used for multiple purposes, including transfers to other users and conversion to and from cash.

These services, that in practice are often found in combination, have different risk profiles. Those who are furthest removed from traditional financial service models (especially mobile money) present the highest risk, but also hold the biggest potential to advance financial inclusion. Such services are not by nature low-risk, but if they are subjected to appropriate control measures, the potential for money laundering or terrorist financing abuse can be limited.

The World Bank paper identifies various mitigation responses appropriate to the specific services. The responses include the following:

- *Anonymity* can be mitigated through enhanced Know Your Customer procedures and identification tools.
- *Elusiveness* can be diminished through transaction limits and enhanced customer profiling, monitoring, and reporting.
- *Rapidity* can be checked by flagging certain types of transactions and managing risks of third-party providers.
- *Poor oversight* can be mitigated by transparent guidelines on mobile services, clearer licensing and regulation of providers, and effective risk supervision and risk management within bank and nonbank mobile financial service providers.

The money laundering and terrorist financing risks posed by different services must be evaluated, but these risks can be managed effectively within the FATF risk-based framework.

Source: Chatain, P-L., R. Hernández-Coss, K. Borowik, and A. Zerzan. *Integrity in Mobile Phone Financial Services,* working paper 146, The World Bank (2008).

Notes

1. See Lyman, T., D. Porteous, and M. Pickens. *Regulating transformational branchless banking: Mobile phones and other technology to increase access to finance.* CGAP Focus Note 43 (2008) (http://www.cgap.org/p/site/c/template.rc/1.9.2583). Ivatury, G. and I. Mas. *The early experience with branchless banking.* CGAP Focus Note 46 (http://www.cgap.org/p/site/c/template.rc/1.9.2640).

2. See D. Porteous. *Just how transformational is m-banking?* (a study commissioned by FinMark Trust) (http://www.finmarktrust.org.za/Documents/transformational_mbanking._pdf). (2007)

3. Lyman, T., D. Porteous, and M. Pickens. *Regulating transformational branchless banking: Mobile phones and other technology to increase access to finance.* CGAP Focus Note 43 (2008) (http://www.cgap.org/p/site/c/template.rc/1.9.2583).

4. Chatain, P-L, R. Hernández-Coss, K. Borowik, and A. Zerzan. *Integrity in Mobile Phone Financial Services,* working paper146, The World Bank (2008).

Annex 3: Risk Management Principles for Low-Risk Products: Some Guidelines

South Africa created a framework that allowed banks to offer basic financial products to enhance financial inclusion. These products are subject to simplified controls. A recent study reviewed the nature and extent of crime experienced in relation to these products. The study found that crime levels were indeed lower for these products compared to other, standard financial products. The study also identified a number of guidelines that may assist regulators that wish to design a similar framework:

Design the Low-Risk Framework with Care

A regulator concerned about the impact anti-money laundering and combating terrorist financing (AML/CFT) may have on access to financial services should create a clear carve-out framework that provides appropriate relief. The design of that framework should be informed by research regarding the reality and needs of the unbanked. Once the low-risk framework is implemented, the regulator must monitor the use and abuse of the relevant products. Criminal abuse that does occur must be analyzed to ensure that the framework does not allow disproportionate risk. If the levels of risk are of concern, appropriate adjustments to the framework will be required.

Assess and Manage the ML/FT Risk of Low-Risk Products

Banks should consciously assess the money laundering and terrorist financing (ML/TF) risk that may be associated with low-risk products. These products are exposed to risk; and even though the level may be low, the risk must be considered and managed. Management of the risk requires monitoring of abuse that occurs and a conscious review of the controls in the light of practical experience. The risk profile of many low-risk products will tend to increase as criminals identify ways to circumvent controls or to abuse a product despite the restrictions imposed. It is therefore important to monitor the risks to ensure that additional or different controls can be imposed when necessary. In this process, it is important to compare the risk profile of the low-risk products with those of standard and higher risk products. A comparative view will ensure that low-level abuse of low-risk products does not lead to the introduction of disproportionate controls.

Profile Customers

Banks must identify customers, and their identities must be verified as required by the national AML/CFT framework. This ensures that the bank knows who the customer is. However, from an AML/CFT risk management perspective the mere identity of the customer is not necessarily very useful. Information such as the source of income of the customer and the expected use of the product is more valuable because it enables the bank to form a picture of the expected transaction profile of the customer. Customer transactions that diverge from that profile would normally trigger a review of the customer and the account, and that may lead to the reporting of a suspicious transaction. Compared to document-based verification, profiling is relatively cheap and less disruptive. The information is simply recorded and is of value whether it is verified or not. Such information not only improves the effectiveness of the monitoring of transactions but also saves costs because it assists forensic investigators to close investigations where unusual transactions can be sufficiently explained by the particular customer's profile.

Consider the Likely Customers

Banks should consider control measures when they allow wealthier clients to use products that were designed for the poor and the socially vulnerable. Where a target customer group was defined and appropriate controls were designed for the target group, care must be taken when persons outside that group are given access to that product. It is not necessary to exclude them from the product, but it may be appropriate to impose additional controls.

Conduct Careful Vetting, Training, and Monitoring of Agents

Banks that use agents to market these products and to assist potential customers to open accounts should manage the risk posed by these agents with care. The agents normally work outside a branch environment and are not integrated into the structure of community of the bank. They may not share the organizational values of the bank or have a particularly strong sense of loyalty to the bank. Agents are therefore more vulnerable to intimidation and corruption. The risk at agent level increases when they work on a commission basis, which can make them more likely to open rather than refuse an account.

It is therefore important to check the background of a potential agent. A check should, for instance, be conducted on the person's criminal record, if any. In addition, newly appointed agents should be introduced to the bank's ethics and values. Ethical orientation should be ongoing to ensure that agents uphold those values and are committed to protecting the bank against abuse by criminals. Agents form part of the control procedures of the bank. It is therefore important to train them on the money laundering control procedures and especially to provide them with the ability to identify fake identification documentation and suspicious clients. Agents often know the clients in their community and are well placed to identify possible client risk once they understand AML/CFT control.

Nonbranch-Based Withdrawal Limit

Criminals seem to be particularly sensitive to daily cash withdrawal limits, especially in relation to ATM withdrawals. Institutions with conservative daily withdrawal limits seem to enjoy more protection against abuse than institutions with more liberal limits. Given the value of most of the transactions with these products, it does not appear as if conservative restrictions will create unnecessary hardship for the majority of the poor who uses these accounts. A general limit may be softened by granting a customer a higher daily withdrawal limit if the customer passes certain controls.

Educate Customers

Many users of low-risk products are new to the banking system. The majority of them would not necessarily understand the dangers of allowing someone else to use their account for transaction purposes. They may have an awareness of the risk of theft but would not necessarily understand how someone could use an account with a nil balance to launder money or how they could be abused as mules to open accounts for criminals. It is therefore important to alert customers to this danger when they open such an account, and this issue should be emphasized as part of the bank's continued communication with its clients.

Source: De Koker, *Money Laundering and Terror Financing Risk Management of Low-risk Financial Products and Services in South Africa.* FinMark Trust (2008).

Annex 4: Preparing and Conducting an On-Site Examination For AML/CFT

It would be difficult to develop examination procedures that would apply to every country, given the differences among their laws, regulations, and policies. One can, nevertheless, provide some examples of examination procedures and examination concepts that jurisdictions can adopt or modify as necessary.

This annex fleshes out many of the ideas presented in the main text, especially in Chapter 5, in a more in-depth and practical way. Many of the procedures have been derived from a handbook used by US bank regulators. This handbook, which can be accessed on the Internet,[1] is very comprehensive and incorporates many of the FATF Recommendations and other international best practices. The specific examples have been modified somewhat by World Bank staff so client countries can more readily apply them in their own banking environment.

Section A4.1 begins with the steps to be taken to organize an examination and includes the scoping and planning process. Section A4.2 describes the review of the bank's anti-money laundering and combating the financing of terrorism (AML/CFT) Risk Assessment. Section A4.3 describes the evaluation of the bank's AML/CFT Compliance Program, and section A4.4 presents other areas to be examined as part of the on-site process, with a special focus on key elements of AML/CFT preventive measures (customer identification, customer due diligence (CDD), suspicious transaction reporting, and so forth). Sections A4.5 and A4.6 focus respectively on Customer Due Diligence, Recordkeeping, and Suspicious Transaction Reporting requirements, while Section A4.7 describes how to assess the bank's compliance with regulatory requirements with respect to foreign correspondent account recordkeeping. Section A4.8 presents the requirements for due diligence in private banking and how to assess them, whereas Section A4.9 focuses on how examiners should pay attention to other risky accounts.

A 4.1   The Examination's Scope and Plan

A 4.1.1   Objectives

The examiner's objectives are to identify the bank's AML/CFT risks, develop the examination scope, and document the examination plan. This process includes determining staffing needs and technical expertise for the examination and selecting the procedures. To facilitate the examiner's understanding of the bank's risk profile, and to establish the appropriate scope of the AML/CFT examination, the examiner, in conjunction with reviewing the bank's AML/CFT risk assessment, should complete the following steps.

A 4.1.2   Steps to Be Followed

Preparatory work to determine the scope of the on-site visit

It is difficult to gauge the scope of the mission at its outset without conducting preliminary activities that help the mission chief determine the length of the mission, the nature of the investigations, the duration of the visit, and the number of assistants. Essentially, the preparatory work entails the review of key documents available either at the off-site department or at the bank. The main tasks to be undertaken are as follows:

1. Review prior inspection reports and the responses of management to previously identified AML/CFT violations, deficiencies, and recommendations. Determine, through discussions with the mission chief, or with the prior mission chief, if there is any additional information or ongoing concerns that have not been documented in the correspondence. Review news articles concerning or pertaining to the bank or its management.
2. Review the prior examination work papers to identify specific AML/CFT examination procedures already completed, obtain AML employee contact information, identify the reports and formats used by the bank to detect unusual activity, identify previously noted high-risk banking operations, and review any prior recommendations for this examination.
3. To the extent needed to gain a proper understanding of the bank's management, including the AML compliance officer, discuss the following with the bank's executives and other counterparts:
   - The AML/CFT compliance program
   - The AML/CFT management structure
   - The ML/FT risk assessment
   - Systems for monitoring and reporting suspicious activity
   - The level and extent of automated AML/CFT systems
4. Inform the bank, in a request letter, when the examination is to begin. The request letter should state what information and records the bank should make

available on the first day of the examination, and what information and records, if any, it should send (and by what date) in advance of the on-site visit.

5. Review the documents provided in the bank's response to the request letter to determine whether it has provided all the requested information and records. If there are any deficiencies, send a follow-up letter, or otherwise communicate with the bank management about them.

6. Read the correspondence between the bank and its primary regulators. The examiner should become familiar with the following, as applicable:
   - Outstanding, approved, or denied bank applications
   - Change of bank control documents, when applicable
   - Approvals of new directors or senior management, when applicable
   - Details of meetings with bank management
   - Other significant activity affecting the bank or its management

7. Review all correspondence between the bank, or the primary regulators, and outside regulatory and law enforcement agencies, on the subject of AML/CFT compliance. Such communications, particularly those from the financial intelligence unit (FIU) and other competent authorities, may document matters relevant to the examination. Some examples are:
   - Filing errors for suspicious activity reports, large cash transaction reports, or other reports required by the jurisdiction
   - Civil money penalties or other sanctions issued by or in process from the FIU or other competent authority
   - Law enforcement subpoenas or seizures
   - Notification that the competent authorities in the jurisdiction have imposed mandatory account closures on noncooperative foreign customers holding correspondent accounts

8. Review suspicious transaction reports (STRs),[2] large cash reports, and other AML/CFT reporting information obtained from the bank's database. The mission chief will determine the length of time for which they will be needed.

   In these documents, take note of the following, and analyze the data for unusual patterns, such as
   - Volume of and types of banking activity, and whether they are commensurate with the customer occupations or types of businesses
   - Number and local currency volume of transactions involving high-risk customers
   - Volume of large cash reports
   - Volume of STRs and cash reports in relation to the bank's size, asset or deposit growth, and geographic location

   Specific targeted volumes, or "quotas," for STR and large cash filings should not be set for any given bank size or geographic location. As part of the examination, however, examiners should review any significant changes in the volume or nature of STRs and large cash reports that have been filed, and should consider possible reasons for these changes.

9. Review internal or external audit reports and work papers in terms of AML/CFT compliance and determine the comprehensiveness and quality of audits, findings, and management responses, and what corrective actions were taken to remedy any deficiencies. A review of the independent audit's scope, procedures, and qualifications will provide valuable information on the adequacy of the AML/CFT compliance program.

10. On the basis of the above examination procedures, and in conjunction with the review of the bank's money laundering/financing of terrorism (ML/FT) risk assessment, develop an initial examination plan. The mission chief should adequately document both the plan and any changes to it that occur during the examination. The process of determining the scope and plan of an examination should ensure that the examiner is aware of the bank's AML/CFT compliance program, its compliance history, and its risk profile, including products, services, customers, and geographic locations.

While the examination plan may change at any time as a result of on-site findings, the initial risk assessment enables the examiner to establish a reasonable scope for the AML/CFT review. For the examination process to be successful, examiners must maintain open communication with the bank's management and discuss relevant concerns as they arise.

A 4.2   The Review of the Bank's ML/FT Risk Assessment

After planning the examination and its scope, another key task at an early stage is a review of the bank's ML/FT risk evaluation. This is because the inspection team needs to understand the banks ML/TF risk exposure.

A 4.2.1   Objectives

If the bank has not prepared the ML/FT assessment, supervisors must complete their own risk analysis using available information. This analysis will be undertaken for the sole purpose of the on-site examination (see chapter 5).

If, on the other hand, the bank does have its own ML/FT risk assessment, the team should then determine whether the bank has given full consideration to all risk areas, including any new products, services, customers, and geographic locations. It is also important to judge the adequacy both of the assessment and of the bank's process for periodically reviewing and updating it. Examiners should also document the bank's ML/FT risk profile, as well as any identified deficiencies in the bank's ML/FT risk assessment process, and discuss them with bank management.

The ML/FT risk assessment is important to the examination; the next few paragraphs discuss the background and procedures needed to ensure its proper review.

A 4.2.2   Steps to Be Followed

1. Background information

   The evaluation of the ML/FT risk assessment is important and should be considered part of the planning process. A well-developed risk assessment helps to define the bank's ML/FT risk profile; it also helps the bank to apply appropriate risk management processes to the AML/CFT compliance program. The result is that management is better able to identify and mitigate gaps in the bank's controls. The assessment should provide a written, comprehensive analysis of the ML/FT risks, and it should be shared with and communicated to all business lines across the bank, as well as the board of directors, management, and appropriate staff. Because there are many effective methods and formats used to complete an ML/FT risk assessment, examiners should not advocate any in particular. It is essential, however, that all parties easily understand the selected format. There are generally two steps in the development of the ML/FT risk evaluation. The first is to identify the specific risk categories unique to the bank (that is, products, services, customers, entities, and geographic locations); the second is to conduct a more detailed analysis of the identified data, so as to assess the risk more accurately within these categories. The examiner should then determine whether management has taken into account all products, services, customers, and geographic locations, and whether its detailed analysis within these specific risk categories was adequate.

2. Evaluating the bank's ML/FT risk assessment
In reviewing the bank's AML/CFT compliance program, an examiner should have sufficient knowledge of the bank's ML/FT risks to determine whether the program is adequate and whether it provides the controls necessary to mitigate risks. During the examination planning process, for example, the examiner may initially determine that the bank has a high-risk profile but, during the examination itself, the examiner may determine that the bank's AML/CFT compliance program adequately mitigates these risks. Alternatively, the examiner may initially determine that the bank has a low or moderate risk profile, but may determine during the examination that the bank's AML/CFT compliance program does not adequately mitigate these risks.

In evaluating the risk assessment, an examiner should not necessarily take any single indicator as determining a lower or higher ML/FT risk. A conclusion regarding the risk profile should be based on a consideration of all pertinent information, and any assessment of risk factors is bank specific because banks may determine that some factors should be weighed more heavily than others. The number of funds transfers is certainly one factor to be considered in assessing risk, for example, but if that risk is to be effectively identified and weighed, the examiner must look at other factors associated with those funds transfers, such as whether they are international or domestic, the local currency amounts involved, and the nature of the customer relationships.

3. Identification of specific risk categories
The first step of the risk assessment process is to identify the specific products, services, customers, entities, and geographic locations unique to the bank. Although, with respect to any bank, attempts to launder money, finance terrorism, or conduct other illegal activities can emanate from many different sources, certain products, services, customers, and geographic locations may be more vulnerable or, historically, have been abused by money launderers and criminals. The risks are not always the same, depending on the specific characteristics of the particular product, service, or customer. When the bank prepares its risk assessment, it should consider various factors, such as the number and volume of transactions, geographic locations, the nature of the customer relationships, and the way it interacts with the customer (face-to-face contact versus electronic banking). Because of these factors, risks will vary from one bank to another. In reviewing the bank's risk assessment, examiners should determine whether management has developed an accurate risk assessment for the bank.

4. Analysis of specific risk categories

The second step of the risk assessment process is to make a more detailed analysis of the data that was obtained during the identification stage, with the object of assessing the ML/FT risk more accurately. This step involves evaluating data pertaining to the bank's activities in relation to the Customer Identification Program (CIP) and customer due diligence information. These data include the number of domestic and international funds transfers, private banking customers, foreign correspondent accounts, payable-through accounts (PTAs), customer transactions, and domestic and international geographic locations of the bank's business area. The level and sophistication of analysis may vary depending on the bank itself. The detailed analysis is important because within any type of product or category of customer there will be account holders whose levels of risk vary.

This step in the assessment process creates a better understanding of the bank's risk profile, and this helps management to develop the appropriate policies, procedures, and processes to mitigate the overall risk. Specifically, the data analysis should consider, as appropriate, the following factors:

- Purpose of the account
- Actual or anticipated activity in the account
- Nature of the customer's business
- Customer's location
- Types of products and services used by the customer

The value of a two-step risk assessment process is illustrated in the following example: In the first step of the risk assessment process, the data collected reveals that a bank sends out 100 international funds transfers per day. Further analysis could show that approximately 90 percent of the funds transfers are recurring, well-documented, transactions for long-term customers. On the other hand, the analysis could equally show that 90 percent of these transfers are nonrecurring or are for noncustomers. While in both cases the numbers are the same, the overall risks are very different.

5. The bank's AML/CFT compliance program based upon its risk assessment

Management should structure the bank's AML/CFT compliance program to address its risk profile in an appropriate manner, in keeping with the findings of the risk assessment. This means that management should understand the bank's ML/FT risk exposure, and should develop the appropriate policies, procedures, and processes necessary to monitor and control those risks. The bank's monitoring systems that identify, research, and report suspicious activity should, for example, be risk based, and should place particular emphasis on those high-risk products, services, customers, and geographic locations identified in the assessment.

Independent testing (audit) should review the bank's risk assessment to confirm that it is reasonable. Additionally, management should consider the staffing resources and the level of training that will be necessary if these policies, procedures, and processes are to be adhered to. Management for those banks that have accepted and assume a higher risk ML/FT profile should provide a more robust program that specifically monitors and controls those higher risks.

A 4.2.3   Bank's Updating of the Risk Assessment

An effective AML/CFT compliance program controls risks associated with the bank's products, services, customers, and geographic locations. An effective risk assessment, therefore, should be an ongoing process, not a one-time exercise. When new products and services are introduced, existing products and services change, high-risk customers open and close accounts, or the bank expands through mergers and acquisitions, management should update its risk assessment to identify changes in the bank's risk profile. Even in the absence of such changes, it is a sound practice for banks to reassess their ML/FT risks at least every 12 to 18 months.

A 4.2.4   Examiner Determination of the Bank's ML/FT Aggregate Risk Profile

In some countries, especially in the US, examiners, during finalizing the examination phase of the AML/CFT inspection, should assess whether the controls of the bank's AML/CFT compliance program are appropriate to manage and mitigate its ML/FT risks, and so determine an aggregate risk profile for the bank. This aggregate risk profile takes into consideration the risk assessment developed by the bank and then factors in the adequacy of the AML/CFT compliance program. Examiners, based on the risk assessment, should determine whether the bank's AML/CFT compliance program will appropriately mitigate the ML/FT risks. As long as the bank's AML/CFT compliance program adequately identifies, measures, monitors, and controls this risk as part of a deliberate risk strategy, the existence of ML/FT risk within the aggregate risk profile should not be criticized. On the other hand, when the risks are not appropriately controlled, examiners must communicate the need to mitigate ML/FT risk to the bank's management and board of directors.

A 4.3   The Evaluation of the Bank's AML/CFT Compliance Program

A 4.3.1   Objectives

After completing the review of the bank's ML/FT risk assessment, the examiners should review the adequacy of the bank's AML/CFT compliance program. From this review, they will determine whether the bank has developed, administered, and maintained an effective program that is in compliance with AML/CFT laws, regulations, and policies (see box A4.1 on evaluation criteria for the existence of an adequate surveillance system). The sequencing is as follows on the next page.

BOX A4.1   **Evaluation Criteria for the Existence of an Adequate Surveillance System**

On-site examiners should conclude that the bank's internal surveillance mechanism is satisfactory if the following criteria are met:

- The surveillance system is properly integrated into the internal monitoring mechanism as a whole.
- The software for identifying large and or complex transactions seems accurate and reliable.
- The software allows for statements to be printed on demand (per customer and transaction type, per amount, per branch, and so forth) for extended periods.
- Alerts are edited regularly (daily, weekly, and so on) and they are acted upon by those responsible.
- The bank's internal inspection monitors compliance with the internal procedures (observance of limits) and thresholds.
- The relevant units (front and back office) examine the unusual transactions and seek further information.
- The internal audits are carried out following strict guidelines.
- The bank's audit/inspection programs cover all areas of activity where there is risk of ML/TF.
- The observations made by internal auditors are communicated to the bank's management.

A 4.3.2   Steps to Be Followed

A 4.3.2.1   Analysis of Board Policies

1. Review the bank's board-approved written AML/CFT compliance program to ensure it contains the following required elements:
   - A system of internal controls to ensure ongoing compliance
   - Independent testing of AML/CFT compliance
   - A designated person or persons responsible for managing AML/CFT compliance
   - Training for appropriate personnel

     A bank's AML/CFT compliance program should be commensurate with its individual AML/CFT risk profile. In addition, a customer identification program should be included as part of the AML/CFT compliance program.
2. Assess whether the board of directors and senior management receive adequate reporting on AML/CFT compliance.
3. On the basis of the examination procedures completed in the planning process, including the review of the risk assessment, determine, first, whether the bank has sufficiently identified the risk within its banking operations (products, services, customers, and geographic locations) and, second, incorporated the risk into the AML/CFT compliance program.

A 4.3.2.2   Analysis of Internal Control Procedures

1. Determine whether the AML/CFT compliance program includes policies, procedures, and processes that
   - Identify high-risk banking operations (products, services, customers, and geographic locations), provide for periodic updates to the bank's risk profile, and provide for an AML/CFT compliance program tailored to manage risks;
   - Inform the board of directors, or a committee thereof, and senior management, about compliance initiatives, identified compliance deficiencies, suspicious activity reports filed, and corrective action taken;
   - Identify a person or persons responsible for AML/CFT compliance;
   - Provide for program continuity despite changes in management or employee composition or structure;
   - Meet all regulatory requirements, meet recommendations for AML/CFT compliance, and provide for timely updates to implement changes in regulations;
   - Implement risk-based customer policies, procedures, and processes demanding due diligence;
   - Identify reportable transactions and accurately file all required reports, including STRs, large cash reports, where applicable and any other nationally required reporting;

- Provide for dual controls and the segregation of duties;
- Provide sufficient controls and monitoring systems for the timely detection and reporting of suspicious activity;
- Provide for adequate supervision of those employees that handle currency transactions, complete reports, grant exemptions, monitor for suspicious activity, or engage in any other activity covered by AML/CFT regulations;
- Train employees to be fully aware of their responsibilities under AML/CFT regulations and internal policy guidelines; and
- Incorporate AML/CFT compliance into job descriptions and performance evaluations of appropriate personnel.

A 4.3.2.3 Examination of Independent Testing Adequacy

1. Determine whether the AML/CFT testing is independent, and is performed by individuals not involved with the bank's AML/CFT compliance staff, and whether persons conducting the testing report directly to the board of directors or to a designated board committee comprised primarily or completely of outside directors.
2. Evaluate the qualifications of the individuals performing the independent testing in order to assess whether the bank can rely upon the findings and conclusions.
3. Review the auditor's reports and work papers to determine whether the bank's independent testing is comprehensive, accurate, adequate, and timely. The independent audit should address the following:
   - The overall integrity and effectiveness of the AML/CFT compliance program, including policies, procedures, and processes
   - AML/CFT risk assessment
   - AML/CFT reporting and recordkeeping requirements
   - Customer identification program implementation
   - The adequacy of CDD policies, procedures, and processes and whether they comply with internal requirements
   - Personnel adherence to the bank's AML/CFT policies, procedures, and processes
   - Appropriate transaction testing, with particular emphasis on high-risk operations (products, services, customers, and geographic locations)
   - Training adequacy, including its comprehensiveness, accuracy of materials, the training schedule, and attendance tracking
   - The integrity and accuracy of management information systems used in the AML/CFT compliance program, such as reports used to identify large currency transactions, to aggregate daily currency transactions, and to identify funds transfer and/or monetary instrument sales transactions
4. If an automated system is not used to identify or aggregate large transactions, determine whether the audit or independent review includes a sample

test check of tellers' cash proof sheets, tapes, or other documentation, to determine whether large currency transactions are accurately identified and reported.

5. Determine whether the audit's review of suspicious activity monitoring systems includes an evaluation of the system's ability to identify unusual activity. Ensure through a validation of the auditor's reports and work papers that the bank's independent testing:

   ■ Reviews policies, procedures, and processes for suspicious activity monitoring

   ■ Evaluates the system's methodology for establishing and applying expected activity or filtering criteria

   ■ Evaluates the system's ability to generate monitoring reports

   ■ Determines whether the system filtering criteria are reasonable

6. Determine whether the audit's review of suspicious transaction reporting systems includes an evaluation of the research and referral of unusual activity. Ensure through a validation of the auditor's reports and work papers that the bank's independent testing includes a review of policies, procedures, and processes for referring unusual activity from all business lines (for example, legal, private banking, foreign correspondent banking) to the personnel or department responsible for evaluating unusual activity.

7. Determine whether the audit addresses the effectiveness of the bank's policy for reviewing those accounts that generate multiple STR filings.

8. Determine whether the audit tracks previously identified deficiencies, and verify that management is correcting them.

9. Review the audit's scope, its procedures, and work papers to determine its adequacy based on the following:

   ■ Overall audit coverage and frequency in relation to the risk profile of the bank

   ■ Board reporting and supervision of, and responsiveness to, audit findings

   ■ Adequacy of transaction testing, particularly for high-risk banking operations and suspicious activity monitoring systems

   ■ Competency of the auditors or independent reviewers regarding AML/CFT requirement

A 4.3.2.4   *Role and Duties Assigned to the Compliance Officer*

1. Determine whether the board of directors has designated a person or persons responsible for the overall AML/CFT compliance program. Determine whether the compliance officer has the necessary authority and resources to execute all duties effectively.

2. Assess the competency of the AML/CFT compliance officer and his or her staff, as necessary. Determine whether the AML/CFT compliance area is sufficiently

staffed for the bank's overall risk level (based on products, services, customers, and geographic locations), size, and AML/CFT compliance needs. In addition, ensure that there is no conflict of interest and that staff are given adequate time to execute all duties.

A 4.3.2.5   Examination of AML/CFT Training Policies and Programs

Banks should establish ongoing employee training programs to ensure that all employees are kept informed of new ML and FT developments. On-site examiners must ensure that the various operational units of the bank do have the internal AML/CFT instructions that set out all prevention and surveillance procedures. It is also paramount to verify that procedures are in place to inform new staff. Examiners should satisfy themselves that the content and frequency of the training sessions are appropriate and that staff are notified of any legislative and regulatory changes (see box A4.2).

1. Determine whether the following elements are adequately addressed in the training program and materials:
   - The importance the board of directors and senior management place on ongoing education, training, and compliance
   - Employee accountability for ensuring AML/CFT compliance
   - Comprehensiveness of training, considering specific risks of individual business lines
   - Training of personnel from all applicable areas of the bank
   - Frequency of training
   - Documentation of attendance records and training materials
   - Coverage of bank policies, procedures, processes, and new rules and regulations

---

BOX A4.2   Evaluation Criteria for Staff Training

On-site examiners should conclude that the bank's staff training policy on AML/CFT is satisfactory if:

- The operational units have an up-to-date manual of procedures containing all the procedures
- The legal provisions, procedures, and updates are annotated by the relevant staff
- Training sessions are comprehensive and delivered on a regular basis
- Training is geared toward all persons involved

- Coverage of different forms of money laundering and terrorist financing as they relate to identification and examples of suspicious activity
- Penalties for noncompliance with internal policies and regulatory requirements

2. As appropriate, conduct discussions with employees such as tellers, funds transfer personnel, internal auditors, and loan personnel to assess their knowledge of AML/CFT policies and regulatory requirements.

A 4.3.2.6   Transaction Testing

While some transaction testing is required, examiners have the discretion to decide the extent of the testing, the activities in which it is performed, as well as the rationale for any changes to the scope of the testing that occur in the examination. Examiners should, of course, document all their transaction-testing decisions. At the outset of their visits, on-site examiners need to obtain key documents in order to perform transactions testing and to examine customers' files. Annex 5 provides an example of the key documents.

A 4.3.3   Other Areas to Be Examined

After completing the review of all four required elements of the bank's AML/CFT compliance program (compliance officer, system of internal control, independent testing of the AML/CFT compliance program, and AML/CFT training program for bank staff), the examiner should document a preliminary evaluation of the bank's in-house AML/CFT apparatus. At this point, the examiner should revisit the initial examination plan to determine whether adjustments to the initially planned scope are warranted as a result of any strengths or weaknesses identified during the review of the institution's AML/CFT compliance program.

Once the examiner has reviewed the scope of the examination, as well as the bank's risk assessment and AML/CFT compliance program the next step is to examine the bank using AML/CFT examination procedures (see sample below). Jurisdictions can adjust these procedures to meet their own requirements relating to laws, regulations, and policies. During the inspection, it is important to scrutinize all significant AML/CFT issues to determine the extent of compliance with the jurisdiction's laws, regulations, and policies, and the effectiveness of the bank's AML/CFT compliance system.

The following important topics require particular attention during an on-site visit:

- Customer identification program
- Due diligence regarding customers
- Suspicious transaction reporting

- Information sharing
- Foreign correspondent accounts
- Private banking

The outcome of these tasks helps examiners to understand the effectiveness and compliance of internal procedures (see box A4.3 on possible shortcoming in practice).

BOX A4.3 **Illustration of Possible Shortcomings in Practice**

- Insufficient recognition of integrity risks, that is, ML/TF, at a strategic level
- Insufficient "know your business" (compliance officer)
- Limited risk analysis, which focuses only on client
- Limited due diligence applied to client characteristics
- Limited analysis of the transaction structure
- Noncompliance with internal client acceptance criteria, and unwilling acceptance of high/unacceptable risk
- Insufficient risk analysis and documentation of risk in client files
- No systematic thinking behind the risk categorization of clients, for example, assumptions that are made with insufficient evidence
- Automated monitoring of clients, accounts, and transactions not yet completed[a]

a. See "Integrity supervision banks and money transaction offices, De Nederlansche Bank," by Petra Steenbakker, Stef Keereweer, Dagmar van Ravenswaay Claasen, Anita Reijnders, and Herman Annink, March 29, 2006.

A 4.4   Customer Identification Program[3]

A 4.4.1   Objectives

"Know Your Customer" (KYC) procedures are at the center of the internal AML/CFT apparatus. It is essential, therefore, that the on-site examiner assesses the bank's compliance with the statutory and regulatory requirements for this program. The key objective is to verify that the bank's internal rules include all customer-identification procedures. The examiner should check file samples for documents that identify natural persons and legal entities and establish that they are convincing and evidentiary. For nonresidents and foreigners (where appropriate), the examiner should verify that supplementary measures, such as a letter of good standing, have been applied. It is also paramount to ascertain the existence (and convincing and evidentiary nature of) documents that identify all occasional customers conducting transactions above a certain threshold. Lastly, an on-site examiner should be satisfied that, when persons opening accounts or making transactions could not act on their own behalf, the bank has taken steps to ascertain their real identities and the identity of the beneficial owner (see box A4.4 for evaluation criteria for KYC).

A 4.4.2   Steps to Be Followed

1. Verify that the bank's policies, procedures, and processes include a comprehensive, written program for identifying customers, and that it is part of the bank's AML/CFT compliance program. At the minimum, this program should include policies, procedures, and processes for the following:
   - Identification of information required, (including name, address, customer identification number, and date of birth, for individuals), and the procedures for risk based identity verification (including procedures to address nonverifiable situations)
   - Procedures for complying with recordkeeping requirements
   - Procedures for checking new accounts against prescribed government lists, where applicable
   - Procedures covering the bank's reliance on another financial institution or a third party, where applicable
   - Procedures for determining whether and when to file a suspicious activity report
2. Determine whether the bank's customer identification program (CIP) has considered the types of accounts offered; the methods of account opening; and the bank's size, location, and customer base.
3. Determine whether the bank's policy for opening new accounts for existing customers appears reasonable.

BOX A4.4 **Evaluation Criteria for KYC**

On-site examiners should conclude that the bank's KYC internal policy and processes is satisfactory if:

- The copies of the official documents produced are systematically kept in the file and are convincing and evidentiary (ID, proof of domicile).
- For foreign[a] (where appropriate) and nonresident customers, the bank applies enhanced due diligence, for example, the presence in the customer's file of a letter of recommendation from another bank.
- The account-opening files for legal entities include certified copies of the articles of incorporation, and from the commercial register for sole traders, proof of power of attorney. The documents should give all information on the name of the legal entity, its legal status, and the address of its registered office.
- For legal entities, files contain evidences that the bank understands the ownership and control structure of the customer.
- The signature cards match those on the powers of attorney and are included in the files.

Note: If during the on-site visit there is repeated, or excessively high, occurrence of missing documents that would have provided convincing proof of identity of the economic beneficiaries, especially if they are foreign-based legal entities, on-site examiners may conclude there is either a significant lack of vigilance or a loophole in the internal procedures.
a. International standards do not necessarily require foreign customers per se to be classified as high risk. See Basel Committee on Banking Supervision, Customer due diligence for banks, paragraph 23, referenced in FATF methodology criteria 5.8.

---

4. Review board minutes, and verify that the board of directors approved the CIP, either separately or as part of the AML/CFT compliance program.
5. Evaluate the bank's audit and training programs to ensure that the CIP is adequately incorporated.
6. Evaluate the bank's policies, procedures, and processes, and verify that all new accounts are checked against prescribed government lists, if such lists are issued, for suspected terrorists or terrorist organizations on a timely basis.
7. Evaluate the bank's policies, procedures, and processes with regard politically exposed persons (PEPs).

A 4.4.2.1 Transaction testing

1. On the basis of risk assessments, prior examination reports, and a review of the bank's audit findings, select a sample of accounts opened since the most recent

examination, and review them for compliance with the bank's CIP. The sample should include a cross-section of accounts such as consumers and businesses, loans and deposits, credit card relationships, and Internet accounts. The sample should also include the following:

- Accounts having incomplete verification procedures
- New accounts opened using both documentary and nondocumentary methods
- Accounts identified as high risk either by the bank or its supervisor
- Accounts opened by existing high-risk customers, for example, Politically Exposed Persons
- Accounts opened with exceptions to policy
- Accounts opened by a third party such as indirect loans

2. From the previous sample of new accounts, determine whether the bank has performed the following procedures:

- Opened the account in accordance with regulatory requirements
- Formed a reasonable belief as to the true identity of a customer, including a high-risk customer
- Obtained from each customer, before opening the account, the identity information required by the CIP such as name, date of birth, address, and identification number
- Within a reasonable time after the opening of the account, verified enough of the customer's identity information to form a reasonable belief as to the customer's true identity[4]
- Appropriately resolved situations in which customer identity could not be reasonably established
- Maintained records of the identity information required by the CIP, the method used to verify identity, and the verification results including results of discrepancies
- Compared the customer's name against the list of known or suspected terrorists or terrorist organizations, when applicable
- Filed STRs, as appropriate

3. Evaluate the level of CIP exceptions to determine whether the bank is effectively implementing its CIP.

4. On the basis of a risk assessment, prior examination reports, and a review of the bank's audit, select, where applicable, a sample of relationships with those third parties on which the bank relies to perform its CIP.

- Determine whether the third party is a regulated institution subject to AML/CFT program requirements.
- Review the contract between the parties and other information, such as the third party's CIP.
- Determine whether reliance on the third party is reasonable.

5. If the bank is using an agent or service provider to perform elements of its CIP, determine whether the bank has established appropriate internal controls and review procedures. These should ensure that its CIP is being implemented in third-party agent or service-provider relationships.

6. Evaluate the bank's CIP record retention policy and ensure that it corresponds to the regulatory requirements to maintain records. The bank should retain the identity information obtained at account opening for five years after the account closes. The bank should also maintain a description of documents relied on and the methods used both to verify identity, and should resolve discrepancies for five years after the records were made.

7. On the basis of examination procedures completed, including transaction testing, determine whether policies, procedures, and processes meet the regulatory requirements associated with CIP.

A 4.5   Customer Due Diligence and Recordkeeping

A 4.5.1   Objective

On-site examiners should assess the appropriateness and comprehensiveness of the policies, procedures, and processes requiring due diligence for obtaining customer information, and for assessing the value of this information in detecting, monitoring, and reporting suspicious activity.

In addition to that, on-site examiners should satisfy themselves that the bank keeps all relevant documents for at least 5 years.

A 4.5.2   Steps to Be followed

1. Determine whether the bank's CDD policies, procedures, and processes are commensurate with the bank's risk profile. Determine whether the bank has processes in place for obtaining information at account opening, in addition to ensuring that current customer information is maintained.
2. Determine whether policies, procedures, and processes allow changes to be made to a customer's risk rating or profile. Determine who is responsible for reviewing or approving such changes.
3. Review the enhanced due diligence procedures and processes the bank uses to identify those customers possibly posing a higher risk for money laundering or terrorist financing.
4. Determine whether the bank provides guidance for documenting the analysis associated with the process of applying due diligence, including guidance for resolving issues when information proves to be insufficient or inaccurate.
5. Determine whether customers' identity documents and business correspondence (whether occasional, whether legal or natural persons) are kept for at least five years after the accounts are closed, or after the business relationship is ended.
6. Determine whether customers' transaction records are kept for five years after transactions are completed.
7. Verify that the bank keeps on file all documents needed to retrace customer transactions that triggered STRs or that have been required to understand the beneficial ownership.

A 4.5.2.1   Transaction Testing

1. On the basis of a risk assessment, prior examination reports, and a review of the bank's audit findings, sample CDD information for high-risk customers. Determine whether the bank collects appropriate information and effectively incorporates this information into the suspicious activity monitoring process.

This sample can be performed when testing the bank's compliance with its policies, procedures, and processes as well as when reviewing transactions or accounts for possible suspicious activity.

2. On the basis of examination procedures completed, including transaction testing, determine the adequacy of policies, procedures, and processes associated with CDD and record keeping.

A 4.6   Suspicious Transaction Reporting

A 4.6.1   Objective

The on-site examiner must ensure that the bank's internal instructions conform to national requirements. Did the bank appoint a correspondent to cope with STR obligations? Was provision made for informing the bank's directorate of all STRs made to the FIU? Is the correspondent sufficiently independent from the operational units? Do the STRs remain confidential (no tipping off)?

Examiners should focus on ascertaining the effectiveness of the bank's decision-making process, rather than on individual STR decisions. Individual STR decisions may be reviewed to confirm the effectiveness of the bank's STR monitoring and reporting procedures (see box A4.5 for evaluation criteria for STRs). Examiners should not, however, be critical of an individual STR decision unless the failure to file an STR is significant or accompanied by evidence of bad faith. It is also important to make sure the information provided by the bank to the FIU is complete and accurate and files were duly received by the FIU and on a timely fashion.

A 4.6.2   Steps to Be Followed

A 4.6.2.1   Review of Policies, Procedures, and Processes

1. Review the bank's policies, procedures, and processes for identifying, researching, and reporting suspicious activity. Determine whether they include the following:

BOX A4.5 **Evaluation Criteria for STRs**

On-site examiners should conclude that the STR management process of the bank being inspected is satisfactory if:

- STR decisions, in the case of large transactions, seem to have been made in a timely fashion and have been based on an organization and set of internal rules designed to ensure compliance with the FIU's regulations
- There is no STR because there is no convincing information
- The STRs appear to be sufficiently documented
- The STRs were made and sent to the FIU in a timely fashion

Note: If during the inspection, inspectors observe that a large number of files and/or a file involving a large sum might have triggered an STR under national requirements, they may conclude that there was significant negligence, or a serious loophole in the internal procedures of the bank's organization.

- Lines of communication for the referral of unusual activity to appropriate personnel
- Designation of individual(s) responsible for identifying, researching, and reporting suspicious activities
- Monitoring systems used to identify unusual activity
- Procedures to ensure the timely generation of, review of, and response to, reports used to identify unusual activities
- Procedures for:
  - Responding to information requests from the competent authorities
  - Evaluating the account of the target for suspicious activity
  - Filing STRs, if necessary
  - Handling account closures
- Procedures for documenting decisions not to file an STR
- Procedures for considering closing accounts subject to continuous suspicious activity
- Procedures for completing, filing, and retaining STRs and their supporting documentation
- Procedures for reporting STRs to the board of directors, or a committee thereof, and senior management
- Procedures for sharing STRs both with head offices and controlling companies

A 4.6.2.2   Evaluating Suspicious Activity Monitoring Systems

1. Review the bank's monitoring systems and how the system(s) fits into the bank's process for overall suspicious activity monitoring and reporting. Complete the appropriate examination procedures that follow. When evaluating the effectiveness of the bank's monitoring systems, examiners should consider the bank's overall risk profile (high-risk products, services, customers, and geographic locations), its volume of transactions, and its adequacy of staffing.

A 4.6.2.3   Reviewing Manual Transaction Monitoring

1. Review the bank's transaction monitoring reports. Determine whether the reports capture all areas posing money laundering and terrorist financing risks. Examples of these reports are currency activity reports, funds transfer reports, monetary instrument sales reports, large item reports, significant balance change reports, nonsufficient funds reports, and nonresident alien reports.
2. Determine whether the bank's monitoring systems use reasonable filtering criteria whose programming has been independently verified. Determine whether the monitoring systems generate accurate reports at a reasonable frequency.

A 4.6.2.4   Automated Account Monitoring

1. Identify the types of customers, products, and services included in the automated account monitoring system.
2. Identify the system's methodology that establishes and applies the criteria for expected activity or profile filtering, and for generating monitoring reports. Determine whether these criteria are reasonable.
3. Determine whether the programming of the methodology has been independently validated.
4. Determine that controls are adequate to ensure limited access to the monitoring system, and to provide sufficient oversight of assumption changes.

A·4.6.2.5   Transaction Testing

1. On the basis of a risk assessment, prior examination reports, and a review of the bank's audit findings, sample the STRs from the bank's internal STR records. Review the quality of STR data to assess the following:[5]
   - STRs contain accurate information.
   - STR narratives are complete and thorough, and clearly explain why the activity is suspicious.

A 4.6.2.6   Testing the Suspicious Activity Monitoring System

Transaction testing of suspicious activity monitoring systems and reporting processes allows the examiner to determine whether the bank's policies, procedures, and processes are adequate and effectively implemented. The examiner should document the factors used to select samples and should maintain a list of the accounts sampled. The size and the sample should be based on the following:

- Weaknesses in the account monitoring systems
- The bank's overall AML/CFT risk profile, such as the number and type of high-risk products, services, customers, and geographic locations
- The quality and extent of review by audit or independent parties
- Prior examination findings
- Recent mergers, acquisitions, or other significant organizational changes
- Conclusions or questions from the review of the bank's STRs

1. On the basis of a risk assessment, prior examination reports, and a review of the bank's audit findings, sample specific customer accounts to review the following:
   - Suspicious activity monitoring reports
   - Large cash reporting information
   - High-risk banking operations (products, services, customers, and geographic locations)

- Customer activity
- Subpoenas received by the bank
- Decisions not to file a STR

2. For customers selected previously, obtain the following information, where applicable:
   - Customer Identification Program and account-opening documentation
   - CDD documentation
   - Two to three months of account statements covering the total customer relationship, and showing all transactions
   - Sample items posted against the account, including copies of checks deposited and written, debit or credit tickets, and funds transfer beneficiaries and originators
   - Other relevant information, such as loan files and correspondence
3. Review the selected accounts for unusual activity. An examiner identifying unusual activity should review customer information for indications that the activity is typical for the customer. When reviewing for unusual activity, consider the following:
   - Individual customers: whether the activity is consistent with CDD information such as occupation, expected account activity, and sources of funds and wealth
   - Business customers: whether the activity is consistent with CDD information including type of business, size, location, and target market
4. Determine whether the manual or automated suspicious activity monitoring system detected the activity that the examiner identified as unusual.
5. Discuss transactions identified as unusual with management. Determine whether the account officer demonstrates knowledge both of the unusual transactions and of the customer. After examining the available facts, determine whether management knows of a reasonable explanation for the transactions.
6. Determine whether the bank failed to identify any reportable suspicious activity.
7. From the results of the sample, determine whether the manual or automated suspicious activity monitoring system is effective in detecting unusual or suspicious activity. Identify any underlying causes of deficiencies in the monitoring systems, such as inappropriate filters, insufficient risk assessment, or inadequate decision making.

A 4.6.2.7   Evaluating the STR Decision-Making Process

1. Evaluate the bank's policies, procedures, and processes that refer unusual activity from all business lines to the personnel or department responsible. The process should ensure that all applicable information from criminal subpoenas and from other official requests is effectively evaluated.

2. When monitoring reports identify unusual activity, determine whether policies, procedures, and processes require appropriate research.

3. Determine whether the bank's STR decision process appropriately considers all the available information about the application of due diligence to customers.

4. From a risk assessment, prior examination reports, and a review of the bank's audit findings, select a sample of management's research decisions to determine the following:

   - Whether management decisions to file or not file a STR are supported and reasonable
   - Whether documentation is adequate
   - Whether the decision process is completed and STRs are filed in a timely manner

5. On the basis of completed examination procedures, including transaction testing, determine the ability of policies, procedures, and processes to meet regulatory requirements associated with monitoring, detecting, and reporting suspicious activity.

A 4.7 Foreign Correspondent Account Recordkeeping

A 4.7.1 Objective

To assess the bank's compliance with statutory and regulatory requirements with respect to correspondent accounts for foreign shell banks, foreign correspondent account recordkeeping, and programs requiring due diligence to detect and report money laundering and terrorist financing.

Documents to request:

- List of all foreign correspondent bank accounts, including a list of foreign financial institutions, for which the bank provides services
- If applicable, documentation to show compliance regarding the prohibition of correspondent accounts with foreign shell banks[6]
- List of all payable-through account relationships[7] with foreign financial institutions
- Access to contracts or agreements with foreign financial institutions that have payable-through accounts
- List of the bank's foreign branches, and the steps the bank has taken to determine that its accounts with its branches are not used to provide services indirectly to foreign shell banks
- Any notice from the national authorities to close foreign correspondent bank accounts.

A 4.7.2 Steps to Be Followed

1. Determine whether the bank engages in foreign correspondent banking.
2. If so, review the bank's policies, procedures, and processes. At a minimum, policies, procedures, and processes should accomplish the following:
   - Prohibit dealings with foreign shell banks, and specify who is responsible for obtaining, updating, and managing information for foreign correspondent accounts
   - Identify foreign correspondent accounts
   - Evaluate the quality of information received in response to requests for information
   - Determine whether and when a suspicious activity report should be filed.
   - Maintain sufficient internal controls
   - Provide ongoing training
3. Determine whether the bank has on file current information for each foreign correspondent account, to determine whether the foreign correspondent is, or is not, a foreign shell bank
4. If the bank has foreign branches, determine whether the bank has taken reasonable steps to ensure that correspondent accounts maintained for its

foreign branches are not used to provide banking services indirectly to a foreign shell bank.

5. Determine whether the bank has established a program requiring due diligence that includes appropriate, specific, risk-based, and, where necessary, enhanced policies, procedures, and controls to address correspondent accounts established, maintained, administered, or managed in the jurisdiction for foreign banks ("foreign correspondent accounts"). Verify that the policies, procedures, and controls requiring due diligence include the following:

  ■ Determining whether any such account is subject to enhanced due diligence
  ■ Assessing the money laundering risks presented by these accounts
  ■ Applying to each foreign correspondent account risk-based procedures and controls reasonably designed to detect and report known or suspected money laundering activity. These procedures and controls include a periodic review of correspondent account activity that is sufficient to determine consistency, using information obtained about the type, purpose, and anticipated activity of the account

6. Review "due diligence" program policies, procedures, and processes governing the AML/CFT risk assessment of foreign correspondent accounts. Verify that the program considers the following factors, where appropriate, as criteria in the risk assessment:

  ■ The nature of the foreign financial institution's business and the markets it serves
  ■ The type, purpose, and anticipated activity of the foreign correspondent account
  ■ The nature and duration of the bank's relationship both with the foreign financial institution and with any of its affiliates
  ■ The AML/CFT and supervisory regime of the jurisdiction issuing the charter or license to the foreign financial institution and, to the extent that information regarding such jurisdiction is reasonably available, of the jurisdiction incorporating or chartering any company that is an owner of the foreign financial institution
  ■ Information known or reasonably available to the bank about the AML/CFT record of the foreign financial institution

7. Ensure that the program is reasonably designed to

  ■ Detect and report, on an ongoing basis, known or suspected money laundering activity
  ■ Perform periodic reviews of correspondent account activity to determine consistency with the information obtained about the type, purpose, and anticipated activity of the account

8. For foreign banks subject to enhanced requirements for due diligence, evaluate the bank's criteria for conducting enhanced scrutiny designed to guard against money laundering in any accounts held by such banks.

9. Review the bank's policies, procedures, and processes for determining whether foreign correspondent banks, subject to enhanced due diligence requirements, maintain correspondent accounts for other foreign banks and, if so, determine whether the bank's policies, procedures, and processes include reasonable steps to ascertain the identity of those foreign banks and fulfill the requirements for due diligence, as appropriate.

A 4.7.3 Other Additional Tasks

A 4.7.3.1 Recordkeeping for Foreign Shell Bank Prohibitions and for Foreign Correspondent Account Records

1. On the basis of a risk assessment, prior examination reports, and a review of the bank's audit findings, select a sample of foreign bank accounts. From the sample determine whether:
   - Information on the accounts is complete and reasonable.
   - The bank has adequate documentation to prove that it does not maintain accounts for, or indirectly provide services to, foreign shell banks.
   - Account closures were made within a reasonable time, and whether the relationship was not re-established without sufficient reason.
   - There are any law enforcement requests for information regarding foreign correspondent accounts. If so, ascertain that requests were met in a timely manner.
   - The bank received any official government notifications to close foreign financial institution accounts. If so, ascertain that the accounts were closed in a timely manner.
   - The bank retains, for five years from the date of account closure, originals of any documents provided by foreign financial institutions, as well as the originals or copies of any document relied on in relation to any summons or subpoena of that institution.
2. Determine whether the bank maintains a special program requiring due diligence for foreign correspondent accounts.
3. From a sample selected, determine whether the bank consistently follows its general policies, procedures, and processes requiring due diligence for foreign correspondent accounts. It may be necessary to expand the sample to include correspondent accounts maintained for foreign financial institutions other than foreign banks (such as money transmitters or currency exchangers), as appropriate.
4. From the original sample, determine whether the bank has implemented enhanced procedures requiring due diligence for higher risk foreign banks, which operate under
   - An offshore banking license,

- A banking license issued by a foreign country designated as noncooperative with international AML/CFT principles or procedures, or
- A banking license issued by a foreign country that has been designated by the jurisdiction as warranting special measures due to AML/CFT concerns.

5. From a sample of accounts that are subject to enhanced due diligence requirements, verify that the bank, in accordance with its policies, procedures, and processes, has taken reasonable steps to
   - Conduct enhanced scrutiny of any accounts held by such banks to guard against money laundering, and
   - Ascertain whether such foreign bank provides correspondent accounts to other foreign banks and, if so, ascertain the identity of those foreign banks and apply due diligence, as appropriate.

6. On the basis of completed examination procedures, including transaction testing, determine the adequacy of policies, procedures, and processes to meet regulatory requirements associated with foreign correspondent account recordkeeping and the need for due diligence.

A 4.8   Requirements for Due Diligence in Private Banking

A 4.8.1   Objective

Assess the bank's compliance with statutory and regulatory requirements to implement policies, procedures, and controls aimed at detecting and reporting money laundering and suspicious activity through private banking accounts, where these are established, administered, or maintained for noncitizens.

A 4.8.2   Steps to Be Followed[8]

1. Determine whether the bank offers private banking accounts. A private banking account means any account (or any combination of accounts) maintained at a bank that satisfies all three of the following criteria:
   - Requires a minimum aggregate deposit of funds or other assets of not less than $1,000,000
   - Is established on behalf of or for the benefit of one or more noncitizens who are direct or beneficial owners of the account
   - Is assigned to, or is administered or managed by, in whole or in part, an officer, employee, or agent of the bank, acting as a liaison between the bank and the direct or beneficial owner of the account

2. Determine whether the bank has implemented policies, procedures, and controls requiring due diligence for private banking accounts it has established, maintained, administered, or managed in the jurisdiction for noncitizens. Determine whether the policies, procedures, and controls are reasonably designed to detect and report any known or suspected money laundering, or any suspicious activity conducted through or involving any private banking account.

3. Review the bank's policies, procedures, and controls to assess whether the bank's due diligence program includes reasonable steps to
   - Ascertain the identity of the nominal and beneficial owners of a private banking account;
   - Ascertain whether any nominal or beneficial owner of a private banking account is a senior foreign political figure;
   - Ascertain the source(s) of funds deposited into any private banking account, and the purpose and expected use of the private banking account for noncitizens; and
   - Review, as needed, the activity of the account, to ensure it is consistent with the information obtained about the client's source of funds, and with the stated purpose and expected use of the accounting order to guard against money laundering, and to report any known or suspected money laundering or suspicious activity conducted to, from, or through a private banking account for noncitizens.

4. Review the bank's policies, procedures, and controls for performing enhanced scrutiny, and assess whether they are reasonably designed to detect and report transactions that may involve the proceeds of foreign corruption, of which a senior foreign political figure is a nominal or beneficial owner.

A 4.8.2.1 Transaction Testing

1. On the basis of a risk assessment, prior examination reports, and a review of the bank's audit findings, select a sample of customer files to determine whether the bank has ascertained the identity of the nominal and beneficial owners of, and the source of, funds deposited into private banking accounts for noncitizens. From the sample selected determine whether
   - The bank's procedures comply with internal policies and statutory requirements;
   - The bank has followed its own procedures governing risk assessments of private banking accounts for noncitizens; and
   - The bank performs enhanced scrutiny, consistent with its policy, regulatory guidance, and statutory requirements, of private banking accounts for which senior foreign political figures are nominal or beneficial owners
2. On the basis of examination procedures completed, including transaction testing, determine the ability of policies, procedures, and processes to meet regulatory requirements associated with practicing due diligence in private banking programs.

A 4.9 Other "Risky" Accounts

A 4.9.1 Objectives

In the course of any on-site visit, examiners should pay attention to certain categories of accounts that represent a higher risk from an ML/TF standpoint. Here, the objective is to verify that the bank has put proper policies and enhanced internal surveillance mechanisms in place to deal with those specific accounts as, for example, accounts with important and frequent cash transactions or securities operations.

A 4.9.2 Steps to Be Followed

The examiner must verify that

- The bank has defined a surveillance policy for high-risk accounts and has put in place a set of indicators (customer's country of origin, profession, and so forth).
- The bank pays attention to all complex, unusually large transactions, and to all unusual patterns of transactions having no apparent economic or visible lawful purpose. It is left to each bank to define the concept of abnormality as it applies to itself. It may be defined in several ways, as for example, by amount, nature, beneficiary, and currency.
- The bank obtains all useful information from the client as to the origin or the destination of the funds, and the identity, and domicile of the beneficiary.
- The characteristics of these transactions are recorded in a confidential register (where applicable).

Notes

1. The full text of the US Bank Secrecy Act/Anti-Money Laundering Examination Manual can be viewed at http://www.occ.treas.gov/handbook/1-BSA-AMLwhole.pdf.
2. Only where access to STRs is permitted by law.
3. Basel Committee, Customer Due Diligence for Banks, para. 20 ff, and FATF recommendation 5.
4. Basel Committee, Customer Due Diligence for banks, para. 22, and FATF Methodology, criteria 5.13 and 5.14.
5. Only if access to STR files is legally permitted by supervisors.
6. Shell bank means a bank incorporated in a jurisdiction in which it has no physical presence and unaffiliated with a regulated financial group. See FATF recommendation 18.
7. This applies mostly to U.S. banks.
8. These steps may not be identical in all jurisdictions.

Annex 5: Key Documents to Obtain at the Outset of the Inspection

The following lists key documents to obtain at the onset of the inspection in order to select the files to be analyzed:

- Accounts opened since (date) in the name of natural persons (with the balances on the request date)
- Accounts opened since (date) in the name of legal persons (with the balances on the request date)
- Accounts opened in the name of foreigners or nonresidents (with the balances on the requested date)
- Accounts opened in the name of offshore companies or nonresident companies (with the balances on the requested date)
- Accounts opened and closed after one year
- Transactions (with the orginators' names) for unit or total amounts over XXX (threshold to be decided by the inspection team leader)
- Personal loans paid off early
- Large exchange transactions handled by tellers
- Large cash deposits
- Transfers to high-risk countries for amounts exceeding a threshold to be set by the mission chief
- Detailed review of accounts where the annual cash deposits and withdrawals exceed a threshold set by inspector; in France, for example, EUR 150,000
- Inactive accounts
- Orders to make funds available to occasional customers
- Customers identified as politically exposed persons (PEPs)

- Statistics: breakdown of customers over the last three years, for example, by business sector, by customer type, by location (distinction between residents and nonresidents)
- Sample of STRs filled out and sent to the FIU
- Safe deposit box holders
- Correspondent banks

Annex 6: List of Areas That Pose Higher Risks

The following areas pose higher risks:

- *Products and Services.* Some products and services offered by banks may pose a higher risk of money laundering or terrorist financing depending on the nature of the specific product or service offered by the bank. Some examples of these products and services are:
  - Electronic funds payment services: electronic cash, stored value cards, funds transfers, third-party payment processors, remittance activities, and automated teller machines
  - Electronic banking
  - Private banking
  - Trust and asset management services
  - Monetary instruments, official bank checks, cashier's checks, money orders, and so forth
  - Foreign correspondent accounts: pouch activity and payable-through accounts[1]
  - International trade finance and letters of credit
  - Lending activities, particularly loans secured by cash collateral and marketable securities
  - Nondeposit account services, nondeposit investment products, insurance, and safe deposit boxes
  - Services identified by regulators, governmental authorities, or other credible sources as being potentially high-risk for ML/FT
- *Customers and Entities.* Any type of account is potentially vulnerable to money laundering or terrorist financing, but certain customers and entities may pose higher money laundering risks. Some examples of possible higher-risk accounts and activities are
  - Foreign financial institutions, including banks and foreign money services providers, exchange houses, money transmitters, and bureaux de change

- Nonbank financial institutions, money services businesses, casinos, brokers/dealers in securities, and dealers in precious metals, stones, or jewels
- Foreign political figures and their immediate family members and close associates and politically exposed persons (PEPs)[2]
- Accounts of foreign individuals
- Foreign corporations with transaction accounts, particularly offshore corporations such as Private Investment Companies and international business corporations located in high-risk geographic locations
- Deposit brokers, particularly foreign deposit brokers
- Cash-intensive businesses such as convenience stores, restaurants, and retail stores
- Nongovernmental organizations and charities
- Professional service providers, attorneys, accountants, or real estate brokers
- Arms dealers
- *Geographic Locations.* Bank management should identify geographic locations that pose a higher risk to the institution and factor that information into its AML/CFT compliance program. It is important that bank management understand and evaluate the specific risks associated with doing business in certain geographic locations. Some examples of high-risk geographic locations can include:
  - Countries subject to international sanctions, including state sponsors of terrorism, issued by organizations such as the United Nations (UN). In addition, in some circumstances, countries subject to sanctions or measures similar to those issued by bodies such as the UN, but which may not be universally recognized, may be given credence by a bank because of the standing of the issuer and the nature of the measures.
  - Jurisdictions determined to be of primary money laundering concern by the government.
  - Offshore financial centers.
  - Other countries identified by the bank as high risk because of the bank's prior experiences.
  - Transaction history or other factors such as legal considerations or allegations of official corruption.
  - Countries identified by credible sources[3] as providing funding or support for terrorist activities.
  - Countries identified by credible sources as having significant levels of corruption or other criminal activity.[4]
  - Domestic high-risk geographic locations such as drug trafficking, financial crime, and other high-crime areas.

Notes

1. Payable-through accounts refers to correspondent accounts used directly by third parties to transact business on their own behalf.

2. Politically Exposed Persons (PEPs) as defined by the Financial Action Task Force (FATF) are individuals who are or have been entrusted with prominent public functions in a foreign country, for example heads of state or of government, senior politicians, senior government officials, judicial or military officials, senior executives of state-owned corporations, and important political party officials. Business relationships with family members or close associates of PEPs involve reputational risks similar to those with PEPs themselves. The definition is not intended to cover middle-ranking or more junior individuals in the foregoing categories.

3. Credible sources refer to information produced by well-known bodies that generally are regarded as reputable and that make such information publicly and widely available. Such sources may include, but are not limited to, supranational or international bodies such as the Organization for Economic Co-operation and Development (OECD) and the Egmont Group of Financial Intelligence units, as well as relevant national government bodies and nongovernmental organizations.

4. Such as Transparency International.

Annex 7: Example of an AML/CFT Questionnaire Used by the French Banking Commission

INTERNAL PROCEDURES	Questions	Answers		
		Yes	No	NA
I – APPOINTMENT OF TRACFIN REPORTING OFFICERS				
1. As soon as they are appointed, are the names of the Tracfin reporting officers transmitted:				
– to TRACFIN?	101	...	...	///
– to the General Secretariat of the Commission bancaire?	102	...	...	///
2. Do your institution's written internal rules stipulate the names of the person or department to contact in order to file a report with Tracfin?	103	...	...	///
3. Were the written internal rules modified immediately to reflect possible changes in information concerning Tracfin reporting officers in the last financial year (appointment of a new officer, change of phone number, etc.)?	104	...	...	...
4. If your institution belongs to a financial group, is the Tracfin reporting officer appointed at the level of the group?	182	...	...	...
II – SYSTEM OF DETECTION OF THE TRANSACTIONS REFERRED TO IN ARTICLES L. 562-2 AND L. 563-3				
1. Do the procedures adopted by your institution allow you to obtain the following information, so that a decision can be made on whether to file a suspicious transaction report (Article L. 562-2) or compile an information file under Article L. 563-3:				
– the size of the transaction...	105	...	...	///
– the type of the transaction (cash deposit, transfer, etc.)	106	...	...	///
– whether the transaction serves an economic purpose..............	107	...	...	///
– whether this economic purpose seems consistent...................	108	...	...	///

Signature of executive manager:

INTERNAL PROCEDURES	Questions	Answers		
		Yes	No	NA
– the currency	109	...	...	///
– the name of the real initiator*	110	...	...	///
– the origin of the transaction (geographical origin, financial institution acting as intermediary, number of account used)*	111	...	...	///
– the name of the beneficiary*	112	...	...	///
– the destination of the transaction (geographical destination, financial institution acting as intermediary, number of account used)*	113	...	...	///
2. Do the procedures adopted permit your institution to report to Tracfin transactions involving sums that might derive from drug trafficking, fraud against the financial interests of European Communities, from corruption or organized crime or which might contribute to financing of terrorism?	114	...	...	///
3. Do the procedures adopted permit your institution to report to Tracfin transactions for which the identity of the initiator or the beneficiary remains doubtful despite customer ID diligences carried out in compliance with the provisions of the Monetary and Financial Code?	115	...	...	///
4. Do the procedures adopted permit your institution to report to Tracfin transactions carried out with a trust fund or other asset management vehicles where the identity of the parties or beneficiaries is unknown?	116	...	...	...
5. Do the procedures permit your institution to detect transactions carried out by persons whose assets have been frozen because of suspected links to terrorist financing or organized crime?	117	...	...	///
6. Does your institution compile an information file on unusually complex transactions not covered by a suspicious transaction report, involve a unit or total amount of over EUR 150,000 and appear to serve no economic or legal purpose?	118	...	...	...
III – CUSTOMER IDENTIFICATION				
1. Before your institution opens an account for a natural person, is this person systematically asked to supply an official and valid identity document bearing his or her photograph?	119	...	...	...
2. Before your institution opens an account for a legal person, is this entity systematically asked to supply an original, authentic, or certified copy of a deed or extract from an official register stating the entity's name, legal form, and headquarters, as well as the identification document and powers of the persons acting in the entity's name?	120	...	...	...

* Special attention should be paid to funds coming from noncooperative countries or territories and persons whose assets have been frozen because of suspected links to terrorist financing or organized crime.

Signature of executive manager:

INTERNAL PROCEDURES	Questions	Answers		
		Yes	No	NA
3. Is there an identification procedure of the person on whose behalf an account is being opened when it appears that the person asking to open the account may not be acting on his or her own behalf?	121	...	...	...
4. Are similar procedures to those referred to in questions 119 and 120 in place when your institution is entering into a business relationship other than opening an account (opening a savings account, providing a service of safe custody of assets, concluding an insurance contract or a capitalization contract giving rise to a mathematical provision, granting a loan, providing a guarantee, transmitting orders)?	122	...	...	...
5. In the case referred to in line 122, is there a procedure of identification of the person who is the beneficial owner of the transaction carried out or asked when the person requesting this transaction does not appear to be acting on his or her own behalf?	123	...	...	...
6. If your institution is a branch of a company whose head office is located abroad, is it in possession of the documents stating the identity of all its customers, including those who have opened an account in another entity of the group?				
– if the customer has already opened an account in another entity of the group located in France or in an another country of the European Economic Area...................................	124	...	...	...
– if the customer has already opened an account in another entity of the group located outside the European Economic Area	125	...	...	...
7. If your institution offers the option of opening an account or carrying out any other transaction with a customer who is not physically present at the moment of its identification, what steps are systematically taken to ascertain the customer's identity:				
get additional written proof to ascertain the customer's identity....................................	126	...	...	...
– implement measures of verification and certification by a third independent person of the official and valid copies of identity document's as referred to in line 119	127	...	...	...
– get a proof of the customer's identity established directly by a financial institution, which states applying identification's measures equivalent to the French ones and based in a Member State of the EEC or party to the EEA agreement or listed as equivalent as referred to in the by-law issued by the minister in charge of economy which includes the member states of the FATF	128	....	...	...
– require the first payment to be carried out from an account opened in a financial institution based in a Member State of the EEC or party to the EEA agreement, as an additional measure to one of the three above-mentioned in the case of an account opening.	183	...	...	...

Signature of executive manager:

INTERNAL PROCEDURES	Questions	Answers		
		Yes	No	NA
8. As referred to in point 7, does the account opened by a non-physically present customer become operational and are any non-face-to-face transactions carried out after the effective implementation of the considered measures and getting the required justificatory documents?	129	...	...	...
9. Are customers' identity documents, stating their name, first names, date, and place of birth, the document's type, number, date, and place of delivery and the authority that issued or certified it, kept for at least five years with effect from the closure of their account or the cessation of the business relationship?	130	...	...	...
10. Are documents pertaining to transactions carried out by customers, including transactions that do not involve a deposit account, kept for at least five years with effect from their execution?	131	...	...	...
11. When entering into a business relationship, does your institution assess the operating profile or other expected transactions from the perspective of money laundering prevention?	132	...	...	...
IV – CUSTOMER IDENTIFICATION–OCCASIONAL CUSTOMER*				
1. Does your institution verify by using an official and valid identity document the identity of any natural persons, as occasional customers, who ask to carry out a transaction involving a sum of more than EUR 8,000, or to rent a safe deposit box, or to carry out a transfer whatever the amount?	133	...	...	...
2. Does your institution verify by the presentation of any deed or extract from an official register the identity of any legal persons, as occasional customers, and the persons acting on their behalf, who ask to carry out a transaction involving a sum of more than EUR 8,000, or to rent a safe deposit box, or to carry out a transfer whatever the amount?	134	...	...	...
3. Is there a procedure of identification of the beneficial owner of a transaction when it appears that the person requesting this transaction may not be acting on his or her own behalf?	135	...	...	...
4. Is a procedure in place for identification of occasional customers asking for carrying out, in a short period of time, several transactions that appear to be linked and whose total amount exceeds EUR 8,000?	136	...	...	...
5. Are occasional customers' identity documents, stating their name, first names, date and place of birth, the document's type, number, date and place of delivery, and the authority that issued or certified it, kept for at least five years with effect from the cessation of the business relationship?	137	...	...	...
6. Are documents pertaining to transactions carried out by occasional customers kept for at least five years with effect from their execution?	138	...	...	...

* Any customers who address a specific / single transaction to a financial institution.

Signature of executive manager:

INTERNAL PROCEDURES	Questions	Answers		
		Yes	No	NA
V – OTHER VIGILANCE REQUIREMENTS				
1. Has your institution adopted procedures for customer profile analysis so it can detect unusual financial flows?	139	...	...	...
2. Are these procedures computerized?	140	...	...	...
3. Is your institution equipped with a computerized system capable of detecting transactions carried out by an occasional customer whose amount exceeds EUR 8,000?	141	...	...	...
4. Is your institution equipped with a computerized system capable of detecting transactions carried out by an occasional customer that appear to b linked and whose total amount exceeds EUR 8,000?	142	...	...	...
5. Is the Tracfin reporting officer appointed by your institution systematically informed of the findings supplied by the systems referred to in lines 139, 140, 141, 142?	143	...	...	...
Vigilance requirements concerning branches and subsidiaries located abroad:				
6. Have you made recommendations to your foreign branches and subsidiaries aimed at helping them to guard themselves against the risk of being used to launder money or finance terrorism and adopted according to Article R. 562-2-1 paragraph 2 of the Monetary and Financial Code, coordinated procedures ensuring a level of vigilance in the group's foreign entities at least equivalent to the French standards?	144	...	...	...
7. Has your institution branches or subsidiaries based in countries whose local provisions prevent the implementation of some or all recommendations set forth in Article 5 of the Regulation No. 91-07 of the Banking Regulation Committee and Article R. 562-2-1 paragraph 2 of the Monetary and Financial Code? (if yes, please fill out form QLB2)	145	...	...	...
8. Has your institution branches or subsidiaries that are hindered to follow the recommendation set forth in Article 4 of the Regulation No. 91-07 of the Banking Regulation Committee, relative to the monitoring of transactions referred to in Article L. 563-3 of the Monetary and Financial Code? (if yes, please fill out form QLB2)	146	...	...	...
9. Has your institution submitted to Tracfin the report referred to in Article 5 of the Regulation No. 91-07 of the Banking Regulation Committee and Article R. 562-2-1 paragraph 2 of the Monetary and Financial Code relative to the branches and subsidiaries concerned by lines 145 and 146?	147	...	...	...
Vigilance requirements with regard to checks:				
10. Has your institution been controlling checks over the past financial year in accordance with the provisions of the Regulation No. 2002-01 of the Banking Regulation Committee?	148	...	...	...

Signature of executive manager:

INTERNAL PROCEDURES	Questions	Answers		
		Yes	No	NA
11. Is the Tracfin reporting officer informed of the results of the checks' control?	149	...	...	...
12. Is the decision-making body informed of the results of the checks' control?	150	...	...	...
13. Has your institution signed agreements under Article 8 of the Regulation No. 2002-01 of the Banking Regulation Committee with foreign institutions to which it offers a check collection or discounting service?	151	...	...	...
Vigilance requirements with regard to electronic money:				
14. Is your institution equipped with a computerized system for monitoring unusual transactions carried out using electronic money?	152	...	...	...
15. If your institution distributes electronic money, are the anomalies linked to the circulation of electronic money submitted to the issuing bank?	153	...	...	...
16. Is the Tracfin reporting officer sent a statement of anomalies at least once a month?	154	...	...	...
VI – STAFF AWERNESS AND TRAINING				
1. Are all new staff members provided with training on prevention of money laundering and terrorist financing when they are recruited or in the weeks following their recruitment?	155	...	...	///
2. Are all staff members regularly updated on this subject?	156	...	...	///
VII – ENSURING PROPER APPLICATION OF THE SYSTEM TO PREVENT MONEY LAUNDERING AND TERRORIST FINANCING				
1. Does your institution have a monitoring system in place to ensure that the internal procedures on money laundering and terrorist financing are observed?	157	...	...	///
2. Does this monitoring system include a regular control mechanism within the framework of the compliance control?	158	...	...	///
3. Does this monitoring system include periodical inspections?	159	...	...	///
4. Does this monitoring system include ensuring compliance with the vigilance requirements provided for under the Regulation No. 2002-01 of the Banking Regulation Committee concerning the control of checks?	160	...	...	///
5. Does the general control system include ensuring compliance with the vigilance requirements provided for under Title I of the Regulation No. 2002-13 of the Banking Regulation Committee concerning the issuance and distribution of electronic money?	161	...	...	///

Signature of executive manager:

INTERNAL PROCEDURES	Questions	Answers		
		Yes	No	NA
6. Is the general management of your institution informed of reports sent to Tracfin and of transactions giving rise to the compilation of an information file as instructed by Article L. 563-3 of the Monetary and Financial Code?	162	...	...	///
7. If your institution is part of a group within the meaning of Article 1 of Regulation No. 2000-03 of the Banking Regulation Committee, is the group management informed of the reports sent to TRACFIN by your institution?	163	...	...	...
8. Is the AML-CFT system included within the scope of the investigations carried out by the person in charge of internal control at your institution?	164	...	...	///
9. Does the internal control function systematically verify that the AML-CFT procedures are being applied when it carries inspections of the branches of your institution?	165	...	...	...
10. Has the compliance control system included an AML-CFT risk assessment in its procedures for systematical preliminary approval of the new products?	184	...	...	...
VIII – EXISTENCE OF WRITTEN INTERNAL RULES COMPLIANT WITH REGULATION				
1. Do your institution's written internal rules indicate				
– the procedure to be followed if it appears that a sum or transaction could likely be reported to TRACFIN ?	166	...	...	///
– the prohibition of the Article L. 574-1 of the Monetary and Financial Code to inform the owner of the funds or the initiator of a transaction that gave rise to a suspicious transaction report of the existence of the declaration made?	167	...	...	///
– the procedure to be followed if, under exceptional circumstances and notably in emergency situations, an unauthorized person is leaded to report the suspicious transaction to Tracfin itself?	168	...	...	///
– the procedures of verification of the customer identity (natural and legal persons)?	169	...	...	///
– the procedure to be followed if the customer does not appear to be acting on its own behalf when it approaches your institution with a request to open an account or execute a transaction?	170	...	...	///
– the nature of and sums involved in transactions that require special vigilance (notably, in case of customers who have opened an account, with respect to the flows usually seen on their account)?	171	...	...	///
– the specific controls to be carried out with regard to checks for the purpose of AML/CFT?	172	...	...	...
– the controls to be carried out if any AML/CFT related anomalies are detected in the circulation of electronic money?	173	...	...	...

Signature of executive manager:

INTERNAL PROCEDURES	Questions	Answers		
		Yes	No	NA
– the indicators making it possible to identify transactions carried out by an occasional customer in a short time period whose total amount exceeds EUR 8,000?	174	...	...	...
– the procedures for compiling the information files referred to in Article L. 563-3 of the Monetary and Financial Code?	175	...	...	...
– the procedures for recording and keeping documents relative to transactions giving rise to compilation of an information file within the meaning of Article L. 563-3 of the Monetary and Financial Code or to suspicious transaction reports to TRACFIN?	176	...	...	///
2. If your institution belongs to a group and if your written internal procedures have been drafted on the basis of a the model prepared for the group as a whole, have the AML/CFT procedures been adapted to the nature of your institution's business?	177	...	...	...
IX – DISSEMINATING THE WRITTEN INTERNAL RULES				
1. Do your operational entities possess a manual of procedures containing all the AML/CFT instructions?	178	...	...	///
2. Does each staff member concerned with the implementation of the AML/CFT measures receive a personal copy of the above-mentioned manual?	179	...	...	///
3. Is each staff member concerned with the implementation of the AML/CFT measures required to acknowledge receipt of the above-mentioned manual?	180	...	...	///
4. If your institution is affiliated to a central body, is this central body informed of the written internal rules adopted by your institution?	181	...	...	...

Signature of executive manager:

DATA ON THE LAST FINANCIAL YEAR	Question	
I – SUSPICIOUS TRANSACTION REPORTS FILED WITH TRACFIN IN THE LAST FINANCIAL YEAR		
1. Reports filed at the initiative of your institution pursuant to points 1 and 2 in the first paragraph of Article L. 562-2 of the Monetary and Financial Code:		
– number	201	.....
– total value of the transactions reported (in EUR thousands)	202	.....
2. Reports filed at the initiative of your institution pursuant to points 1 and 2 of the second paragraph of Article L. 562-2 of the Monetary and Financial Code:		
– number	203	.....
– total value of the transactions reported (in EUR thousands)	204	.....
3. Reports filed by the TRACFIN reporting officer appointed by your institution on behalf of other institutions belonging to the same group pursuant to points 1 and 2 of the first paragraph of Article L. 562-2 of the Monetary and Financial Code:		
– number	205	.....
– total value of the transactions reported (in EUR thousands)	206	.....
4. Reports filed by the TRACFIN reporting officer appointed by your institution on behalf of other institutions belonging to the same group pursuant to points 1 and 2 of the second paragraph of Article L. 562-2 of the Monetary and Financial Code:		
– number	207	.....
– total value of the transactions reported (in EUR thousands)	208	.....
5. As regards suspicious transaction reports filed with Tracfin in the last financial year pursuant to points 1 and 2 of the first paragraph of Article L. 562-2 of the Monetary and Financial Code, what has been the average lag between executing transactions and reporting transactions (in days)?	209	.....
6. Number of anomalies detected when controlling checks? which have given rise to a suspicious transaction report or the compilation of information file?	215	.....

Signature of executive manager:

DATA ON THE LAST FINANCIAL YEAR	Question	
II – INFORMATION FILES COMPILED IN THE LAST FINANCIAL YEAR ON TRANSACTIONS REFERRED TO IN ARTICLE L. 563-3 OF THE MONETARY AND FINANCIAL CODE		
1. Number	210	.....
2. Largest value of a transaction covered by such a file (in EUR thousands)	211	.....
III – TRAINING		
1. Number of staff members having received an AML/CFT training in the last financial year..............................	212	.....
IV – MONITORING SYSTÈM		
1. Date of the last inspection of the AML/CFT system carried out by your internal control function (year, month)	213	.....
V – WRITTEN INTERNAL RULES		
1. Date of the last update of the AML/CFT procedures (year, month)	214	.....

Name and job title of signatory:

Date: Signature:

Annex 8: Example of Sanctions Applied by the French Banking Commission

(Source: Commission bancaire, annual report.)

No. 8 CALYON, formerly known as CREDIT AGRICOLE INDOSUEZ
Fine – October 11, 2004
(1,000,000 euros)

Whereas […]

The Banking Commission members, Mr. Hannoun, Chairman, Ms. Barbat-Layani, Mr. Jurgensen, M.r LaPommé, Mr. Léonnet, Mr. Robert, and Mr. Touzéry;

Having heard at its meeting of September 17, 2004, Mr. […], Chairman of the Calyon Board of Directors, with his legal counsel Mr. […];

And after deliberations by the Committee members alone;

Due diligence with regard to the identification of customers and information on the true beneficiary:

Whereas based on the relevant wording of the provisions of Article L. 563-1 of the *Monetary and Financial Code* in force when the acts being inquired into occurred, and under the terms of Article 3 of Decree 91-160 of February 13, 1991, financial entities shall confirm the identity of the cocontracting party through presentation of documentary proof before opening an account which, in the case of a legal entity, means the original or certified copy of any deed or extract from the official register showing the name, type of legal organization, and headquarters, together with all the powers of persons acting on behalf of the legal entity, that they should retain the references or copy of the documents; whereas they must ascertain the true identity of the persons for whom an account is opened or a transaction is carried out when it appears to them that the persons opening the accounts or requesting the transactions may not be acting on their own behalf; whereas this obligation imposes a duty on the institution to request any document or written proof that it deems necessary;

Whereas the inspection reports and responses submitted by the institution reveal that the ships' financial transactions were structured in a complex manner that did not disclose a direct legal link to the true beneficiary of the transaction; whereas, therefore, the institution should have obtained the necessary documentary proof to identify the real beneficiary in order to fulfill its vigilance obligations; whereas, had such steps been taken and it had proven impossible to obtain proba- tive documents, written documentation external to the institution establishing with reasonable certainty the identity of the real beneficiary could have been considered for at least two of the eight ship financing files examined in the July 19, 2001, report [companies A and B]; whereas at the time of the investigation, *Crédit Agricole Indosuez* (CAI) did not have any information that would have identified the real beneficiaries of the transaction, the persons entitled to the financial benefits derived from the activities of the ad hoc entities used; whereas the documents furnished by the institution in its submission as information on the real beneficiaries of these transactions were done so after the date of the report; whereas an offense has there- fore been committed;

Whereas the CAI is the agent for a loan granted to company [C] to purchase an airplane operated by [company D], and the inspection report of March 31, 2004 and the documents submitted on September 2, 2004 indicate that CAI did not ascer- tain the identity of the shareholders of company [E], the holder of 100 percent of the shares of [C]; whereas [C] and [E], both being companies registered in Delaware, having a share capital of US$1.00, domiciled with a "Corporation Service Company," or a "Corporation Trust Company," with their only known activity being that of holding assets, do not appear to be the real beneficiaries of the transaction; whereas, consequently, even though CAI has identified the company operating the aircraft that was financed, the institution did not ascertain the real beneficiaries of the transaction, who in this case are the persons having the right to benefit from the profits realized by these entities; whereas an offense has been committed;

Whereas at the time of the investigation CAI did not appear to have information on the real beneficiaries of the nine investment funds set up at [bank F] domiciled in country Z, whose assets have been deposited at CAI in France; whereas the fact that this country belongs to the Gulf Cooperation Council, and is also a member of the international coordination and cooperation entity established to combat money laundering (FATF), is not sufficient to establish that the financial institutions had at that time implemented any anti-money laundering mechanism similar to that to which French financial institutions are subject; whereas, therefore, the documents produced by the defense, especially the FATF 2003-2004 annual report, show that a comprehensive mechanism to combat money laundering consistent with the FATF recommendations was implemented in 2003; whereas, under these circumstances, the institution, where the practice of having subaccounts bearing the name of the various investment funds demonstrates that it was aware that [bank F] was not acting on its own behalf but on behalf of those funds, cannot therefore invoke the benefit of the last paragraph of Article 3 of Decree 91-160 to exempt itself from its obligations; whereas an offense has been committed;

Obligation to apply special scrutiny and make a written report on the characteristics of transactions covered by Article L. 563-3 of the Monetary and Financial Code:

Whereas under the terms of the provisions of Article L. 563-3 of the *Monetary and Financial Code*, any large transaction involving unitary amounts of more than 150,000 euros and which, without being covered by the requirements for suspicious transaction reports, involve unusually complex conditions and do not seem to have any economic justification or lawful purpose, must be subject to special scrutiny by the financial entity; whereas, in this case, the financial entity shall make inquiries of the customer as to the origin and destination of the funds, the purpose of the transaction, and the identity of the recipient, and shall then make a written record of the characteristics of the transaction;

Whereas CAI has granted a loan of US$57 million to company [G] to finance an aircraft leased to company [H], registered in Bermuda and 100 percent owned by [company I], also registered in Bermuda; whereas the aircraft lease charges were paid by company [J]; whereas the beneficiary of the transaction was supposedly [person/entity K] according to a written statement issued by company [J] in February 1998; whereas this individual gave a rental security and pledged US$20 million from his/her account at CAI Switzerland as a deposit; whereas the report of July 19, 2001, revealed that CAI did not have the essential facts to establish a formal link between [company J] and the beneficiary, nor sufficient information on the origin of the funds; whereas the documents submitted on December 24, 2002, revealed that the additional information on the transaction was only provided in October 2002 by [company J] and CAI Switzerland; whereas, at the time of the first inspection, CAI had not applied special scrutiny as required under Article L. 563-3, even though the transaction was unusually complex and no economic justification was apparent; whereas an offense has been committed;

Whereas in the first half of 2000, six transfers from CAI Geneva amounting to over 820,000 euros were deposited by an unknown originator into the CAI Paris account of [company L]; whereas customer [M] received over this same period two transfers of almost 2 million euros from CAI Geneva, without any indication of the originator; whereas in the absence of any mention of the originator of transfers of very large sums and where the institution has no information on the origin of the customer's funds nor the economic justification for the transactions, the institution should have scrutinized these transactions carefully and requested that the customer provide information on the origin of the abovementioned sums; whereas with respect to [company L] it was only on February 5, 2001, at the request of the Banking Commission Inspection Team that CAI Paris asked CAI Geneva about the identity of the originator of the transfer; whereas with regard to [customer M], it is clear from the documents submitted by CAI, and the March 31, 2004, inspection report that in 2000, the customer file at CAI Paris did not contain any information on the originator, who was simply believed to be the customer himself, and the earliest note produced by CAI containing information furnished by *Credit Agricole Indosuez Cheuvreux Gestions* only dates from July 12, 2001; whereas, with regard to these two customers, CAI Paris did not ascertain the origin of the sums in a timely manner; whereas, therefore, a violation of Article L. 563-3 has been committed in respect to these customers.

Vigilance procedures

Whereas under Article 2 of Regulation 91-07 financial institutions must exercise constant vigilance and establish appropriate internal structures and procedures to ensure compliance with Title V1 of Book V of the *Monetary and Financial Code*; whereas the annual review of private banking customers referred to in Circular 00/11 of July 11, 2000, only involved customers who deposited sums over 15 million euros, a threshold lowered to 7.5 million for customers considered most apt to arouse the suspicion of CAI; whereas vigilance measures implemented were inadequate bearing in mind the risks inherent in the activity; whereas in its last submission, the institution indicated that it had conducted an annual review of files having no threshold amount; whereas an offense has nevertheless been committed in respect of the preceding period;

Whereas CAI Paris accounts for the Jersey registered company [N] showed activity in the first half of 2000—five credit transfers for a total of more than 150 million euros and three debit transfers for a total of more than 100 million euros; whereas, nevertheless, CAI Paris did not have any information on transactions recorded in the accounts; whereas the institution declared that the account was managed from London, where the orders of the customer were received and where the group had a complete file, including legal information and annual reports of the company; whereas, nevertheless, in order to exercise vigilance over the account transactions of its own customers, CAI Paris should have had information on transactions involving large sums in Paris, furnished, where applicable, by the institution of the group which had contact with the customer; whereas an offense has been committed;

Prevention of money laundering in foreign subsidiaries and branches:

Whereas under Article L. 563-3 of the *Monetary and Financial Code*, credit institutions must ensure that their foreign branches and subsidiaries comply with the obligations to establish and retain written records for five years from the date of the special scrutiny of large transactions which involve unusually complex conditions and do not appear to have any economic justification or lawful purpose;

Whereas the inspection report of July 19, 2001 reveals that the procedures applicable to CAI Gibraltar, CAI Switzerland, and CAI Luxembourg did not cover the obligation imposed under Article L. 563-3; whereas the procedures established by the institution either were implemented after July 2001 or do not address the aforementioned obligation; whereas, furthermore, the fact that the laws of the States concerned could have imposed equivalent obligations does not exempt CAI from ensuring compliance by its foreign subsidiaries and branches; whereas an offense has been committed;

Whereas under Article 5 of Regulation 91-07, credit institutions domiciled in France shall make all helpful recommendations to their foreign subsidiaries and branches so that they may protect themselves appropriately against the risk of being used to launder money; whereas, consequently, the institutions must ensure that their entities abroad have procedures that are at least similar to those provided for under French law and implement a control system to ensure compliance;

Whereas the entities of the CAI Group in Gibraltar, Monaco, and Switzerland did not carry out regular second-level internal controls with respect to money laundering prevention from 1997 to 2000; whereas the CAI general inspection reports tendered in evidence by the institution in its December 22, 2002, submission, for Gibraltar in 1996 and 2000, for Monaco in 1997, and for the Swiss subsidiary company FICAI in 2000, are not proper second level controls as they were not carried out regularly; whereas the institution affirms that second level controls took place in those entities without specifying whether they dealt with money laundering or providing documents in proof;

Whereas the lack of controls did not allow the group to monitor the money laundering risk to a sufficient extent; whereas, indeed, in the trust department at Gibraltar, the 1996 CAI general inspection report revealed that customers were not always known before an instrument was created; whereas the report also revealed that in the private banking department, the opening of accounts as well as transactions effected in relation to 100 customers originally from the former Soviet Union were insufficiently monitored; whereas in the April 2000 report of the same entity, it was stated that knowledge of some current Russian customers was still inadequate; whereas the specific report of June 2000 on Nigerian accounts reveals that 15 accounts received US$38 million from March 1999 to March 2000, and for 75 percent of these amounts, the originator of the transfers was unknown, that the real beneficiary of most of these accounts was allegedly a former oil minister, and that the sums in question could have been proceeds from corruption; whereas the reports also state that these accounts began to be used in Switzerland before they were transferred to Gibraltar on letters of introduction drafted by the Swiss companies of the group without providing complete information to the Gibraltar institution;

Whereas the 1997 CAI report on CFM Monaco revealed that lax oversight of the opening of accounts resulted in many accounts being opened without sufficient documentation; whereas the CNCA [*Caisse Nationale de Crédit Agricole*] inspection report of January 11, 2000, states that "the bank manages the assets (416 billion French francs) and financial flows of three groups of customers, whose economic sources are unknown to it and who are, furthermore, close to 'controversial' political regimes, and also has customers (2 billion French francs of managed assets) whose profiles remain suspicious, even if the doubt is not at the same level;"

Whereas the Banking Commission Inspection report of March 4, 2002, reveals that the shortcomings in organizing the dissemination and use of lists of individuals linked to the Taliban regime leading CAI Hong Kong in one case on November 15, 2001, to execute a SWIFT transfer of over US$250,000 indicating as the Afghan originator of the transfer "[Mr. O.], son of [Mr. P.]," which has a close homonymy with [names of two persons], appearing on the list of persons linked to the Taliban regime under EC Regulation 1354/2001 of July 4, 2001; whereas although it was the institution's submission that the funds recently blocked in the United States of America were ultimately unblocked by US authorities, the failure to detect such a level of homonymy, which was in fact detected by its correspondent, constitutes an unacceptable lack of organization of anti-money laundering measures by the CAI group at the international level;

Whereas all these facts highlight significant failures in the effectiveness of the recommendations and in monitoring compliance with them; whereas in these circumstances, the provisions of Article 5 of Regulation 91-07 were violated;

Whereas, in light of the foregoing, the institution has violated several key provisions of the regulations applying to it with regard to the fight against money laundering, particularly in terms of monitoring group entities abroad, which is particularly serious, bearing in mind the characteristics of the activity and the size of the group; whereas in respect of the other complaints against CAI, there are no grounds to impose sanctions;

Whereas the offenses were committed prior to major changes in the management and organization of the institution and prior to substantial efforts to strengthen its anti-money laundering system; whereas, in these circumstances, there are grounds to impose a fine only; whereas, consequently, Article L. 613-21 of the *Monetary and Financial Code* should be applied and a fine in the amount of 1 million euros (1,000,000 euros) be imposed on Calyon;

Whereas Calyon has requested that notice of the Banking Commission's decision not be published in connection with the bank's name; whereas, in view of the serious nature of the offenses committed, this request must be refused;

Decides:

Article 1:   A fine of 1 million euros (1,000,000 euros) shall be imposed on Calyon;

Article 2:   Public notice shall be given of this decision;

Decision read out in a public session held on October 11, 2004.

Annex 9: FATF 40+9 Recommendations

40 Recommendations on Money Laundering

Legal Systems

• Scope of the criminal offence of money laundering

Recommendation 1

Countries should criminalize money laundering on the basis of United Nations Convention against Illicit Traffic in Narcotic Drugs and Psychotropic Substances, 1988 (the Vienna Convention) and United Nations Convention against Transnational Organized Crime, 2000 (the Palermo Convention).

Countries should apply the crime of money laundering to all serious offences, with a view to including the widest range of predicate offences. Predicate offences may be described by reference to all offences, or to a threshold linked either to a category of serious offences or to the penalty of imprisonment applicable to the predicate offence (threshold approach), or to a list of predicate offences, or a combination of these approaches.

Where countries apply a threshold approach, predicate offences should at a minimum comprise all offences that fall within the category of serious offences under their national law or should include offences which are punishable by a maximum penalty of more than one year's imprisonment or for those countries that have a minimum threshold for offences in their legal system, predicate offences should comprise all offences, which are punished by a minimum penalty of more than six months imprisonment.

Whichever approach is adopted, each country should at a minimum include a range of offences within each of the designated categories of offences [3].

Predicate offences for money laundering should extend to conduct that occurred in another country, which constitutes an offence in that country, and which would have constituted a predicate offence had it occurred domestically.

Countries may provide that the only prerequisite is that the conduct would have constituted a predicate offence had it occurred domestically.

Countries may provide that the offence of money laundering does not apply to persons who committed the predicate offence, where this is required by fundamental principles of their domestic law.

Footnotes:

[3] See the definition of "designated categories of offences" in the Glossary.

Recommendation 2

Countries should ensure that:

a) The intent and knowledge required to prove the offence of money laundering is consistent with the standards set forth in the Vienna and Palermo Conventions, including the concept that such mental state may be inferred from objective factual circumstances.

b) Criminal liability, and, where that is not possible, civil or administrative liability, should apply to legal persons. This should not preclude parallel criminal, civil or administrative proceedings with respect to legal persons in countries in which such forms of liability are available. Legal persons should be subject to effective, proportionate and dissuasive sanctions. Such measures should be without prejudice to the criminal liability of individuals.

- Provisional measures and confiscation

Recommendation 3

Countries should adopt measures similar to those set forth in the Vienna and Palermo Conventions, including legislative measures, to enable their competent authorities to confiscate property laundered, proceeds from money laundering or predicate offences, instrumentalities used in or intended for use in the commission of these offences, or property of corresponding value, without prejudicing the rights of bona fide third parties.

Such measures should include the authority to: (a) identify, trace and evaluate property which is subject to confiscation; (b) carry out provisional measures, such as freezing and seizing, to prevent any dealing, transfer or disposal of such property; (c) take steps that will prevent or void actions that prejudice the State's ability to recover property that is subject to confiscation; and (d) take any appropriate investigative measures.

Countries may consider adopting measures that allow such proceeds or instrumentalities to be confiscated without requiring a criminal conviction, or which require an offender to demonstrate the lawful origin of the property alleged to be liable to confiscation, to the extent that such a requirement is consistent with the principles of their domestic law.

Measures to be taken by Financial Institutions and Non-Financial Businesses and Professions to prevent Money Laundering and Terrorist Financing

- Customer due diligence and record-keeping

Recommendation 4

Countries should ensure that financial institution secrecy laws do not inhibit implementation of the FATF Recommendations.

Recommendation 5

Financial institutions should not keep anonymous accounts or accounts in obviously fictitious names.

Financial institutions should undertake customer due diligence measures, including identifying and verifying the identity of their customers, when:

- establishing business relations;
- carrying out occasional transactions: (i) above the applicable designated threshold; or (ii) that are wire transfers in the circumstances covered by the Interpretative Note to Special Recommendation VII;
- there is a suspicion of money laundering or terrorist financing; or
- the financial institution has doubts about the veracity or adequacy of previously obtained customer identification data.

The customer due diligence (CDD) measures to be taken are as follows:

a) Identifying the customer and verifying that customer's identity using reliable, independent source documents, data or information [4].

b) Identifying the beneficial owner, and taking reasonable measures to verify the identity of the beneficial owner such that the financial institution is satisfied that it knows who the beneficial owner is. For legal persons and arrangements this should include financial institutions taking reasonable measures to understand the ownership and control structure of the customer.

c) Obtaining information on the purpose and intended nature of the business relationship.

d) Conducting ongoing due diligence on the business relationship and scrutiny of transactions undertaken throughout the course of that relationship to ensure that the transactions being conducted are consistent with the institution's knowledge of the customer, their business and risk profile, including, where necessary, the source of funds.

Financial institutions should apply each of the CDD measures under (a) to (d) above, but may determine the extent of such measures on a risk sensitive basis depending on the type of customer, business relationship or transaction. The measures that are taken should be consistent with any guidelines issued by competent authorities. For higher risk categories, financial institutions should perform enhanced due diligence. In certain circumstances, where there are low risks, countries may decide that financial institutions can apply reduced or simplified measures.

Financial institutions should verify the identity of the customer and beneficial owner before or during the course of establishing a business relationship or conducting transactions for occasional customers. Countries may permit financial institutions to complete the verification as soon as reasonably practicable following the establishment of the relationship, where the money laundering risks are effectively managed and where this is essential not to interrupt the normal conduct of business.

Where the financial institution is unable to comply with paragraphs (a) to (c) above, it should not open the account, commence business relations or perform the transaction; or should terminate the business relationship; and should consider making a suspicious transactions report in relation to the customer.

These requirements should apply to all new customers, though financial institutions should also apply this Recommendation to existing customers on the basis of materiality and risk, and should conduct due diligence on such existing relationships at appropriate times.

Footnotes:

[4] Reliable, independent source documents, data or information will hereafter be referred to as "identification data".

(See also Interpretative Notes Recommendation 5 and Interpretative Note to Recommendations 5, 12 and 16)

Recommendation 6

Financial institutions should, in relation to politically exposed persons, in addition to performing normal due diligence measures:

a) Have appropriate risk management systems to determine whether the customer is a politically exposed person.

b) Obtain senior management approval for establishing business relationships with such customers.

c) Take reasonable measures to establish the source of wealth and source of funds.

d) Conduct enhanced ongoing monitoring of the business relationship.

(See also Interpretative Note to Recommendation 6)

Recommendation 7

Financial institutions should, in relation to cross-border correspondent banking and other similar relationships, in addition to performing normal due diligence measures:

a) Gather sufficient information about a respondent institution to understand fully the nature of the respondent's business and to determine from publicly available information the reputation of the institution and the quality of supervision, including whether it has been subject to a money laundering or terrorist financing investigation or regulatory action.

b) Assess the respondent institution's anti-money laundering and terrorist financing controls.

c) Obtain approval from senior management before establishing new correspondent relationships.

d) Document the respective responsibilities of each institution.

e) With respect to "payable-through accounts", be satisfied that the respondent bank has verified the identity of and performed on-going due diligence on the customers having direct access to accounts of the correspondent and that it is able to provide relevant customer identification data upon request to the correspondent bank.

Recommendation 8

Financial institutions should pay special attention to any money laundering threats that may arise from new or developing technologies that might favour anonymity, and take measures, if needed, to prevent their use in money laundering schemes. In particular, financial institutions should have policies and procedures in place to address any specific risks associated with non-face to face business relationships or transactions.

Recommendation 9

Countries may permit financial institutions to rely on intermediaries or other third parties to perform elements (a) – (c) of the CDD process or to introduce business, provided that the criteria set out below are met. Where such reliance is permitted, the ultimate responsibility for customer identification and verification remains with the financial institution relying on the third party.

The criteria that should be met are as follows:

a) A financial institution relying upon a third party should immediately obtain the necessary information concerning elements (a) – (c) of the CDD process. Financial institutions should take adequate steps to satisfy themselves that copies of identification data and other relevant documentation relating to the CDD requirements will be made available from the third party upon request without delay.

b) The financial institution should satisfy itself that the third party is regulated and supervised for, and has measures in place to comply with CDD requirements in line with Recommendations 5 and 10.

It is left to each country to determine in which countries the third party that meets the conditions can be based, having regard to information available on countries that do not or do not adequately apply the FATF Recommendations.

(See also Interpretative Note to Recommendation 9)

Recommendation 10

Financial institutions should maintain, for at least five years, all necessary records on transactions, both domestic or international, to enable them to comply swiftly with information requests from the competent authorities. Such records must be sufficient to permit reconstruction of individual transactions (including the amounts and types of currency involved if any) so as to provide, if necessary, evidence for prosecution of criminal activity.

Financial institutions should keep records on the identification data obtained through the customer due diligence process (e.g. copies or records of official identification documents like passports, identity cards, driving licenses or similar documents), account files and business correspondence for at least five years after the business relationship is ended.

The identification data and transaction records should be available to domestic competent authorities upon appropriate authority.

(See also Interpretative Note to Recommendation 10)

Recommendation 11

Financial institutions should pay special attention to all complex, unusual large transactions, and all unusual patterns of transactions, which have no apparent economic or visible lawful purpose. The background and purpose of such transactions should, as far as possible, be examined, the findings established in writing, and be available to help competent authorities and auditors.

(See also Interpretative Note to Recommendation 11)

Recommendation 12

The customer due diligence and record-keeping requirements set out in Recommendations 5, 6, and 8 to 11 apply to designated non-financial businesses and professions in the following situations:

a) Casinos—when customers engage in financial transactions equal to or above the applicable designated threshold.

b) Real estate agents—when they are involved in transactions for their client concerning the buying and selling of real estate.

c) Dealers in precious metals and dealers in precious stones—when they engage in any cash transaction with a customer equal to or above the applicable designated threshold.

d) Lawyers, notaries, other independent legal professionals and accountants when they prepare for or carry out transactions for their client concerning the following activities:

- buying and selling of real estate;
- managing of client money, securities or other assets;
- management of bank, savings or securities accounts;
- organisation of contributions for the creation, operation or management of companies;
- creation, operation or management of legal persons or arrangements, and buying and selling of business entities.

e) Trust and company service providers when they prepare for or carry out transactions for a client concerning the activities listed in the definition in the Glossary.

(See also Interpretative Note to Recommendation 12 and Interpretative Note to Recommendations 5, 12 and 16)

- Reporting of suspicious transactions and compliance

Recommendation 13

If a financial institution suspects or has reasonable grounds to suspect that funds are the proceeds of a criminal activity, or are related to terrorist financing, it should be required, directly by law or regulation, to report promptly its suspicions to the financial intelligence unit (FIU).

(See also Interpretative Note to Recommendation 13)

Recommendation 14

Financial institutions, their directors, officers and employees should be:

a) Protected by legal provisions from criminal and civil liability for breach of any restriction on disclosure of information imposed by contract or by any legislative, regulatory or administrative provision, if they report their suspicions in good faith to the FIU, even if they did not know precisely what the underlying criminal activity was, and regardless of whether illegal activity actually occurred.

b) Prohibited by law from disclosing the fact that a suspicious transaction report (STR) or related information is being reported to the FIU.

(See also Interpretative Note to Recommendation 14)

Recommendation 15

Financial institutions should develop programmes against money laundering and terrorist financing. These programmes should include:

a) The development of internal policies, procedures and controls, including appropriate compliance management arrangements, and adequate screening procedures to ensure high standards when hiring employees.

b) An ongoing employee training programme.

c) An audit function to test the system.

(See also Interpretative Note to Recommendation 15)

Recommendation 16

The requirements set out in Recommendations 13 to 15, and 21 apply to all designated non-financial businesses and professions, subject to the following qualifications:

a) Lawyers, notaries, other independent legal professionals and accountants should be required to report suspicious transactions when, on behalf of or for a client, they engage in a financial transaction in relation to the activities described in Recommendation 12(d). Countries are strongly encouraged to extend the reporting requirement to the rest of the professional activities of accountants, including auditing.

b) Dealers in precious metals and dealers in precious stones should be required to report suspicious transactions when they engage in any cash transaction with a customer equal to or above the applicable designated threshold.

c) Trust and company service providers should be required to report suspicious transactions for a client when, on behalf of or for a client, they engage in a transaction in relation to the activities referred to Recommendation 12(e).

Lawyers, notaries, other independent legal professionals, and accountants acting as independent legal professionals, are not required to report their suspicions if the relevant information was obtained in circumstances where they are subject to professional secrecy or legal professional privilege.

(See also Interpretative Notes to Recommendation 16 and Interpretative Note to Recommendations 5, 12, and 16)

- Other measures to deter money laundering and terrorist financing

Recommendation 17

Countries should ensure that effective, proportionate and dissuasive sanctions, whether criminal, civil or administrative, are available to deal with natural or legal persons covered by these Recommendations that fail to comply with anti-money laundering or terrorist financing requirements.

Recommendation 18

Countries should not approve the establishment or accept the continued operation of shell banks. Financial institutions should refuse to enter into, or continue, a correspondent banking relationship with shell banks. Financial institutions should also guard against establishing relations with respondent foreign financial institutions that permit their accounts to be used by shell banks.

Recommendation 19 (This Recommendation was Revised and the Following text was Issued on 22 October 2004)

Countries should consider the feasibility and utility of a system where banks and other financial institutions and intermediaries would report all domestic and international currency transactions above a fixed amount, to a national central agency with a computerised data base, available to competent authorities for use in money laundering or terrorist financing cases, subject to strict safeguards to ensure proper use of the information.

Recommendation 20

Countries should consider applying the FATF Recommendations to businesses and professions, other than designated non-financial businesses and professions, that pose a money laundering or terrorist financing risk.

Countries should further encourage the development of modern and secure techniques of money management that are less vulnerable to money laundering.

- Measures to be taken with respect to countries that do not or insufficiently comply with the FATF Recommendations

Recommendation 21

Financial institutions should give special attention to business relationships and transactions with persons, including companies and financial institutions, from countries which do not or insufficiently apply the FATF Recommendations. Whenever these transactions have no apparent economic or visible lawful purpose, their background and purpose should, as far as possible, be examined, the findings established in writing, and be available to help competent authorities. Where such a country continues not to apply or insufficiently applies the FATF Recommendations, countries should be able to apply appropriate countermeasures.

Recommendation 22

Financial institutions should ensure that the principles applicable to financial institutions, which are mentioned above are also applied to branches and majority owned subsidiaries located abroad, especially in countries which do not or insufficiently apply the FATF Recommendations, to the extent that local applicable laws and regulations permit. When local applicable laws and regulations prohibit this implementation, competent authorities in the country of the parent institution should be informed by the financial institutions that they cannot apply the FATF Recommendations.

- Regulation and supervision

Recommendation 23

Countries should ensure that financial institutions are subject to adequate regulation and supervision and are effectively implementing the FATF Recommendations. Competent authorities should take the necessary legal or regulatory measures to prevent criminals or their associates from holding or being the beneficial owner of a significant or controlling interest or holding a management function in a financial institution.

For financial institutions subject to the Core Principles, the regulatory and supervisory measures that apply for prudential purposes and which are also relevant to money laundering, should apply in a similar manner for anti-money laundering and terrorist financing purposes.

Other financial institutions should be licensed or registered and appropriately regulated, and subject to supervision or oversight for anti-money laundering purposes, having regard to the risk of money laundering or terrorist financing in that sector. At a minimum, businesses providing a service of money or value transfer, or of money or currency changing should be licensed or registered, and subject to effective systems for monitoring and ensuring compliance with national requirements to combat money laundering and terrorist financing.

(See also Interpretative Note to Recommendation 23)

Recommendation 24

Designated non-financial businesses and professions should be subject to regulatory and supervisory measures as set out below.

a) Casinos should be subject to a comprehensive regulatory and supervisory regime that ensures that they have effectively implemented the necessary anti-money laundering and terrorist-financing measures. At a minimum:

- casinos should be licensed;
- competent authorities should take the necessary legal or regulatory measures to prevent criminals or their associates from holding or being the beneficial owner of a significant or controlling interest, holding a management function in, or being an operator of a casino;
- competent authorities should ensure that casinos are effectively supervised for compliance with requirements to combat money laundering and terrorist financing.

b) Countries should ensure that the other categories of designated non-financial businesses and professions are subject to effective systems for monitoring and ensuring their compliance with requirements to combat money laundering and terrorist financing. This should be performed on a risk-sensitive basis. This may be performed by a government authority or by an appropriate self-regulatory organisation, provided that such an organisation can ensure that its members comply with their obligations to combat money laundering and terrorist financing.

Recommendation 25

The competent authorities should establish guidelines, and provide feedback which will assist financial institutions and designated non-financial businesses and professions in applying national measures to combat money laundering and terrorist financing, and in particular, in detecting and reporting suspicious transactions.

(See also Interpretative Note to Recommendation 25)

Institutional and other measures necessary in systems for combating Money Laundering and Terrorist Financing

- Competent authorities, their powers and resources

Recommendation 26

Countries should establish a FIU that serves as a national centre for the receiving (and, as permitted, requesting), analysis and dissemination of STR and other information regarding potential money laundering or terrorist financing. The FIU should have access, directly or indirectly, on a timely basis to the financial, administrative and law enforcement information that it requires to properly undertake its functions, including the analysis of STR.

(See also Interpretative Note to Recommendation 26)

Recommendation 27

Countries should ensure that designated law enforcement authorities have responsibility for money laundering and terrorist financing investigations. Countries are encouraged to support and develop, as far as possible, special investigative techniques suitable for the investigation of money laundering, such as controlled delivery, undercover operations and other relevant techniques. Countries are also encouraged to use other effective mechanisms such as the use of permanent or temporary groups specialised in asset investigation, and co-operative investigations with appropriate competent authorities in other countries.

(See also Interpretative Note to Recommendation 27)

Recommendation 28

When conducting investigations of money laundering and underlying predicate offences, competent authorities should be able to obtain documents and information for use in those investigations, and in prosecutions and related actions. This should include powers to use compulsory measures for the production of records held by financial institutions and other persons, for the search of persons and premises, and for the seizure and obtaining of evidence.

Recommendation 29

Supervisors should have adequate powers to monitor and ensure compliance by financial institutions with requirements to combat money laundering and terrorist financing, including the authority to conduct inspections. They should be authorised to compel production of any information from financial institutions that is relevant to monitoring such compliance, and to impose adequate administrative sanctions for failure to comply with such requirements.

Recommendation 30

Countries should provide their competent authorities involved in combating money laundering and terrorist financing with adequate financial, human and technical resources. Countries should have in place processes to ensure that the staff of those authorities are of high integrity.

Recommendation 31

Countries should ensure that policy makers, the FIU, law enforcement and supervisors have effective mechanisms in place which enable them to co-operate, and where appropriate co-ordinate domestically with each other concerning the development and implementation of policies and activities to combat money laundering and terrorist financing.

Recommendation 32

Countries should ensure that their competent authorities can review the effectiveness of their systems to combat money laundering and terrorist financing systems by maintaining comprehensive statistics on matters relevant to the effectiveness and efficiency of such systems. This should include statistics on the STR received and disseminated; on money laundering and terrorist financing investigations, prosecutions and convictions; on property frozen, seized and confiscated; and on mutual legal assistance or other international requests for co-operation.

- Transparency of legal persons and arrangements

Recommendation 33

Countries should take measures to prevent the unlawful use of legal persons by money launderers. Countries should ensure that there is adequate, accurate and timely information on the beneficial ownership and control of legal persons that can be obtained or accessed in a timely fashion by competent authorities. In particular, countries that have legal persons that are able to issue bearer shares should take appropriate measures to ensure that they are not misused for money laundering and be able to demonstrate the adequacy of those measures. Countries could consider measures to facilitate access to beneficial ownership and control information to financial institutions undertaking the requirements set out in Recommendation 5.

Recommendation 34

Countries should take measures to prevent the unlawful use of legal arrangements by money launderers. In particular, countries should ensure that there is adequate, accurate and timely information on express trusts, including information on the settlor, trustee and beneficiaries, that can be obtained or accessed in a timely fashion by competent authorities. Countries could consider measures to facilitate access to beneficial ownership and control information to financial institutions undertaking the requirements set out in Recommendation 5.

   • International co-operation

Recommendation 35

Countries should take immediate steps to become party to and implement fully the Vienna Convention, the Palermo Convention, and the 1999 United Nations International Convention for the Suppression of the Financing of Terrorism. Countries are also encouraged to ratify and implement other relevant international conventions, such as the 1990 Council of Europe Convention on Laundering, Search, Seizure and Confiscation of the Proceeds from Crime and the 2002 Inter-American Convention against Terrorism.

   • Mutual legal assistance and extradition

Recommendation 36

Countries should rapidly, constructively and effectively provide the widest possible range of mutual legal assistance in relation to money laundering and terrorist financing investigations, prosecutions, and related proceedings. In particular, countries should:

   a) Not prohibit or place unreasonable or unduly restrictive conditions on the provision of mutual legal assistance.

b) Ensure that they have clear and efficient processes for the execution of mutual legal assistance requests.

c) Not refuse to execute a request for mutual legal assistance on the sole ground that the offence is also considered to involve fiscal matters.

d) Not refuse to execute a request for mutual legal assistance on the grounds that laws require financial institutions to maintain secrecy or confidentiality.

Countries should ensure that the powers of their competent authorities required under Recommendation 28 are also available for use in response to requests for mutual legal assistance, and if consistent with their domestic framework, in response to direct requests from foreign judicial or law enforcement authorities to domestic counterparts.

To avoid conflicts of jurisdiction, consideration should be given to devising and applying mechanisms for determining the best venue for prosecution of defendants in the interests of justice in cases that are subject to prosecution in more than one country.

Recommendation 37

Countries should, to the greatest extent possible, render mutual legal assistance notwithstanding the absence of dual criminality.

Where dual criminality is required for mutual legal assistance or extradition, that requirement should be deemed to be satisfied regardless of whether both countries place the offence within the same category of offence or denominate the offence by the same terminology, provided that both countries criminalise the conduct underlying the offence.

Recommendation 38

There should be authority to take expeditious action in response to requests by foreign countries to identify, freeze, seize and confiscate property laundered, proceeds from money laundering or predicate offences, instrumentalities used in or intended for use in the commission of these offences, or property of corresponding value. There should also be arrangements for co-ordinating seizure and confiscation proceedings, which may include the sharing of confiscated assets.

(See also Interpretative Note to Recommendation 38)

Recommendation 39

Countries should recognise money laundering as an extraditable offence. Each country should either extradite its own nationals, or where a country does not do so solely on the grounds of nationality, that country should, at the request of the country seeking extradition, submit the case without undue delay to its competent authorities for the purpose of prosecution of the offences set forth in the request. Those authorities should take their decision and conduct their proceedings in the same manner as in the case of any other offence of a serious nature under the domestic law of that country. The countries concerned should cooperate with each other, in particular on procedural and evidentiary aspects, to ensure the efficiency of such prosecutions.

Subject to their legal frameworks, countries may consider simplifying extradition by allowing direct transmission of extradition requests between appropriate ministries, extraditing persons based only on warrants of arrests or judgements, and/or introducing a simplified extradition of consenting persons who waive formal extradition proceedings.

- Other forms of co-operation

Recommendation 40

Countries should ensure that their competent authorities provide the widest possible range of international co-operation to their foreign counterparts. There should be clear and effective gateways to facilitate the prompt and constructive exchange directly between counterparts, either spontaneously or upon request, of information relating to both money laundering and the underlying predicate offences. Exchanges should be permitted without unduly restrictive conditions. In particular:

a) Competent authorities should not refuse a request for assistance on the sole ground that the request is also considered to involve fiscal matters.

b) Countries should not invoke laws that require financial institutions to maintain secrecy or confidentiality as a ground for refusing to provide co-operation.

c) Competent authorities should be able to conduct inquiries; and where possible, investigations; on behalf of foreign counterparts.

Where the ability to obtain information sought by a foreign competent authority is not within the mandate of its counterpart, countries are also encouraged to permit a prompt and constructive exchange of information with non-counterparts. Co-operation with foreign authorities other than counterparts could occur directly or indirectly. When uncertain about the appropriate avenue to follow, competent authorities should first contact their foreign counterparts for assistance.

Countries should establish controls and safeguards to ensure that information exchanged by competent authorities is used only in an authorised manner, consistent with their obligations concerning privacy and data protection.

(See also Interpretative Note to Recommendation 40)

9 Special Recommendations on Terrorist Financing

Recognizing the vital importance of taking action to combat the financing of terrorism, the FATF has agreed these Recommendations, which, when combined with the FATF Forty Recommendations on money laundering, set out the basic framework to detect, prevent and suppress the financing of terrorism and terrorist acts. For further information on the Special Recommendations as related to the self-assessment process, see the Guidance Notes.

I.   Ratification and Implementation of UN Instruments

Each country should take immediate steps to ratify and to implement fully the 1999 United Nations International Convention for the Suppression of the Financing of Terrorism.

Countries should also immediately implement the United Nations resolutions relating to the prevention and suppression of the financing of terrorist acts, particularly United Nations Security Council Resolution 1373.

II.   Criminalising the Financing of Terrorism and Associated Money Laundering

Each country should criminalise the financing of terrorism, terrorist acts and terrorist organisations. Countries should ensure that such offences are designated as money laundering predicate offences.

(See also Interpretative Note to SRII and Best Practices Paper)

III.   Freezing and confiscating terrorist assets

Each country should implement measures to freeze without delay funds or other assets of terrorists, those who finance terrorism and terrorist organisations in accordance with the United Nations resolutions relating to the prevention and suppression of the financing of terrorist acts.

Each country should also adopt and implement measures, including legislative ones, which would enable the competent authorities to seize and confiscate property that is the proceeds of, or used in, or intended or allocated for use in, the financing of terrorism, terrorist acts or terrorist organisations.

(See also Interpretative Note to SRIII and Best Practices Paper)

IV. Reporting suspicious transactions related to terrorism

If financial institutions, or other businesses or entities subject to anti-money laundering obligations, suspect or have reasonable grounds to suspect that funds are linked or related to, or are to be used for terrorism, terrorist acts or by terrorist organisations, they should be required to report promptly their suspicions to the competent authorities.

V. International co-operation

Each country should afford another country, on the basis of a treaty, arrangement or other mechanism for mutual legal assistance or information exchange, the greatest possible measure of assistance in connection with criminal, civil enforcement, and administrative investigations, inquiries and proceedings relating to the financing of terrorism, terrorist acts and terrorist organisations.

Countries should also take all possible measures to ensure that they do not provide safe havens for individuals charged with the financing of terrorism, terrorist acts or terrorist organisations, and should have procedures in place to extradite, where possible, such individuals.

VI. Alternative remittance

Each country should take measures to ensure that persons or legal entities, including agents, that provide a service for the transmission of money or value, including transmission through an informal money or value transfer system or network, should be licensed or registered and subject to all the FATF Recommendations that apply to banks and non-bank financial institutions. Each country should ensure that persons or legal entities that carry out this service illegally are subject to administrative, civil or criminal sanctions.

(See also Interpretative Note to SRVI and Best Practices Paper)

VII. Wire transfers

Countries should take measures to require financial institutions, including money remitters, to include accurate and meaningful originator information (name, address and account number) on funds transfers and related messages that are sent, and the information should remain with the transfer or related message through the payment chain.

Countries should take measures to ensure that financial institutions, including money remitters, conduct enhanced scrutiny of and monitor for suspicious activity funds transfers which do not contain complete originator information (name, address and account number).

(See also Interpretative Note to VII and Best Practices Paper)

VIII.   Non-profit organisations

Countries should review the adequacy of laws and regulations that relate to entities that can be abused for the financing of terrorism. Non-profit organisations are particularly vulnerable, and countries should ensure that they cannot be misused:

by terrorist organisations posing as legitimate entities;
to exploit legitimate entities as conduits for terrorist financing, including for the
   purpose of escaping asset freezing measures; and
to conceal or obscure the clandestine diversion of funds intended for legitimate
   purposes to terrorist organisations.

(See also Interpretative Note to SRVIII and Best Practices Paper)

IX.   Cash couriers

Countries should have measures in place to detect the physical cross-border transportation of currency and bearer negotiable instruments, including a declaration system or other disclosure obligation.

Countries should ensure that their competent authorities have the legal authority to stop or restrain currency or bearer negotiable instruments that are suspected to be related to terrorist financing or money laundering, or that are falsely declared or disclosed.

Countries should ensure that effective, proportionate and dissuasive sanctions are available to deal with persons who make false declaration(s) or disclosure(s). In cases where the currency or bearer negotiable instruments are related to terrorist financing or money laundering, countries should also adopt measures, including legislative ones consistent with Recommendation 3 and Special Recommendation III, which would enable the confiscation of such currency or instruments.

(See also Interpretative Note to SRIX and Best Practices Paper)

Note

With the adoption of Special Recommendation IX, the FATF now deletes paragraph 19(a) of Recommendation 19 and the Interpretative Note to Recommendation 19 in order to ensure internal consistency amongst the FATF Recommendations. The modified text of recommendation 19 reads as follows:

Recommendation 19

Countries should consider the feasibility and utility of a system where banks and other financial institutions and intermediaries would report all domestic and international currency transactions above a fixed amount, to a national central agency with a computerised data base, available to competent authorities for use in money laundering or terrorist financing cases, subject to strict safeguards to ensure proper use of the information.

Index

transaction testing, 200, 203, 204, 206, 207, 208*b*, 218
BCCI (Bank of Credit and Commerce International), 46*b*
BCP. *See Core Principles for Effective Banking*
Belgium
  external auditors, 19*b*
  on-site examinations, 113n16
  organizational approaches, 11*b*
  sanctions, 133
branchless banking, 7, 179–181

C

Canada
  cooperation, scope, 151, 152
  on-site examinations, 86, 87*b*
  organizational approaches, 11*b*, 14*b*
  supervisors, accountability, 16
CDD. *See customer due diligence*
CIP. *See customer identification program*
collaboration requirements
  AML/CFT regimes, 3, 9, 10
  off-site supervision, 72–75
compliance
  low compliance, xii, 107*b*
  risks, 28
  sanctions compliance, 117*f*
consequences of money laundering, financing terrorism
  adverse consequences, xxiii
  banking issues and, 5–7
  risks generally, 28–30, 29*b*
cooperation
  AML/CFT regimes, 3, 9, 10
  cross-border cooperation, xii, 112n13, 161, 162
  domestic cooperation, 150*f*
  importance of, 148
  international cooperation, 160–165
  law enforcement authorities, with, 152, 153*b*, 154
  national cooperation, 149–159
coordination, interagency, 9, 10
Core Principles for Effective Banking Supervision (BCP), 6, 47–49
credit risks, 30

criminal activities
  banks controlled by criminals, 46, 46*b*, 47, 47*b*
  criminalization of, 5, 6
  low-risk products and, 183–186
  prevention through bank licensing, 45
  reduction of, 6
  scope, purpose of guide, xi
cross-border cooperation
  scope, purpose of guide, xii, 112n13
  supervisors, among, 161, 162
customer due diligence (CDD), 6, 41n6
  compliance, 94*f*
  cooperation, scope, 149
  enhanced due diligence requirements, 105–108
  international cooperation, 162
  low-risk products and, 183–186
  obligations generally, xi, xii
  on-site examination evaluation of, 206–207
  on-site examination requirements, 93, 94*f*
  on-site examinations and, 84
  private banking for noncitizens, 217–218
  requirements generally, 103, 104
  risk categories and, 34, 35
customer identification, xi, xii, 6
customer identification program (CIP)
  on-site examination evaluation of, 202–205, 203*b*
  on-site examination requirements, 93
  requirements generally, 103, 104
  risk categories and, 34, 35
customer risk assessment, 32, 33

D

domestic agenda, advancing, 5

E

entities, risk assessment, 32, 33
European Union (EU), international cooperation, 163*b*–164*b*
examiners
  off-site examiners, duties, 63, 65, 66, 67, 68